ped 2/4/08

Listening
to Children

University of
Chester
Warrington Campus

of related interest

Kids Need...
Parenting Cards for Families and the People who Work With Them
Mark Hamer
ISBN 978 1 84310 524 4 (Card Game)

Speaking Up: Introducing Advocacy; Rules and Standards; Listen Up! Speak Up!;
Advocacy in Action
A Plain Text Guide to Advocacy 4-volume set
John Tufail and Kate Lyon
ISBN 978 1 84310 474 2

See You in Court
A Social Worker's Guide to Presenting Evidence in Care Proceedings
Lynn Davis
ISBN 978 1 84310 547 3

Young Children's Rights
Exploring Beliefs, Principles and Practice
2nd Edition
Priscilla Alderson
ISBN 978 1 84310 599 2
Children in Charge series

Children Taken Seriously
In Theory, Policy and Practice
Edited by Jan Mason and Toby Fattore
Foreword by Mary John
ISBN 978 1 84310 250 2
Children in Charge series

Developing Advocacy for Children and Young People
Current Issues in Research, Policy and Practice
Edited by Christine M. Oliver and Jane Dalrymple
ISBN 978 1 84310 596 1

Learning Through Child Observation
Mary Fawcett
ISBN 978 1 85302 288 3

Listening
to Children

A Practitioner's Guide

Alison McLeod

Jessica Kingsley Publishers
London and Philadelphia

The author and publishers are grateful to the proprietors listed below for permission to quote the following material: extract from *The House at Pooh Corner*. Text by A.A. Milne. Copyright © The Trustees of the Pooh Properties. Published by Egmont UK Ltd London and used with permission, and by permission of the Pooh Properties Trust. From *The House at Pooh Corner* by A.A. Milne, copyright © 1928 by E.P. Dutton, renewed © 1956 by A.A. Milne. Used by permission of Dutton Children's Books, A Division of Penguin Young Readers Group, A Member of Penguin Group (USA) Inc., 345 Hudson Street, New York, NY 10014. All rights reserved.

First published in 2008
by Jessica Kingsley Publishers
116 Pentonville Road
London N1 9JB, UK
and
400 Market Street, Suite 400
Philadelphia, PA 19106, USA

www.jkp.com

Library of Congress Cataloging in Publication Data
McLeod, Alison, 1950-
  Listening to children : a practitioner's guide / Alison McLeod.
    p. cm.
  ISBN 978-1-84310-549-7 (pb : alk. paper) 1. Listening. 2. Attention. 3. Children. I. Title.
  BF323.L5M365 2008
  158'.3083--dc22

                                              2007043132

British Library Cataloguing in Publication Data
A CIP catalogue record for this book is available from the British Library

ISBN 978 1 84310 549 7

Printed and bound in Great Britain by
Athenaeum Press, Gateshead, Tyne and Wear

Contents

Part 4: Particular Conversations – Interviews for Specific Purposes

Part 5: Young People and Participation

Your children are not your children. They are the sons and daughters of life's longing for itself. They come through you but not from you, and though they are with you yet they belong not to you.

You may give them your love but not your thoughts, for they have their own thoughts. You may house their bodies but not their souls, for their souls dwell in the house of tomorrow, which you cannot visit, not even in your dreams. You may strive to be like them, but seek not to make them like you. For Life goes not backward, nor tarries with yesterday.

From **The Prophet** by Kahlil Gibran [1883–1931]
Gibran [1923] 1995, (p.5)

First Words

Everything, you know, finally, the lot, this is all *my* meeting, it's about *my life*. You lot are just doing your jobs, but it's all pertinent to me and it's all mine.

So said 17-year-old Anna when talking to me about her statutory review – the meeting that has to be held regularly for all children in public care to check that the plans for looking after them are on track. Her words are a salutary reminder to professionals that what may be all in a day's work for them can have long-term consequences for the children and young people they work with. I wanted to let Anna speak first in this book because she taught me so much about listening to children. She was one of the young people I worked with in a project that aimed to improve standards of care for children looked after by local authorities. One of the central principles of the project was that it would consult with young people, take notice of their views and actively involve them in its planning and management throughout, and I must confess that I approached this agenda with some scepticism: consultation exercises were always tokenistic, I thought. Would teenagers really want to attend boring meetings, serve on committees? Did they have the confidence, the skills or the knowledge to present their views in a public forum? My thoughts echoed those of Keay (2006, p.2): 'If I cast my mind back to my distant childhood, this worthy agenda would have come a very poor second best to playing football.' Anna and her colleagues proved me wrong. They entered into the project with a passion and commitment that put the professionals to shame. Their 'lived in' experience of the care system gave a whole new perspective that I could not provide, despite my years of experience of social work: it was their burning sense of injustice that made an impact on staff, and their enthusiasm for building a better future that engaged other young people so that we began to see real changes in attitudes and practices as a result.

I say Anna taught me much, but there is still much for us all to learn about listening to children and young people. I first decided to find out more about the topic in the early 1990s, one long afternoon as I sat in a chilly courtroom listening to arguments fly back and forth about whether a baby boy would rather return to his parents or be placed for adoption. The option he would almost certainly have preferred, had he been able to voice an opinion – that of remaining with his foster carers – was not on offer. I reflected as I listened to the pros and cons, that although the law says we must consider children's wishes and feelings before making decisions that will affect them, this is often easier said than done. I decided then to investigate how social workers go about listening to children and how effective they are at doing it.

My first move was to read all I could about how to communicate with children but at that time I could find very little published on the subject. Things have changed over the last decade. There has been an explosion of interest in children's rights and participation in recent years and forests have been felled to provide the paper for all the words written on the subject, yet we are still only in the early stages of beginning to understand how to do it. Indeed, when Luckock *et al.* (2006) reviewed the evidence on the teaching of skills in communication with children and young people on social work training courses, they found no consensus about how this should be done, nor indeed any guarantee that a qualified social worker would have received any training on the topic at all. As Clark and Moss (2001, p.1) comment, in the field of listening to children 'the rhetoric outpaces the practice'. So this book, while it aims to guide the uninitiated through the maze of conflicting views, theories and advice on listening to children, and to arm them with some tools for practice, does not claim to have all the answers. Readers should approach the book with critical self-awareness, considering their own practice and be prepared to develop their own views. They can expect to use it as a jumping-off point for the more technical literature in this ever-expanding field. And they would be well advised to take note of the views of children printed in these pages, since they are the real experts on their own lives.

How to read this book

The book is arranged in themed sections. This introductory section explains what the book is about, who it is for and what it consists of. It introduces the reader to the young people whose comments complement my text. Parts 1 and 2 address the theory of listening to children while Parts 3, 4 and 5 look at how to apply this theory to practice.

Part 1 starts by considering why we should listen to children. It asks whether and how listening may make our interventions with young people more effective. It discusses the ethical and human rights angles and explains the legal background from a UK perspective, demonstrating how far recent policy initiatives have moved on from earlier legislation. It questions, however, how much change there has really been in practice.

Part 2 sets out what we know about communicating with children. In it I summarize what research tells us about children and communication. How do they learn language? What is the relationship between thought and memory? What are the roles of culture and context in an interaction? Key concepts such as attachment are examined and criticisms of developmental psychology are debated. The contributions of sociology and social work theory to our understanding of how to communicate with children are discussed.

In Part 3 I move on from the theory to the question of how to put listening into practice. A range of practical techniques are described for building rapport, encouraging children and young people to talk to us, understanding what they say and eliciting their views. The importance of being aware of power dynamics in a relationship is highlighted and there is advice on bringing an intervention to a close.

This is followed in Part 4 by advice on managing more technical or specialist contexts: interviewing children who may have been abused, sharing difficult and complex information with them, helping them to express their feelings and to come to a positive understanding of who they are.

Part 5 concerns taking young people's views seriously. It discusses how to promote children's rights (individually and as a group) by offering them choices, involving them in age-appropriate ways in decision-making, consulting with them and assisting them to participate in the development and evaluation of policies and services. In the brief concluding chapter I sum up some of the main points already made, and let the young people's comments speak for me.

Throughout the book I consider how our attitudes to the agency of young people have changed and raise questions about how they may develop in future. I argue that we need to learn to treat children with respect, help them develop a voice as young citizens and then take their views seriously, both because they are human beings in their own right every bit as much as adults are, and also since the future is in their hands.

Each part of the book is self-contained. It may make most sense to read it in the order it is written, but this is not essential and the reader may wish to go straight to the part that interests them most. For example, the teacher charged with setting up a school council might start with Part 5, whereas the adoptive parents who have to explain to their seven-year-old about his birth parents' drug addiction might only be interested in Part 4, and the student writing an essay on children's rights would find the most relevant material in Part 1. A newly qualified social worker working in a children and families team, on the other hand, might want to start at the beginning and read the book through to the end.

Throughout the book, alongside the text, you will find inserted material. This material falls into four categories. First, there are verbatim quotes in speech bubbles from young people giving their views and comments on the issues discussed in the text. Second, there are checklists of pointers for good practice. Third, there are practice examples taken from my research, my experience as a social worker, teacher and parent, or drawn from the literature. These illustrate how professionals have attempted to listen to children and young people in real life. Although they are mostly chosen to illustrate good practice, since they are real – not imaginary – examples, the practice in the examples is not flawless: there will always be aspects that could have been handled better. Finally, there are reflective activities for the reader to engage in (see Reflective Exercise 0.1 below for example). I believe that thoughtfulness and sensitive self-awareness are essential characteristics of the practitioner who listens effectively to service-users. These qualities are not innate and can be developed by those who practise them; they are more akin to skills than to personality traits.

The young people and their stories

Following my reflection in the courtroom described at the beginning of this chapter, I carried out a piece of research (McLeod 2001, summarized in McLeod 2006) into how effectively social workers listen to children who are in public care – 'looked after by the local authority' as the Children Act 1989 describes it. I will refer to this as the 'Listening but not Hearing' study. It demonstrated that, although the social workers believed they were making strenuous efforts to listen to what the children said to them, the young people I interviewed in the course of the research did not feel as though anyone was hearing them. I use the words of ten of these young people to illustrate my points throughout this book. I introduce them to you here with a pen picture, a little about their history and a flavour of their views. Then, when you read their comments you can have some idea of who it was that said it. Although they were all in public care and I was asking them to tell me particularly about whether their social workers listened to them, I believe that many of their comments are applicable to any situation where a practitioner is listening to a child.

I have changed all the young people's names, and any details of their circumstances from which they might be identified. I have decided not to say why each child came to be living away from home, but the reasons included physical or sexual abuse; neglect; domestic violence; parents who misused drugs or alcohol or were mentally ill; breakdown of family relationships; the child's behaviour being beyond the parents' control; and the death of one or both parents. In most cases more than one of these factors applied.

Reflective Exercise 0.1

As you read the case studies below, ask yourself the following questions:

- What does this young person's story tell me about communicating with children?
- How do I feel, reading their story?
- How might these feelings influence me if I were working with this young person?

Alistair (15 years) had come into local authority accommodation 18 months earlier. He had lived in two children's homes and had had three unsuccessful foster placements before moving to the foster home where he now was, and which he said suited him well. He was very critical of the organization that was then known as Social Services but is now called Children's Services, and of both the social workers he had had: 'The system is shite. Always has been and always will be.' Among his complaints were that his social worker never explained things to him and did nothing to help him; he had been victimized in foster care and ill-treated in residential care; planning meetings that should have been held had not been. However, he also said he hated meetings and form-filling and thought formal complaints procedures were a waste of time. On the other hand, he showed an understanding of the need for rules and give and take in his current foster placement; he appeared to trust his foster carers and felt he could rely on them to speak up for him and represent his interests.

Alistair had a great sense of humour and his account of his time in the care system was colourful and entertaining. He did not, however, appear to take the interview very seriously: much of what he said seemed calculated to shock or impress me, and a lot of it stretched the bounds of my credulity. If the information from his social worker or that in Social Services records were to be believed, much of it was indeed fantasy, exaggerated or untrue. This left me with a dilemma over how much weight to accord his views.

I have already introduced *Anna* on page 9. She was aged 17 when I interviewed her for the 'Listening but not Hearing' study, though we had previously met on the care standards project and knew each other quite well. Anna was an articulate and confident young woman from a professional family who was hoping to go to university the following year. She had started to be looked after some four years previously.

Even though she was now doing well, Anna's time in care had not been easy for her. She had experienced a lot of change: she had lived for spells with two relatives, in two children's homes and in at least two foster homes before moving out into her own flat. She had changed schools several times and was on to her fifth social worker. Anna was critical of the care system, though she was moderately positive about her current social worker. Children's rights was a passion for her: she had startled her social worker when, aged 13, she had demanded her own copy of the Children Act so she could check out just what her legal rights were! Anna had strong and well-thought-out views about listening to children. She was convinced that young people in Britain were routinely discriminated against, and not given adequate control over their lives or allowed appropriate choices. She had detailed proposals for how to explain the system better to looked-after children, how to involve them more effectively in planning for their care, how records should be kept and on many other subjects. When she didn't get satisfaction from her social worker she rang up the director: 'I believe in going to the top!'

I found 11-year-old *Ben* wary, but keen to be helpful. He had come into care a year earlier and had been placed together with his younger brother in a foster placement. They were now living with relatives, still technically in care, but with a plan to discharge the care orders. These boys had not suffered the many moves of the teenagers described above, but Ben had still found the experience of being removed from home deeply distressing. He had not liked being in foster care, saying he had been bullied by the foster carers' children and that, although his social worker had listened when he had complained about it to her, she had not succeeded in stopping it. He felt he had been allowed to have a say in planning meetings and that people listened when he said he was happy where he was now and wanted to stay. He spoke highly of his social worker, who he said had done everything she could to help him. However, she had now left and had not yet been replaced.

Karen was almost 18, and the oldest of these young people, but she was also the least forthcoming. She was very guarded: finding out what she thought was like getting blood out of a stone. She told me that everything about Social Services and the work of the social workers she had known was fine, but it seemed to me she was only saying it because she thought that was what I wanted to hear.

Karen, after many years in care, was now living independently with her boyfriend and baby. She had had numerous placements in children's homes and foster homes, and although she said she had been unfairly treated by some of her foster carers she said she had never complained: 'I just don't want to cause trouble really.' She could no longer remember all the social workers she had had. She was much more interested in asking me for advice about paying her electricity bill than in talking about whether social workers took notice of her views: 'Social workers always listen, really, to me. They ask me if anything is troubling me and I always say "No", so they're wasting their time really.'

Kerry (15) was very different. Stopping her talking was the main problem. She had plenty to say that was relevant (much of it concerning social workers' nosiness and young people's powerlessness) and a lot more that for my purposes was less so (for example, about the inadequacy of her pocket money and what clothes she would buy if she had more money). It would have been easy to dismiss everything she said as adolescent discontent. This would have done her an injustice, however. Among her complaints about the unfairness of life – and, to be fair, life had treated her badly – she made some very good points: how young children communicate their feelings; how adults should behave if they want to gain a child's trust; how intimidating it can feel as a teenager to take part in a formal meeting with a roomful of strangers. Kerry had been in public care for about ten years, had lived in numerous foster homes and had had several changes of social worker.

Patrick was 12, and small for his age so he looked younger, but his responses were thoughtful and mature. He considered each question carefully, pondering before giving a response. He drew me a detailed 'life-map', talking through for me who had or had not listened to him at different stages of his life. Patrick had been looked after since the age of eight. After a couple of false starts he was now in a very settled long-term foster placement. He was broadly positive about the series of social workers he had had, though he did object to their intrusive questioning, saying that he preferred to keep his personal feelings private. He complained about social workers who visited infrequently or arrived late for appointments and said he hated to be patronized, stressing that adults should adjust their language appropriately for the age and ability level of children they are talking to. Mainly he felt his views had been adequately taken into account when decisions had been made about his care.

Like Patrick, *Robert* (aged 14) was in a stable long-term foster home. He had been there for about five years having come into care as a small child. He had had several foster home breakdowns in his early years, and although the plan had initially been to place him for adoption, this had never come to fruition. Robert acknowledged that he had been a very mixed up child who had been confused about what was happening and who expressed his distress through difficult behaviour. He felt workers should have tried harder to explain to him what was going on and they should have realized that some of his behaviour stemmed from his unhappiness with the foster homes he was placed in. One of his social workers had done life-story work with him; he had found this helpful and felt very let down when she left. He had also done a course of work with a play therapist and he felt that this had been extremely helpful.

Robert was quite content with his current situation. He felt his wishes and views were listened to and taken account of and that he had channels for redress available to him should he have a complaint. He hated feeling different because of being in care, and wanted to be 'normal' like his friends and not to have social workers and review meetings and all the things that make the life of a youngster in care different from that of other teenagers. For this reason he was keen to be able to leave care soon. However, he was also anxious about leaving his foster home and hoped he would still have some support available to him once he moved out.

Steven (16) was in residential care and on the day of our interview was in a state of uncertainty since the children's home was about to close and he did not know where he would go next. Anxiety might go some way to explaining his antagonistic demeanour and the stream of invective he came out with, though according to his social worker this was his normal style of communication: 'Have you any advice for social workers?' 'Yeah. Fuck off out of our lives!' His opinion of his current social worker, as expressed to me, was that she was a complete waste of space. Interestingly, though, he had warm praise for his previous social worker (like Robert he felt upset that she had left) and was able to articulate clearly what a good social worker would do; one of his chief complaints about the current one was that she did not visit him often enough!

Steven had come into care as a toddler. A series of foster placements had failed, and, as in the case of Robert, early plans for him to be adopted had never been implemented. Unlike Robert, however, no family placement had lasted for him and he had ended up in a residential school with holidays in a children's home. Steven could be described as a casualty of the system, having spent almost all his life in care, lurching from crisis to crisis without ever having achieved a stable living situation. He was extremely negative about his experience of the care system: 'Social Services has caused all the trouble in my life.' He alleged he had been ill-treated or unfairly treated wherever he had lived, said no one had ever listened to his concerns and that he had no faith in any of the formal channels for redress. His view was that it would be better if children remained with their families whatever their circumstances.

Tammy, a 15-year-old girl who was living in a children's home, was a lively and engaging young person with a graphic turn of phrase. She had only been accommodated by the local authority for six months. She was particularly incensed that, since they had sole parental responsibility for her, her parents' permission had to be sought for a range of day-to-day decisions: 'That gets on my nerves, because I've *disowned* them!' She thought that being looked after was infinitely better than being at home and was warm in the praise of her social worker. Tammy had lots of practical ideas for how social workers could build constructive relationships with young people, prime among which were to take them out and not to 'pry'. Like a number of the other young people, she felt her feelings were her private affair and she had no wish to share them with anyone else. She would have preferred to have been living in a foster home. However, she did not accuse anyone of failing to take her wishes on board: she accepted that her social worker could not help there being a shortage of foster placements for teenagers.

Wayne was 14. Coming into care some five years earlier had been sudden and traumatic for Wayne, who had then had a number of unsuccessful placements but was now doing well with a single male foster carer with whom he had lived for three years. Wayne had no social worker: his case was currently unallocated. He had complained about this without getting any response and had a generally jaundiced view of Social Services, which he felt did not listen to his concerns at all. He was particularly critical of the failure of staff to sit down and talk with him about the plans for his care when he had first been looked after, and he described with some bitterness being moved around from foster home to foster home with nothing but a bin bag containing a few possessions, getting more bewildered at each move. Wayne did, however, feel well supported by his current foster carer, who he felt he could turn to at any time for help, and who he thought compensated for the failings of the system.

Issues of autonomy came up a lot in the interview with Wayne: he wanted more say in the decisions about his life than he felt he was getting. He believed that he was old enough to know what was good for him: 'I can look after myself. I'm 14 and I feel strongly I'm old enough to understand the risks I'm taking and make my own mind up... I mean, it seems I have to ring up the Social to see if I can go to the toilet!' Social workers, he said, shouldn't 'try to lead your life for you... They should be your equal, not your master.'

Wayne was not the only one of the young people I interviewed to raise the issue of autonomy and how much control children can appropriately exercise over the direction of their own lives. Practitioners and academics debate the matter hotly too. It lies at the heart of the disputed theory and practice of listening to children. In Part 1 this is one of the key topics to address as I attempt to answer the question: why should we listen to children?

Part 1: The Voice
of the Child

Children have as much need for a revolution as the
Proletariat has.

William Morris [1834–1896] (quoted in Berger 1971, p.179)

Chapter 1

Why Listen to Children?

What is 'listening'?

A fundamental question is to ask why we should listen to children and I will argue that this is a question not just of common sense, or indeed of legal obligation, but ultimately one of human rights. However, before going any further we need to pause and consider what 'listening' actually means. This may seem self-evident, but, in fact, the word can mean different things to different people, and unless it is clarified this can lead to misunderstandings. In the 'Listening but not Hearing' study (Mcleod 2001; see First Words, p.12) I found that while the social workers thought they were trying hard to listen to looked-after children, the youngsters I interviewed nearly all complained that their social workers didn't listen to them. Part of the reason for this difference of view was that the adults and the children were using the word differently. 'It's just hearing her, being respectful', said Tammy's social worker, explaining to me how she had responded when Tammy asked to move and there was nowhere else for her to go. As she and the other social workers saw it, listening to a child meant paying attention to what they said, having an open attitude, respecting and empathizing with their feelings, but not necessarily doing as they asked. For the young people on the other hand, if no action followed, the adults had not really been listening. As Alistair put it: 'Half the time they aren't listening. Especially Veronica. She used to look like she was listening, but she never was. She used to just look and nod and *do* nothing.'

I knew the social worker I have named 'Veronica' well, as it happened, and couldn't help feeling that Alistair had a point. Forever after when I saw her I had to control my smiles as a vision intruded of one of those nodding dogs people keep on the parcel shelves of their cars!

In the literature on listening to children one can find the same distinction between writers who define listening in terms of attitude and those who argue that 'true' listening implies action. In the interesting collection of essays on listening to pre-school children, *Beyond Listening* (Clark, Kjørholt and Moss 2005), for example, one finds the former view: listening is 'a value in the ethics of an encounter' '[it] is first and foremost about an ethic of openness to and respect for the other' (Kjørholt, Moss and Clark 2005, pp.176, 178). Claims about children's rights, the authors argue, should be evaluated critically: choice, independence and responsibility for decision-making should not be assumed to be good for children in every context. Cairns and Brannen (2005, p.78), on the other hand, adopt the latter construction. They present a view of children and young people as: 'active citizens, who are knowledgeable about their world and able to play a full part in decision-making processes that affect them'. They relate an anecdote of how adults in a powerful position (regional transport policy-makers) paid lip-service to consultation by meeting with young people but then ignoring their views. However, when the same young people armed themselves with in-depth knowledge of the topic at issue they were able to challenge the expertise of the adults effectively, who were then forced to take their views more seriously. 'This…made the difference between having a say, which happened at the first meeting, and being listened to and achieving change, which happened at the second meeting' (Cairns and Brannen 2005, p.81). The way these writers use the words 'listened to' reflects the view of the young people I interviewed: listening involves more than just paying attention to what young people say; it involves taking it seriously and acting in response.

> 'When you're young they tend not to listen to you because they think they know better all the time.' (Steven)

The concepts of listening as an attitude or listening that leads to action are each grounded in an underlying value. In the case of listening as an ethic of openness, the primary underlying value is respect. In the case of listening as a means of achieving change, the primary value is empowerment. Much that is written about listening to children concerns effective and respectful communication, and much concerns empowering children through promoting their rights and participation. My interpretation of 'listening' encompasses both: true respect for another person, in my view, implies that you will do what you can to empower them. This book will therefore address listening to children both at the micro level – how to promote effective communication in the context of a respectful one-to-one relationship with a child (Parts 3 and 4) – and also at the macro level – how we can empower young people to participate meaningfully in decisions that affect their lives, both at an individual level and as members of society (Part 5).

What is a child?

This second question may seem even more obvious, but if anything, the concept of 'childhood' is even more hotly contested than that of 'listening'. Childhood is a concept that is relative, culture-bound and consequently hard to define. In many countries today people may take on adult responsibilities at a much younger age than is generally the case in Europe. For example, from my own experience of working in Papua New Guinea in the 1970s, children under ten looked after younger siblings, wielded machetes, lit fires and walked miles to school without adult supervision. The age at which children are viewed as responsible for criminal actions, on the other hand, varies enormously across the world, a higher age of criminal responsibility being by no means confined to the West. For example, in Scotland it is 8, in Belgium, 18, in India, 7 and in Egypt, 15. What 'childhood' means has changed throughout history too: some writers argue that the concept of a child is a modern one and that in earlier times younger people were not perceived as a separate group from adults: 'In medieval society the idea of childhood did not exist' (Aries 1962, p.128). Though this view has not gone unchallenged (Thomas 2002) there is little doubt that children in Britain nowadays have a longer apprenticeship for adulthood than was the case in the past, or is the case in many cultures in the present. It can be argued that this makes growing up harder for today's teenagers: there is no defining moment at which one becomes an adult in our society since adult responsibilities and privileges in law are gained in an incremental and not always obviously logical way. Why should one be old enough to join the army before one is permitted to vote, for example? (Take a look at the age quiz in Reflective Exercise 1.1. The answers may be found at the end of this chapter.)

So, when does a child in our society stop being a child and become an adult? There is no simple or clear-cut answer, which complicates questions about how, whether and when adults should listen to children. In this book, when I refer to 'children', in general I use the term 'child', as it is used in the Children Act 1989, meaning any person who is under the age of 18. Where age makes a significant difference to the question under consideration I will specify, otherwise 'child' can be taken to mean anyone who is a child in law.

'The age when you leave care is too high. You're old enough to get married and have children at 16 but not old enough to leave care.' (Robert)

Reflective Exercise 1.1

Answer the quiz below (answers at the end of this chapter). Then reflect: at what age do you feel you yourself 'grew up'? Was this related to attaining the legal age of majority? To leaving home? To a significant personal experience? Or was there no specific moment at which you feel you left your childhood behind you?

At what age, in the United Kingdom (2007), may a person legally:

- marry
- be employed to work for money
- buy cigarettes
- get tattooed
- vote
- adopt a child
- hold a shotgun certificate
- buy fireworks
- drive a car?

How logical do these different ages appear to you?

If you are not from the United Kingdom you could research the ages in your own country and compare. Are there any major differences?

The rationale for listening
Because it works

In a family I once worked with, the mother was busily packing for a family holiday when her small daughter wandered up to her and started chatting:

'You've finished painting in the den', said the little girl.

'Mm', said her mother, absently.

'It's going to be Robbie's bedroom, isn't it?'

'Yes, love.'

'So he won't be sleeping in my bedroom any more.'

'No, love.'

'That's good. We won't have to play sausages any more.'

This was the critical moment. The mother could so easily have said 'No, love' again, got on with her packing, and the opportunity would have passed. Instead she said:

'Sausages? What's that?', and her daughter replied:

'Oh, you know, it's that horrid game Robbie likes. The one where he puts his willy in my fanny. I don't like it. Can you tell Robbie I don't want to play it any more?'

The child was too young to have any conception of what it was she was telling her mother, that this was not a game that all big brothers played with their little sisters, that not everyone called it 'sausages'. Her mother could so easily have failed to ask the right question at the right moment and so would not have found out what it was the child had to tell her; the little girl would have gone away believing that she had told her mother what was going on and that her mother had not thought it was important and had done nothing to stop it happening. Was it chance that the mother asked that critical question, or did her intuition and knowledge of her daughter tell her that something important was troubling her, something important enough to interrupt business as pressing as holiday preparations? Whichever it was, she demonstrated here the essential attributes of effective listening: the ability to keep an open mind, to tune into the other person's agenda and to be prepared for the unexpected. And how vital that proved for her ability to protect her young daughter from harm.

I tell this anecdote to make a point: that we should listen to children because it makes our work with them more effective. The most compelling reason for professionals to take notice of what children say is perhaps the pragmatic one: we waste our own time if we do not.

A dismal series of child death enquiries from Dennis O'Neill (Monckton 1945) to Victoria Climbié (Laming 2003) testifies to the dire consequences that can follow when professionals fail to hear the child's voice. On the positive side, a range of evidence also links effective listening with better outcomes for children. For example, Bell's (2002) study of children who were subject to child protection investigations found that where the social worker supported, listened and explained, the children's needs were better met and their situations improved. Similarly, Triseliotis *et al.* (1995), in their study of Scottish teenagers receiving social work services, found that where there was good communication between social worker, young person and parents, better progress was achieved, and where the young person participated in the choice of placement, outcomes were more successful.

Why should this be? Better results may follow on from professionals listening, simply because young people who do not like the decision an adult has made may choose deliberately to undermine it. Excluding children from decisions that affect them can thus be counterproductive. Veeran (2004) provides examples from work with street children in South Africa and South Asia: removing girls from the street where they were working as prostitutes without consulting with them only led to them going straight back. It was essential rather to find out what the child's view of the problem was and what they themselves saw as the solution. Providing their families with support or protecting the girls in situ might turn out to be more constructive solutions than removing them to a refuge where they did not want to be.

It is axiomatic that adults cannot make a reliable judgement about what is best for a child without exploring the child's perspective, but there may be additional psycho-social benefits for young people that arise from playing a role in decision-making. It has been argued that even very young children will benefit simply from being consulted: 'telling who you are – presenting yourself and your views and being heard – is one of the most important issues in identity construction' (Eide and Winger 2005, p.76). Research shows that children whose parents are divorcing feel less upset and more in control if they are consulted about what is happening (Butler *et al.* 2002) and that 'children with positive feelings of self-esteem, mastery and control can more easily manage stressful experiences' (Munro 2001, p.134). Skills such as communication, debate, negotiation and prioritization can be learnt from engagement in decision-making processes, which can help the child with problem-solving in other areas of their life (Sinclair 2000). It is also claimed that involvement can promote young people's social inclusion (Spicer and Evans 2006). There is thus broad support in the literature for the value of participation for the young, and though much of this is based on personal opinion and anecdote, there is some supporting evidence from research.

PRACTICE EXAMPLE 1.1 THE 'STUDENT VOICE' RESEARCH PROJECT

This consultation exercise sought the views of 1800 students from six secondary schools in a town in Northwest England on the question: 'If you had the chance to make changes to education in the future, what recommendations would you make and why?' The research was carried out by a team of 18 young people aged between 14 and 16 years from the schools, supported by seven students aged between 17 and 18 years from local colleges and a sixth form. Research methods included an online questionnaire and structured interviews, and data was collected that was both quantitative and qualitative. Three adult researchers trained the students in research methods and coordinated the project, but the student research team was given as much control as possible. They identified the topics, designed the survey questions, wrote the interview frameworks and decided who to interview; they carried out the analysis of the data they had gathered and they decided on the key messages and recommendations they wanted to communicate.

Among the wealth of data they amassed was the worrying statistic that 114 young people (6.5%) who responded to the survey said they never felt safe in school. The young researchers comment: 'Because of the urgency of these statistics...we think that this area – how to ensure students feel safe at school, and what feeling safe actually means – needs to be considered immediately by our head teachers and teachers, and could form the basis of further research in the future' (Carr 2007, p.14).

The report's full recommendations were:

- A variety of different teaching and learning approaches.
- More opportunities for working with other schools and other organizations.
- Rules, rewards and sanctions need to be consistent and fair.
- There should be more emphasis on positivity.
- Students should feel safe all of the time.
- Students want to feel that they can participate actively and authentically in the decision-making process. (Carr 2007 p.3)

The acid test is what difference the consultation exercise made. There was, of course, significant personal learning for the individuals who took part in the project. Evidence that anything changed within the schools was harder to come by, but one school was reported to be undertaking further enquiries into bullying in the school, and another had made improvements to the physical environment (state of the toilets) in response to the survey findings.

Being heard, then, benefits children. There is also some evidence that advantages of listening to children can be felt at a service-wide level (Carr

nney (2005) found that a Scottish project that consulted with
an early years centre led to improvements in staff working practices. Cairns and Brannen (2005) report on how young people in Northeast
England were enabled to exert a positive influence on issues from local
transport policy to medical facilities and treatment (see also Practice
Example 1.1 – the 'Student Voice' Research Project). It is evidence of all
three kinds – that listening to children can protect children, can enhance
their well-being and can lead to improvements in services – that has led governments to legislate on the child's right to be heard.

Because it's the law

This brings us to the second reason why professionals should listen to
children: in most parts of the world the law says they must. After a decade of
negotiation the United Nations passed the UN Convention on the Rights of
the Child (UNCRC; United Nations 1989). Britain ratified the Convention
in 1991 and it has also been ratified by every other member state of the UN
bar two: Somalia and the United States of America. Article 12 of the Convention assured:

> to the child who is capable of forming his or her own views the
> right to express those views in all matters affecting the child, the
> view of the child being given due weight in accordance with the
> age and maturity of the child.

This right has been interpreted in widely varying ways in the many states
that are party to the Convention. Some take a broad interpretation of what is
meant by 'matters affecting the child'. In Scandinavia, for example, parents
are required by law to consult with their children before making decisions
that will affect them. In Britain the interpretation is somewhat narrower, but
expanding.

The first piece of UK legislation incorporating the Convention's
requirement to listen to the child's voice was the Children Act 1989, which
applies to England and Wales. It was followed a few years later by the
broadly similar Children (Scotland) Act 1995. Perhaps the most significant
achievement of the 1989 Children Act can be seen, in retrospect, to be its
contribution to children's rights. Since it was enacted, young people in
Britain have had by law a right to be heard, and this is a very significant step
towards their emancipation.

The child's voice is a central thread running throughout the Act. The
crucial sections are Section 1(3)a, which requires courts to consider the
wishes and feelings of children involved in legal proceedings and to give

them due consideration (having regard to the child's age and understanding), and Sections 22(4)a and 22(5), which make the same requirements when any decision is made about a child who is, or may be, looked after by a local authority. The Act also established independently investigated complaints systems for children receiving services from local authorities. Regulations and guidance (Department of Health 1991) stipulate in greater detail how children's wishes and feelings are to be elicited and specify that young people must be informed about their rights and about options available to them. They are to be encouraged and enabled to attend case conferences and reviews concerning them and are to participate in the planning for their own care, as far as their age and understanding allow. The Children Act 1989 thus gave children a voice in several different ways: it required practitioners to enter into a dialogue with children and gave children the right to be heard; it enhanced their powers of self-determination by giving them the right to participate in decisions that might affect them; it gave them a right to redress against injustice. Freeman (1992, p.52) commented at the time that the Children Act 1989 was: 'not only more child-centred [than earlier legislation] but the clearest recognition yet of the decision-making capacities of children'.

The 1989 Children Act was not, however, the last word on children's legal rights in England and Wales. The Family Law Act 1996 extended the requirement to consider children's wishes and feelings to private as well as public law and in 2002 the Adoption and Children Act extended this to cover adoption proceedings too. This also required local authorities to set up advocacy services to assist children wanting to make a complaint under the provisions of the Children Act 1989. The 'Quality Protects' initiative (Department of Health 1998) required local authorities to consult with young people on the overall design and provision of services as well as on the conduct of individual cases and this approach was taken further in the Children Act 2004 and its associated guidance.

The Children Act 2004 followed in the wake of the Climbié enquiry (Laming 2003), which broke the mould of previous child abuse enquiries by blaming system failure rather than individuals for the tragedy and demanding sweeping reforms to children's services. The Act established a Children's Commissioner for England, to raise awareness of the best interests of children by looking at how government and public and private sector bodies listen to children and by highlighting failures in complaints procedures. It also extended the requirement to elicit and consider wishes and feelings to cover all children in need. The guidance to the 2004 Act and ensuing policy documents gave a high profile to the voice of children and young people. For example, *Change for Children* (Department for Education and Skills 2004b) listed 'engage in decision-making' as a targeted outcome for children. It also required Children's Trusts to consider the views of children and young people before drawing up strategic plans. The *National Services Framework* (Department of Health 2004) required National Health Service staff to provide appropriate information for children about health care services, listen and respond to their views and seek explicit consent before treatment. Simultaneously, schools were exhorted to encourage greater participation by pupils (Department for Education and Skills 2004a).

It can thus be seen that people who work with children, not just in the United Kingdom but in most parts of the world, are legally obliged to take children's views seriously. It can be argued, however, that there is a higher order of moral justification for listening to children than mere national legislation: that it is an ethical issue, a question of human rights.

Because it is (their) right

It is curious that in English the word 'right' can have so many meanings. If I say we should listen to children 'because it is right', I mean because it is a morally good thing to do. If, on the other hand, I say 'because it is *their* right', what I now mean is 'because it is children's just entitlement'. Both of course are true.

If we consider first the assertion that we should listen because it is a good thing to do, we have to bear in mind that no professional intervention with a child or young person exists in a moral vacuum. If it is possible to have a positive impact on a child's life, it follows that it must also be possible for our influence to be harmful. Each profession therefore has its separate, but overlapping codes of ethics. For some international examples, see Canadian Nurses Association (2002); Irish Sports Council (2000); New Zealand Teachers' Council (2004) and, from the United States, National Association of Social Workers (2006). In any of these documents one will find that a central place is given to respect: professionals who practise ethically will treat their patients, pupils or clients with respect, whether they are adults or children, and respecting a person requires one to listen to what the other person says. Similarly, in the guidance document *Common Core of Skills and Knowledge for the Children's Workforce* (Department for Education and Skills 2005, p.7) listening is identified as the first skill for those working with children, and respect as the first prerequisite of listening.

As we have already observed, another value fundamental to social work is empowerment. To quote the code of ethics of the US National Association of Social Workers (NASW):

> The primary mission of the social work profession is to enh
> human well-being and help meet the basic human needs o. ...
> people, with particular attention to the needs and empowerment
> of people who are vulnerable, oppressed, and living in poverty.
> (NASW 2006, p.1)

Again, listening is inextricably linked with empowerment: to ignore a person disempowers them. Taking notice of their views and allowing them to influence decision-making is empowering. Listening is thus central to ethical practice.

Looking now at the second assertion, that we should listen to children because it is their right, we move to the second meaning of the word 'right': as an entitlement in law, or as a matter of natural justice. We have already seen above that ratification of the UN Convention does indeed mean that in most countries in the world children are now legally entitled to have their say, but why should the Convention lay such a stress on the voice of the child?

A fundamental argument in favour of children's right to speak out is that to have a voice is an essential step in the liberation of an oppressed group. No one can count on having their needs met if they are unable to express those needs. That is why freedom of speech as well as the vote is central to democracy: both give the individual a voice within the apparatus of the state. There is more to democracy than just speaking one's mind, but the right to self-expression is a necessary condition (Turner 1990).

'I think children are treated very much in this society as incapable, the same way mentally ill or elderly people are treated.' (Anna)

It may seem unexpected to hear children referred to as an 'oppressed' group, but it can be argued that politically they have always been so. They have been described as: 'the largest minority group that has no voice, no vote, very little influence and – with a few exceptions – very few rights in law' (Pringle 1979, p.193). Children are a group defined by age, and like oppressed groups defined by gender, race or other characteristics, as a body they lack the power, influence, wealth and independence that are generally enjoyed by other members of society. UK law still treats children in many ways less favourably than adults. For example, while an assault is a criminal offence, there is a specific exclusion clause for adults in charge of children administering 'reasonable' physical punishment (Children Act 2004, Section 58; see also Reflective Exercise 1.2). Where adult and child views diverge, it is generally the adult's view that prevails. Kellet (2006) relates how the Scottish parliament in 2002 planned to legislate against adults hitting children but first studied public opinion. They found that while 95 per cent of children surveyed were in favour of the proposed law, the majority of adults were against. The measure was subsequently dropped.

Reflective Exercise 1.2

According to a pamphlet from the Children Are Unbeatable! Alliance: 'The current law allowing "reasonable punishment" of children…undermines the work of all professionals working to support families… Equal protection from assault for children is the only just and safe way to clarify the law and meet human rights obligations. The law should send the clear message that hitting children is as unacceptable and unlawful as hitting anyone else' (Parenting UK 2007, p.2).

The British government does not, apparently, agree. What arguments justify physical punishment of children? Where do you stand on this issue?

Cairns and Brannen argue that discrimination against children and young people on grounds of age alone is endemic in British society:

> From policies banning all young people from public leisure centres from 7pm, to buses refusing to stop to pick up young passengers, from the arbitrary authority and discipline of school regimes to the restrictions on the number of young people allowed in some shops, the discrimination is so pervasive as to affect all young people. The extent and effect of this varies according to circumstances, and those who are already disadvantaged by other factors, such as poverty or disability, suffer greater oppression than those who are better resourced. (Cairns and Brannen 2005, p.85)

Children's dependent legal status evolved from their dependent biological position. The assumption is that, as they depend on their parents for care, they can count on having their political needs met for them by proxy too, and that they can acquire full adult rights once they become fully capable of exercising adult responsibilities. Under Greek and Roman law, from which our own legal system developed, a child was regarded as a possession of the parent. A comment of Aristotle illustrates the attitude: 'The justice of a father is different towards his own children than an ordinary citizen because one can do no injustice to one's own property' (cited in Pringle 1979, p.194). This attitude may appear to us extreme, but the view still persists today. 'He's my kid: I can do what I like with him!' is a retort often heard by social workers making enquiries about alleged ill-treatment. So long as children have no rights themselves, and are seen merely as appendages of the adults who look after them, the belief can flourish that adults can treat or mistreat children as they like, and there may be no redress.

There will be times, of course, when it may be better for children that adults take responsibility for decision-making away from them: it may be necessary to protect children, because of their vulnerability, from the damaging consequences of freedoms that they are too young to handle. The right to free speech would be of no benefit to a baby, but would do it no harm. The right to dash into the street free from adult restraint, on the other hand, might lead to a toddler not being around long to enjoy any freedoms at all. However, a compelling argument can be made to support the view that children in our risk-averse society are over-protected and that this prevents them from learning from their own mistakes, and so may ultimately be harmful to them (Gill 2006; Hillman 2006).

'You should be given freedom to do what you want as long as you don't get stupid and start messing around.' (Robert)

Failure to listen to children can be unjust, dangerous and counterproductive. At a deeper level, there is a philosophical weakness too, which is that ignoring the child's voice denies the child's humanity. Campbell comments:

> It is as if the significance of the child could be captured in the image of the adult-to-be, who will one day have an important role to play in society. In the shadow of this future, children's lives are governed and moulded, often to an extent which involves real suffering in the years of childhood. (Campbell 1992, p.16)

If it is wrong to subjugate the needs of a child to those of the adult who is her parent, may it not also be wrong to subjugate them to the needs of the adult who is her future self? There has been a growing view over the last quarter of a century that, to quote Newell (1989), 'Children are people too' and that, if human rights are universal, children, being human, should enjoy them in their own right. Thus, it is as a question of human rights that we find the essential justification for the stress on the voice of the child in national and international law.

What do we mean by human rights?

The concept of human rights has come to be a central one in modern democratic societies. A right lays down a standard of fair treatment that an individual can legally expect. 'Rights are important moral coinage. To have rights is to have dignity and respect. The possessor of rights does not have to grovel. He can demand what is his due' (Freeman 1983, p.212). Human rights, according to Freeman, are necessary to the creation of a fairer society that stresses human dignity; they are mechanisms for empowering the vulnerable, since without rights one cannot count on redress from injustice.

Human rights, as Rosenbaum (1980) has demonstrated, are valued by nations with very different political and cultural systems. This does not mean, however, that we all understand the same thing by the term. Three quite distinct philosophical strands go to make up the meanings underlying the notion of human rights in modern thought: strands associated with liberty, with self-determination and with equality, which themselves can be mutually incompatible (Turner 1990). Human rights have been variously interpreted as political, sociological, moral or religious principles, as opportunities, obligations, benefits, freedoms, powers, and, as a result, such different meanings have accrued to the term that it could be regarded as meaningless outside of the particular historical and political framework in which it is used.

To try to make sense of these diverse understandings human rights are often subdivided by type. Writers on children's rights sometimes talk about the '3 Ps': protection, provision and participation (Bell 2002). 'Protection' covers safeguarding from any type of harm; 'provision' refers to the right to services such as education or health care; 'participation' rights are those under the heading of listening to children: the right to be heard and to take part in decision-making. Freeman (1983) describes the supporters of children's rights as falling into several camps: 'child savers', 'welfarists', 'child liberators' and 'child empowerers'. The 'child savers' are those concerned with protection rights. 'Welfarists' concern themselves with improving the physical conditions of children's lives: their provision rights. Freeman's other two categories, the 'liberators' and the 'empowerers' are the ones who are concerned with participation rights. An example of a 'liberator' would be John Holt. In Holt's (1975) blueprint for how children should be treated in society Freeman (1983) argues that Holt went way beyond what was sensible. Essentially, Holt advocated giving children equal rights with adults. For example, he proposed removing bars on the age at which a person could drive a car, work for money or engage in sexual activities with scant attention to the risks this might entail. Freeman (1983, p.33) concludes that the 'child-liberating' approach is 'politically naive and psychologically wrong'. Freeman's final group are those who support extending children's decision-making powers and giving them a greater say in their lives, but in a gradual way that recognizes the limited capacity of younger children. Children's rights in this sense he sees as part of a good society that values and respects all its members, and develops their potential in the hope of a brighter future.

The most contentious issues in children's rights concern the question of capacity. Can children be entitled to rights that they are not capable of exercising? Should they be permitted to make decisions before they are able to choose responsibly? It can be argued that it is only by being given the freedom to make choices (and perhaps mistakes) that young people can learn to act responsibly: responsibility has been compared with a muscle that has to be exercised if it is to develop (Timms 1997). It is ultimately a question of balance: some protection is necessary if vulnerable young human beings are to survive infancy, but there must be limits to both paternalism and autonomy. Thomas's conclusion is to 'allow that every person has full human rights, but that the *exercise* of those rights varies with the circumstances' (2002, p.47). To demonstrate that this applies to adults as it does to children he gives the example of an adult who is in a coma following a head injury: the adult now needs to exercise rights to protection that he had no need for the day before; conversely, he is suddenly unable to exercise the rights to self-determination that he had previously taken for granted. Reviewing the evidence on children's decision-making capabilities, Thomas concludes that allowing children more self-determination will, overall, lead to better decisions, but that exercising choice has to be practised incrementally. He argues for a concept of 'dynamic self-determination', in which a child's voice is constantly heard but involvement in decision-making grows as the child grows, with his or her wishes being given increasing weight in line with the child's developing competence. A balanced approach to children's rights will thus seek to empower young people, but in a gradual, incremental, age-appropriate manner.

Children's rights, in any case, appear set to be an important influence on child-care thinking into the new century. The challenge will be to achieve a balance: between parents' and children's rights, between self-determination and protection. The child's voice is central to the process, but it has taken a century of public child-care for this to have become accepted.

Answers to quiz in Reflective Exercise 1.1

In the United Kingdom (2007) a person may legally:

- marry at 16 with parental consent or at 18 without
- be employed at 13, or younger in theatre or agriculture
- buy cigarettes at 16
- get tattooed at 18
- vote at 18
- adopt a child at 21
- have a shotgun certificate at 14
- buy fireworks at 18
- drive a car at 17.

Chapter 2

Children's Rights Through History

Children as chattels

It has been a long road to bring children's rights as far as they have come. Centuries-old attitudes that saw youth as a potentially dangerous, subversive force requiring containment had to be overcome, and this did not happen overnight. (Nor are such attitudes yet completely dead.)

In ancient Rome, a father had the right to kill, sell or abandon his child. Under the Massachusetts 'Stubborn child' law of 1646 a child who cursed a parent could face the death penalty, and similar acts remained on the statute books in a number of US states into the 19th century. In 18th-century Australia, the law 'did not recognise children as separate legal persons. Rather, children were seen simply as the property of their fathers…there was no legal interference in the rights of the father over his child' (Sidoti 2005, p.17). Legislation to outlaw abuse of animals (the Cruelty to Animals Act 1829), predated child protection legislation in Britain by 60 years. In 1874 in the United States a similar situation existed. There being no law against cruelty to children, an outraged neighbour brought an action against the parents of the child Mary Allen, who had been savagely beaten, under the legislation on cruelty to animals: the justification used was that a child, as a human, was a member of the animal kingdom and so was covered by the law! This case was an important landmark in the achievement of rights to protection for children in the United States and opened the door for legislation against child maltreatment.

Meanwhile, in Britain, the patriarchal state allowed children very little control over their own destiny. The Agar Ellis case in 1878 was an important test case, which established how few rights children (or, for that matter, women) had. The mother in the matter had custody of the children following divorce but her ex-husband wanted to dictate what religion they were to be brought up in. The judge found for the father and against the wishes of both mother and children. He refused in fact even to hear what the wishes of the children were (they were aged 9, 11 and 12, and were all female) as he ruled their views were not relevant to his decision, and stated in his summing up: 'The right of a father to the…control of his children is one of his most sacred rights' (cited in Berger 1971, p.158).

The rise of children's rights in Britain

The Cruelty to Children Act of 1889 outlawed ill-treatment, neglect or abandonment of children by parents in England and Wales and as such was hailed as a 'Children's Charter'. Berger (1971, p.161) describes it as 'the first glimmering of an idea that children had any rights at all'. Subsequent child-care legislation over the next century added to its provisions but did little to assist young people's self-determination:

> The whole wording of the Acts is in terms of acting on behalf of children and not in supporting a child in its efforts to grow up… Legislation which had respect for children as full human beings would…have written into it the right of children to be consulted directly about their situations. (Berger 1971, p.164)

The concept of a 'Children's Charter' surfaces again and again in the children's rights movement. As long ago as 1924 Eglantyne Jebb, the founder of the Save the Children Fund, drew up a *Declaration of the Rights of the Child*, which was subsequently adopted by the League of Nations (Fuller 1951). Although it talks of 'rights', it is entirely concerned with rights to protection and provision. It is noticeable that it is written throughout in the passive voice: the child must *be helped, be fed, be protected*. These rights are ascribed to children by adults. There is nothing for children to do for themselves: there are no participation rights here, no voice, no self-determination. Nevertheless, asserting a right to services was a necessary step on the road, and its significance should not be denied.

For the United Nations to come out in support of a more political definition of children's rights took several more decades. The idea was first floated in 1979 but from first draft to adoption took ten years of negotiation. The United Nations Convention on the Rights of the Child (United Nations 1989) was ratified by an unprecedented number of states, and this was a 'Children's Charter' with a commitment to all three types of right. Lansdown (1992, p.4) summarizes what was new about it: 'Perhaps the most radical feature of the UN Convention is its acknowledgment of children's civil and political liberties and their rights to participation in society'.

Article 12, which guarantees to children the right to be heard, is described by Lansdown as the Convention's 'lynchpin'.

Unfortunately, though described as 'binding' on all signatories, the Convention lacks teeth: there are no effective sanctions if states sign up but then flout its principles. Domestic legislation, on the other hand, does have a binding effect on the citizens of a country, and so the changes in laws of individual states may prove of more lasting significance for the children of the world. In the case of the United Kingdom, by the time it ratified the UN Convention, national legislation giving children a voice was ready for implementation: the Children Act 1989. The international negotiation that culminated in the Convention was one influence on the British government. More significant were domestic pressures.

By the late 1970s it had become clear that child-care law was excessively complex and shot through with contradictions. The Short Committee was set up by the government to look into the possibilities for reform. Its report gives clear indications of how the tide was turning towards allowing more civil rights to minors:

> The idea that a child belongs to his family, to the extent that it denotes ownership, is no longer generally accepted as valid. Children belong to families by virtue of identifying with them, not by virtue of ownership. However young, a child is an independent person with a complete and separate identity. The State exercises a protective function over the child's right to the extent that a child is less than fully capable of self-determination as an individual. (Social Services Committee 1984, Para. 16)

The Short Report advocated greater involvement of children in decision-making processes and access to a complaints procedure.

Most of the recommendations of the Short Report were incorporated into the 1989 Act or its accompanying regulations and guidance. Other issues intervened, however, that ensured that children's rights were not as central an issue for the legislators as they had been for the members of the Short Committee. During the 1980s in Britain, there were a series of well-publicized child-abuse scandals: notably Jasmine Beckford, Tyra Henry and Kimberley Carlile (London Borough of Brent 1985; London Borough of Greenwich 1987; London Borough of Lambeth 1987), which put child protection right back centre-stage, and ensured that

'I wanted to go and live with my dad. I was seven or eight. I wasn't that young. At that age I should have been listened to but I wasn't.'
(Kerry)

strengthening powers of local authorities and clarifying inter-agency procedures in child-abuse investigations would be high on the agenda for the
Children Bill. As an aside, it is notable that in each of these cases a failure to
listen to the voice of the child contributed to the tragedy.

Perhaps the most significant influence of all, however, was Cleveland.
In a few months in 1987, sexual abuse was diagnosed by two paediatricians
in 121 children from 57 families in the county of Cleveland in Northeast
England, and most were removed from home and taken into care.
Child-care services in the area virtually collapsed under the weight of
numbers and most of the children eventually returned home. The main issue
arising from this child-care scandal in the eyes of the public was essentially
one of parents' rights. The media presented an image of rampant, unbridled
social workers snatching hapless children from loving families and
whisking them into care. That the ensuing enquiry report (Secretary of State
for Social Services 1988) demonstrated that a lot of the media reporting to
have been inaccurate made no difference. The image stuck. Gledhill (1989,
p.27), of the right-wing Centre for Policy Studies, probably spoke for the
public mood of the time when he asserted that there was 'a widespread
acceptance of the need to curb social workers' arrogation of powers to
themselves' and that more power needed to be returned to parents. This
view had the effect of increasing the stress on parents' rights and constrain-
ing local authorities' powers in the legislation that eventually emerged.

For professionals working in the field of child sexual abuse there were
lessons to be learnt from the Cleveland debacle too, but not necessarily the
same ones. One was the crucial importance for all agencies involved in the
investigation of allegations of child sexual abuse to cooperate closely.
Another was that dire consequences can ensue for a child who is not
respected – who is treated as 'an object of concern' rather than as a person.
Cleveland provided devastating evidence of the suffering it could cause
children if their civil rights were disregarded. The report gave examples of
children not being consulted, of their wishes and feelings being ignored, of
them being medically examined against their will. There were accounts of
children repeatedly interviewed or examined and feeling under pressure to
make 'disclosures'. There was moving testimony from the young people of
their distress, confusion and anger at their treatment – all of which was
unquestionably well-intentioned and meant by the harassed and over-
whelmed social workers, police and health care staff to be for their protection. Perhaps Gledhill (1989, p.18) has a point when he talks about: 'the
tyranny of the compassionate mind'.

The Cleveland Report (Secretary of State for Social Services 1988)
probably had a greater bearing on the emphasis on children's civil liberties

in the Children Act 1989 than any other single influence. Among its recommendations were listening carefully to children, respecting their wishes and feelings, explaining to them what is happening and seeking their consent before interviewing or examining them. All of these recommendations were written into the legislation or the accompanying regulations and guidance. The eventual formulation of the Act was in essence a compromise between competing interest groups. Children's rights perhaps came out as well as it did because it appealed to opposing groups for different reasons. Thus, while the left sees service-user rights as a means to the end of empowering the dispossessed (Newell 1989), the right champions them as a means of disempowering professionals (Gledhill 1989). Since both these outcomes may ensue, either side may find they have got more than they bargained for when they try to put children's rights into practice.

The Children Act 1989 aimed to set the scene for child-care practice into the next millennium and obviate the need for further legislation. It achieved the former but not the latter. Since then, we have seen a series of enactments in the United Kingdom on family law, youth offending, education, child protection, young carers, care standards and adoption, culminating with a whole new Children Act only 15 years later in 2004. Several new influences affected the way legislation developed. The first was the body of research evidence (Department of Health 1995), which drew attention to the fact that all the hostile media attention received by social workers as a result of child-abuse scandals had led to increasingly defensive practice with an excessive reliance on procedures in an attempt to cover agencies' backs. Official policy since 1995 has been to encourage a 'refocusing' of services towards prevention. However, there is room for scepticism as to how far this has been achieved (Hobbs, Kaoukji and Little 2006).

The second influence on recent legislation has been a move towards managerialism. International evidence, for example from Australia and the United States (Fattore and Turnbull 2005; Mayall 2005), would suggest that this trend has not only been apparent in the United Kingdom. The managerial approach stresses accountability and focuses on measurable outcomes in an attempt to drive performance up. Not all commentators are impressed by its impact, however. Jordan (2006) argues that it warps the priorities of schools; Bell (2002)'s view is that it devalues the relationship skills that are central to listening to children and Munro (2001, p.130) claims that it 'limit[s] the power of social workers to respond to children's individual preferences…[and so] may paradoxically be creating obstacles to their empowerment'.

The most significant influence on the Children Act 2004, however, was the death of Victoria Climbié, a little girl from West Africa ironically sent to

Britain by her parents for a better future than they could give her themselves. She was tortured and murdered by the couple caring for her, numerous agencies having had contact with the family without recognizing the danger Victoria was in. It was identified in the ensuing enquiry report (Laming 2003) that there had been a failure to focus on Victoria as an individual and to hear her voice, but the main thrust of the report was the fragmented structure of the agencies providing children's services and the poor communication between professionals, hence the emphasis of the report on the need for changes in the structures for service delivery. The central feature of the ensuing Children Act 2004 thus became proposals for new service structures, rather than for how services are delivered. It was refreshing to see systems and management held primarily accountable for a child's death rather than individual front-line workers. However, this approach also may produce unintended consequences since a 'focus on structures, not skills, not only curtails professional involvement, but also militates against skill development' (Morris and Shepherd 2000, p.171). Guidance on consulting with and listening to children notwithstanding, The Children Act 2004 thus continues the move towards a procedural and managerial rather than a professional approach, which may have the effect of detracting from rather than enhancing children's rights.

Dissenting views

Legislation increasing children's rights has not been universally applauded. One view is that children's wishes have been given too much influence. Increasing children's power can, of course, bring them into head-on conflict with other interest groups. More control for children means less for adults, hence the backlash against increased rights for children that ensued as the public belatedly caught on to the implications of some of the changes brought in, or thought to have been brought in, by the Children Act 1989. For example, much hostile publicity was given in the press to the suggestion that children could 'divorce' their parents, while there was never any such provision in the Act. Parents blamed the Act for their lack of control over their teenagers: 'The Children Act 1989 allowed [my 14-year-old daughter] the right to make the reckless and dangerous decision to leave home while I as her mother had no rights and no control…[because] the "rights" of the child were paramount' (Lloyd Scott 2000, p.2). This indicates a misunderstanding of the law: it is not children's rights but their welfare that is paramount, and the Children Act did not change the perennial problem that it is sometimes hard to make adolescents behave as their parents would wish. Legislation does sometimes, however, provide a useful scapegoat for the trials of parenting.

The rights to complaint that young people have gained can be unpopular with social care staff (Aiers and Kettle 1998), and teachers and police can feel they are losing control when young people 'know their rights' (Bennett 1994). These groups betray a fear of children as a destabilizing force felt by many adults in Britain and worldwide. (See Bolzan 2005 for an Australian perspective on this phenomenon.) They are not alone, however, in feeling that the legislation gives an unhelpful degree of self-determination to young people. O'Quigley (2000) examined the evidence on whether children's voices were heard in private law cases, as they should be under the Family Law Act 1996, and concluded that they were not. The view of the judiciary, solicitors and Divorce Court Welfare Officers (now known as Children's Guardians) responsible for implementing the law appeared to be that it might put children under too much pressure to attempt to ascertain their views. The requirements of the legislation were therefore quietly ignored.

The Children Act 1989 has also been criticized on the opposite grounds: that its provisions do not empower children enough. As King and Piper (1990) argue, the appeal to 'rights' in legal proceedings rarely clarifies matters, given that child-care disputes are generally messy affairs of conflicting opinions rather than clear-cut cases of right and wrong. The court's authority is undermined by the dependence on expert opinion, since what has to be decided is not really a question of rights at all, but of 'whose conception of the child's needs should prevail' (p.70). The fact that the child's welfare is accorded a higher priority than his or her wishes causes them to question how much the legislation really does empower children.

The UN Convention on the Rights of the Child also has its detractors: Boyden (1990) points out that the globalization of the children's rights discourse through the UN Convention means that children are increasingly seen internationally to be entitled to welfare rights as defined by Western welfare professionals. 'Rights', however, like 'childhood' and indeed 'welfare' are culturally relative terms. The ideal of education for all may not be welcomed by the Third World family dependent on a working child's earnings, nor indeed by the child who gains status and independence through earning power (Miljeteig 2005). It is for this reason that Stephens (1995) describes the UN Convention as 'colonizing': exporting a Eurocentric view of childhood. The Convention is Western also in its stress on the individual rather than the collective, which as Kjørholt et al. (2005) argue is philosophically based in a neo-liberal view of market forces and risks undervaluing the importance of interdependence and mutual support. John

(1995) attacks the Convention from another angle: she asks why children were not involved in writing it and why it does not give them more political rights, including the right to participate in running their schools.

The implication of these arguments is that the claims of the children's rights discourse should, like all claims, be viewed critically and not accepted wholesale. These critics of the Convention do not reject the concept of rights for children, or all attempts to promote children's rights through legislation. They support any attempt to combat oppression while pointing out that each approach has its limitations and may be capable of operating oppressively in unintended ways. My view is that we should continue to respect young people and to do our honest best to empower them, while recognizing that meaningful involvement of the powerless is very difficult to achieve. The next chapter considers what we mean by participation and how far current policy and practice have actually gone in achieving it for children.

Chapter 3

Listening to Children Now

As already noted, there is more to listening than simply hearing what someone says. Children themselves want to be able not only to express their views but also to see changes result from them. Article 12 can be seen as the cornerstone of the UN Convention on the Rights of the Child (UNCRC), yet according to John (2005, p.11): 'the most challenging aspect of the realization of the UNCRC for governments, policy-makers, researchers and practitioners alike, has been how to honour and facilitate participation by children'. Why should this be?

Eating spinach

Participation, as Arnstein (1969) observed in a seminal article four decades ago, is rather like eating spinach. Everyone is in favour of eating spinach in principle, because it is well known to be good for you. The problem is that, Popeye aside, many of us don't actually like spinach all that much. So it is with participation. The UK government has brought out a 'torrent of initiatives' (Lewis and Porter 2004, p.191) on children and participation in recent years so that things have reached the stage where listening to children can be described as the new orthodoxy (McLeod 2007b). Social work training courses are full of rhetoric about anti-oppressive practice and empowerment, partnership and participation, but when researchers look at the work actually carried out by social work agencies in Britain, true examples of partnership practice turn out to be thin on the ground. This is not just an issue for British social work. Te One, writing about education in New Zealand, says teachers claim to be in favour of children's participation in the educational process but 'teachers' talk and teachers' actions are not the same thing' (2006, p.19) Policy-makers talk of participation rights but fail to ensure they are implemented: 'It is not enough to say what the child's rights are – the child's experience is what matters' (Te One 2006, p.19). What, then, do we mean by 'participation', and what evidence is there that the rights given to children by the legislation are actually being realized in practice?

Ladders of participation

Arnstein, in her 1969 article on citizen participation in urban planning processes drew up what she called a 'ladder of participation'. This was a diagram illustrating how many purposes and activities could be graced with the title of 'participation' and how these could be ordered into a hierarchy with the least true involvement of participants on the bottom rungs of the ladder and the most at the top. A number of writers have made attempts to adapt Arnstein's model to the field of children's rights (Sinclair 2000). One of the simplest and clearest of these attempts is that of Shier (2001) as shown in Figure 3.1.

Children share power and responsibility for decision-making
Children are involved in decision-making processes
Children's views are taken into account
Children are supported in expressing their views
Children are listened to

Figure 3.1 Shier's ladder

Shier omits Arnstein's lowest rungs, relating to tokenistic activities that are not really participation at all, and then distinguishes between the steps on the way to fully involving a child in a decision. He starts from the point at which adults listen to what children have to say about an issue, since without this first step no real involvement can happen (though without further action this too can be perceived as tokenistic). Shier's next stages lead through supporting children to express their views, taking these views into account and involving them in decision-making processes, up to the point where power and responsibility for making a decision is fully shared between adults and children.

Not everyone agrees that it is helpful to view participation as a hierarchy: activities represented by lower rungs, such as consultation, may be more appropriate ways of participating than those on higher rungs in certain circumstances (Spicer and Evans 2006). Some writers prefer to describe participation as a 'continuum' (Franklin and Sloper 2006), a circle (North West Quality Protects Reference Group 2002), or a jigsaw puzzle, all pieces of which have to be present and fit correctly with each other if the process is to work (Wright *et al.* 2006). What is attractive about Shier's model, though, is that it highlights how it is possible for participation to occur at different levels, while to an extent each level is dependent on those beneath. It would not be possible, for example, for children to take part in decision-making processes without their views being taken into account, whereas their views could be taken into account by adults making a decision without the children having any direct involvement in the making of that decision at all.

Bottom up or top down?

A number of writers on participation unfavourably compare projects where the impetus for children's involvement comes from above (for example, from a government directive to include children more) with those where it comes from below (for example, from young people organizing themselves around a common cause and demanding changes) (Dalrymple 2003; Ward 2000). The implication is that grassroots pressures will be truer to what the proponents really want and need, and that adult-directed initiatives will be built on adults' terms, which will skew the outcomes. Badham (2004) cites as an example a UK government-funded project established to promote young people's active democratic involvement as young citizens, which refused to support these same young people when they wished to protest against the government's policy in Iraq!

The user-led bottom-up model may not always be effective when one is dealing with the most vulnerable and least powerful groups in society, however. Jacobs (2006), in an article on participation in health care in the Netherlands, acknowledges that the requirement for bureaucracies to make their services reliable and predictable, conflicts with the maverick results of following service-users' agendas and that true bottom-up initiatives are impossible when funding priorities are decided from the top. Nevertheless, she argues, what matters most is outcome rather than process, and people can be empowered by taking part even when someone above has decreed the limits of their participation. Ethnic minority children in the Netherlands were a group that was hard to reach, was not organized and had no collective voice. Their participation in health-care planning was minimal and to wait for them to organize themselves and demand better services could have taken forever. They were not recruited directly to the health-care project she describes but through their parents, and the children had no involvement in the project design, which she acknowledges could have been disempowering. Nevertheless, there was evidence from outcomes that the children who participated in the project benefitted in terms of control over their own health care and that they were also able to have an influence on service provision.

A question of relationship

Another way of asking 'When is participation not participation?' involves looking at the relationship between the adult or organization encouraging the activity and the child who is, or is not involved. Bell (2002) uses a model of relationship culled from attachment theory to explain why the children and young people involved in child protection procedures in her study did not feel empowered. Relationships between infants and their parents or other primary attachment figures can be described as 'supportive/compan-ionable' (SC) or 'dominant/submissive' (DS). The former is characterized by secure, mutually responsive and unthreatening interactions, with the child seeking care when needed; the latter by defensive and controlling approaches from the adult demand-ing compliance from the child, a lack of trust and unmet needs. SC relation-ships are associated with securely attached children and DS ones with insecure patterns of attachment.

'Sometimes social workers can be quite intimidating: "Come over here! We want to ask these questions!" I've got a teacher like that: she just looks at me and I think I must have done something wrong.' (Patrick)

Bell's (2002) research demonstrates that where social workers related to children in SC ways the children were more likely to feel that the social worker had helped them, and outcomes for them were better. However social workers operate within systems and 'the dominant value-base of social services departments today is business efficiency rather than the human rights of children' (p.2). The child protection procedures required by their organizations tended to discourage SC behaviours and encourage DS ones. Children caught up in investigations did not understand what was happening, they were afraid and felt they had lost control of their lives. Structures for involving children in child protection conferences disempowered the children, making them less rather than more able to fight their own corner. 'Situations where adults are perceived as controlling the interaction and holding power reinforce and reactivate the child's sense of powerlessness, making it even more difficult for them to express their wishes and feelings' (Bell 2002, p.6).

The implications of this research are important: it is not enough for individual professionals to try to listen to the young people they work with; they also need also to be located within listening organizations (Wright *et al.* 2006). And there is another significant point that arises from Bell's work: the essence of relationship is that it is a two-way process. The young people who had the worst outcomes in Bell's study were those who trusted nobody enough to form a relationship of any kind with them; for them the only way they could find of taking some control over the process was to refuse to engage with it. It is not enough for professionals to offer a supportive and companionable relationship to help young people through their difficulties; the young people also have to accept the offer; they have to choose to participate. Thus, effective participation has to be *both* a top-down *and* a bottom-up process.

While most of the literature extols the value of participating as against *not* participating, Kelley (2006) is more concerned with the quality of the experience and warns that if young people's willingness to take part is exploited by the unscrupulous or the misguided, only

> 'I can say whatever I want but I'm wasting my breath – nobody listens. There isn't any point when it's all decided.'
> (Steven)

disillusion and cynicism will result. Involving children and young people is not, she argues, a binary question of whether children are heard or not heard. The crucial questions concern how well they are heard and how adults respond to the views they express. The evidence, however, suggests that adults' responses are as yet sadly inadequate.

Current participation practice

In the remainder of this chapter I will summarize what research can tell us about how well adults listen to children, focusing mainly on UK evidence, but with some reference to international experiences. I will consider what we know about children's involvement in decision-making in their own families, in formal contexts such as child protection procedures or court hearings, in schools and in the wider political sphere.

Decision-making in families

Participation, you might think, should begin at home. However, despite Article 12 of the UNCRC having been in place for a decade and a half, it would appear that children's involvement in decisions that affect them in their daily lives remains limited. Hillman (2006) argues that children are overprotected: one in two children in Britain is now driven to school; one in three children under 11 never plays outside; adults increasingly monitor and control all children's activities. The result, he asserts, is that children cannot learn to assess risks or make their own decisions. Christensen (1998), in a Danish study of children's day-to-day involvement in their own health care, concluded that even where children were competent to make decisions, adults rarely allowed them to do so. Families, however, vary widely, and generalizations should not be too sweeping. Leach (2003), in a review of European research on children's participation in family decision-making, identifies significant variations culturally in attitudes to children's decision-making. Parents' views shape the amount of influence allowed to a child; Chinese and Muslim young people have both been found to be more accepting of their parents' judgements than those from other communities. Children are more likely to be given a say in trivial matters than important ones. For example, they might be allowed to choose their own clothes but their parents would decide whether or not they moved house. This parental power to control the level and spheres of children's participation means that the structure of families, even the most liberal ones, is inherently unequal, leading Leach to conclude that the European family cannot be described as democratic.

Conflict resolution

Formal situations involving professional interventions into children's lives require more structured decision-making processes than take place in families, and official guidance is that children should be involved at an age-appropriate level in these processes (Children and Young People's Unit 2001; Department for Education and Skills 2004a; Department of Health 2004). However, there is little consensus, even among child-care professionals, on when to involve children in making decisions. Shemmings (2000) illustrates how widely professionals' attitudes towards children and decision-making can vary: in a questionnaire sent to health visitors and social workers involved in child protection, he asked for their views on the age at which children should be allowed to make a range of decisions, from choosing what television programmes to watch to getting tattooed. There was a striking dichotomy in their answers between those in favour of children's decision-making powers (what Shemmings calls the 'rights' position) and those against (the 'rescue' position). For example, in the case of agreeing to medical treatment the range of answers was from 5 to 18 years, with individuals' answers tending to cluster at the lower or the higher end of the range rather than to fall in the middle. Social workers and health visitors were as likely as each other to fall into either the 'rights' or the 'rescue' camp.

The 'rescue' mentality perhaps explains why practice in involving children does not yet appear to have caught up with policy-makers' aspirations: as already noted, Bell's (2002) research indicates that being involved in child protection procedures can still be a deeply disempowering experience for children. Shemmings (2000) found that while the majority of social workers thought children should attend child protection conferences, many of them believed that children's influence on decisions should be strictly limited. It is questionable therefore how positive an experience of attendance at the meetings could have been for the children.

The Family Group Conference (FGC) is supposed to be a more inclusive and strengths-based model for resolving family disputes, in which the expertise of family members is recognized, so one might expect young people to play a more active role in the way they reach decisions. Both Kiely (2005), writing about the United Kingdom and Standbu (2004) in Norway, found that most children over ten attended FGCs but that few younger ones did, and that, particularly where children were not present, their voices were not always clearly heard, which could lead to worse decisions.

'I was invited to the beginning of the conference but when they actually decided whether you were going to be on the child protection register you had to leave the room, which I found absolutely **awful**. I thought it was so **rude**. They were talking about me!' (Anna)

When child-care issues are so serious that they reach court there is again much evidence suggesting that young people's involvement in decision-making is not optimized. Thoburn (2004) found that few young people involved in care proceedings attended court, though many said they would have liked to; less than half felt they had been listened to or had their rights respected in the court process; less than half of those who attended court said they had been able to speak to the judge.

Care planning

Most research regarding looked-after children's involvement in decision-making has focused around review meetings (see Practice Example 3.1). There has clearly been progress if one takes the long view: in Sinclair's 1984 research, young people were present at only 2 per cent of their reviews. By 1998 this had risen to 55 per cent. Nevertheless, she questions how much real involvement the young people had in the meetings: only one young person in five acted at any point in the meetings she observed as a full partner with the adults. 'Every enhancement in standards simply serves to show how much there is still to achieve', she observes (Sinclair 1998, p.138), concluding: 'While [adults] may feel they are listening, young people do not feel as though they are heard' (Sinclair 1998, p.139).

PRACTICE EXAMPLE 3.1 THE 'CHAIR YOUR OWN REVIEW' PROJECT

An Independent Reviewing Officer (IRO) assisted two teenagers who were looked after in a local authority in Northern England to chair their own review meetings (the statutory meeting to check on the progress of a child in care). They gained so much from this experience that she persuaded managers to agree to a pilot project to extend the experiment to other young people. In partnership with Pathway (leaving care) staff she developed a peer-led programme. Nine looked-after young people aged between 13 and 17 worked with them to draw up and deliver presentations to staff. The young people were trained as trainers and group-work facilitators and they then led training for managers, IROs, other staff and carers and put on a group-work programme for looked-after young people in the 12–15 age group. This addressed the topics: 'Why review?' 'Understanding adults', 'Decision-making and negotiating' and 'Chairing skills'. Materials were produced with tips on managing meetings, entitled *Do you want to be a chair?* and illustrated with different sorts of chairs (armchairs, deckchairs, kitchen chairs).

After this the programme was rolled out into practice and in time could be seen as embedded in the agency's culture, with many looked-after teenagers expecting to chair their own reviews. Implementation was patchy, however, depending on attitudes of staff locally, and it was found essential to have a rolling programme of training to keep it going: meetings did not work well where young chairs were not well prepared. However, evaluation demonstrated that where they were properly prepared and well supported by the adults around them, participating young people benefitted enormously in terms of increased confidence and self-esteem. The leader of the project comments: 'The overall impact of this work has been to alter the balance of power in decision-making with young people. The reason for the young people feeling more confident is due to their experience of being listened to, taken seriously and influencing decisions that directly affect them.'

The review is not, of course, the only point in a child's life in care at which decisions are made, and what research there is suggests that there is scope for developing practice across the board. Leeson's recent study (2007) of the experiences of a small group of adolescent boys in residential care suggests that practice is as poor as ever. She describes a lack of involvement in decisions at all stages of the care-planning process, from coming into care, to choice of placement, to plans about contact with family: 'All reported a feeling that formal processes happened around them with an expectation that they would passively go along with the resultant decisions' (p.273). As a result the young people experienced: 'overwhelming feelings of helplessness' (p.272), together with a lack of self-esteem or sense of agency. 'The boys were all scared of making decisions, did not know how to make them and did not know whom to trust to help them in that process' (Leeson 2007, p.272).

> 'I was asked did I want to go there. I'm not good at making decisions and I didn't want to have to say. But I did think it was good they asked me.' (Patrick)

Schools and participation

Not all children go to court or come into care but almost all attend school, and the opportunities for participation here are manifold. There is evidence that school councils can have benefits for pupils and schools alike: 'Effective class/school councils have a positive impact on the general atmosphere in the school, pupils' behaviour, commitment to learning, and exclusions' (Department for Education and Skills 2004a, p.8). It is also possible, however, for such bodies to be tokenistic, having little influence (Begg 2004). Leoni (2006), p.123) locates the inadequacies of many school councils in their failure to address unequal power relations: '[they] replicate the power dynamic of the classroom where teacher knows the answer and pupils listen'. May (2005, p.30) puts forward a linked argument: 'Whose participation is it anyway?' she asks. More and more detailed guidance has been produced for local authorities on how to involve pupils, and pupil participation is now a statutory requirement in England and Wales under the Education Act 2002. However, the emphasis is always on what the professionals should elicit or promote: 'Ultimately the publications empower practitioners to ascertain, manage and represent the pupils' voice, rather than encouraging practitioners to empower the pupils themselves' (May 2005, p.30).

Involvement in policy and politics

When one looks at the literature on children's involvement in the wider community, policy development and politics, it is the same picture: enthusiastic accounts of inspiring small projects, but larger-scale research indicating that these are the exception and have little impact. A study of young people's contributions to planning processes at a local level in various parts of England and Wales describes a number of promising initiatives: young people as consultants in the development of a parish plan; a children's section in a district plan; teenagers' involvement in planning sports facilities and a local transport strategy; the setting up of a Youth Town Council. Overall, however, it found 'little concrete evidence that adults have taken steps to ensure young people's real involvement in planning' (Forum for Rural Children and Young People 2005, p.7).

Germany appears on the face of it to have a better record than the United Kingdom on involving children in democratic processes: young people's participation has been considerably developed there since the ratification of the UN Convention (see also Practice Example 3.2 on Slovenia). A national children's committee represents children's interests in parliament, young people's representatives are built into local council structures and open fora are organized where any child can express their views. Nevertheless Swiderek (2004, p.88) expresses scepticism about how much influence younger members of the community actually have. Young people's representation is 'not necessarily a confirmation of effective power nor of the quality of children's participation'. Views expressed tend to be filtered and manipulated by adults rather than feeding straight into decision-making processes, with the result that the young people have a 'feeling of being powerless and unable to change anything' (Swiderek 2004, p.93).

PRACTICE EXAMPLE 3.2 THE SLOVENIAN CHILDREN'S PARLIAMENT

Slovenia, a country the size of Wales between Austria, Italy and Croatia, has only had a national government of its own since 1991, and since that time it has had a children's parliament as well as an adult one. The Children's Parliament meets once a year with 100 teenagers representing local communities. A specific topic is chosen each year for debate (issues chosen have included bullying and drug use), schools organize events around the theme and local delegates are selected to attend the country-wide meeting. This is held in the debating chamber of the National Parliament building and is attended by representatives of the government. The young people debate the chosen topic, put questions to ministers and make proposals. They also select the following year's topic. Papers of debates and proposals are published.

Although the young people's views and the publicity they are accorded in the media can have some influence on government thinking, and the process can be seen as 'a foundation course in parliamentary democracy' (Dekleva and Zorga 2004, p.143), the Children's Parliament lacks any power to make decisions, so as an institution it can be seen as educational rather than political.

Involving children effectively depends on being able reliably to identify their views. However, the evidence suggests that lip-service is often paid to the need for consultation with children. Research across a spectrum of services suggests consultation exercises are often poorly designed and/or tokenistic. Cavet and Sloper (2004), in a review of children's involvement in local government, found that consultation was limited and patchy, tended to be confined to trivial issues, its methodology was weak and there was little evidence of impact on the decisions eventually made. Like Franklin and Sloper (2006) they found that socially excluded groups such as disabled children were less likely to be included. Elsey (2004) studied urban planning processes in Scotland and found that young people were largely excluded when the local community was consulted, and where their views were considered they were compartmentalized into areas seen as 'children's issues', such as playgrounds. It was not recognized that the young people, like their parents, had a stake in wider community issues such as housing, transport or leisure facilities. LeFrancois (2007), in an ethnographic study of young people in hospital found that although staff claimed to listen to children's views, they defined the contexts and language in which the views were to be expressed and screened out views seen as unacceptable. Lest it be thought that these disappointing findings apply only to the United Kingdom, Worrall-Davies and Marino-Francis (2007) reviewed all published surveys of user views across child and adolescent mental health services in the United States and Canada, as well as the United Kingdom, and concluded that methodology was unsound and there was very little evidence of them influencing service delivery.

It is easy to feel discouraged by the weight of these findings. Nevertheless, though progress is slow, some writers find grounds for optimism. Cavet and Sloper (2004), while finding only limited examples of good participation practice, detected a movement in attitudes:

> despite shortcomings in the evidence base, the literature reviewed was virtually unanimous in its support for the involvement of young people in public decision-making... Very few major public/voluntary sector organizations serving young people...do not have a policy-level commitment to their participation. (p.618)

Overall, then, despite anecdotal accounts of imaginative initiatives, research would suggest that we are not yet very good at listening to children in practice, whatever the government and professional rhetoric would have us believe. It is against this rather pessimistic backdrop that I present my guide for the professional who wants to learn more about how to listen to children. Communication has emerged as the necessary basis for all listening so in the next part of the book I will move on to what research can tell us about adult–child communication: what promotes it and what gets in the way.

Part 2: Communicating with Children

When I was a child I spake as a child, I understood as a child, I thought as a child; but when I became a man I put away childish things.

1 Corinthians 13:11

Chapter 4

The Developing Child

How can we learn to communicate with children?

Legislation and the imperatives of both ethics and pragmatism may tell us to listen to what children have to say but putting this instruction into practice is not always straightforward. How can one ascertain the wishes and feelings of a baby, a young person with disabilities affecting their ability to communicate, or a truculent teenager who doesn't want to talk to you? Some children have learnt never to trust adults, or have been taught to fear people in authority. When a child refuses to speak it can be, as the Cleveland Report puts it: 'a difficult matter of judgement to know whether the child is not telling because of some sort of pressure, such as fear of the consequences, or because there is nothing to tell' (Secretary of State for Social Services 1988, p.207). Where a child has a disability, or uses a language other than that of the interviewing adult, there may be a need for an interpreter, augmentative communication systems (boards, symbol cards, special computer software systems etc.) or assistance from someone with specific skills or knowledge. Even when children can understand and will talk, they may not give direct answers to direct questions. They may not understand or be able to express clearly the strong but conflicting emotions they are experiencing (Schofield 2005).

'At that time I was very confused. I had sort of a life to sort out again. I sort of wasn't very straight with everything in my head. I wasn't caring about anyone because I was so angry.' (Patrick)

Advice on communicating with children is often unhelpfully vague:

> The key to ascertaining the wishes and feelings of the child is to have the time, skills and patience to really listen to what the child has to say... The issue is...one of the right chemistry between the child and the adult. (Cross, Goosey and James 1991, pp.43–4).

This hardly takes us far enough: how does one 'really' listen? What exactly is 'chemistry'? What are the skills a good communicator requires? To answer these questions we must explore what research can tell us about the nature of communication and the working of human minds.

The study of communication with children crosses the boundaries between psychology, sociology and linguistics, as well as education, social work and the psychotherapies. None of these disciplines can tell us everything about how to communicate with children, and what each says may be disputed by adherents of opposing perspectives. However, a rounded understanding of the topic is more likely to come from considering the different accounts of how human beings communicate, and the criticisms that have been made of each of these accounts, than from assuming that any one perspective has all the answers. This part of the book will therefore look at research on child development, at the sociology of childhood and at theories of direct work with children for the light that each can shed on how we can achieve successful communication with children and young people.

Developmental psychology and its detractors

It is widely argued that staff working with children must have a good grounding in knowledge of child development: the British government clearly thinks so, since it names 'child and young person development' as the second core knowledge area for the child-care workforce, after 'communication and engagement' (Department for Education and Skills 2005). Jones's thorough guide *Communicating with Vulnerable Children* (2003) is solidly based in developmental psychology, as is Garbarino and Stott's useful work *What Children Can Tell Us* (1992). Both these books argue that a professional must have an understanding of all aspects of child development to know what can be expected of a child at a given age and stage of development, and that this knowledge can then be utilized for more effective practice.

The child development model of psychology has, however, been attacked by both feminists and sociologists (Burman 1994; Prout and James 1990). Taylor (2004) summarizes the objections to this model of child development. First, it makes claims to universal truth for its findings on parenting, without acknowledging its own historical and cultural bias or the possibility that its findings may be politically motivated – Bowlby's (1969, 1973, 1980) early findings on 'maternal deprivation' for example, from which attachment theory developed, have been interpreted as a ploy to get women out of the workforce and back into the home in a post-war period of high male unemployment (Rutter 1972). A second criticism is that child development theory has an 'individualizing' tendency, rooted in Western philosophy, which devalues the collective and mutual – individuals then tend to be blamed for problems that may in fact be the result of external forces, such as poverty. Third, it 'operates with a "deficit model" in relation to children, concentrating attention on their limitations and lack of competence' (Taylor 2004, p.229) and consequently underestimates children's capabilities as 'socially competent actors' (Taylor 2004 p.230). Finally, many would argue that evidence based on laboratory experiments into human behaviour (as most of the findings of developmental psychology are) is not transferable to real life contexts. Taylor attacks the government's espousal of child development theory as an underpinning for evidence-based practice by pointing out that the link between the theory and the practice is far from straightforward or clear. For example, she quotes research showing that social workers assessing parenting were less influenced by their knowledge of child development and their observations of parenting practice than by the quality of the relationship they were able to establish with the children's parents and their perception of how cooperative the parents were.

'The older you get, the more likely they are to take note of what you say. Though actually I think a five-year-old knows just as well what they want as a 15-year-old.' (Anna)

Taylor's conclusion is not, however, to deny the relevance of information about child development for child-care professionals, but rather to suggest that they should approach this knowledge in a more critical way, analyse and question it rather than accept it wholesale. With this stricture in mind I therefore present here what research has identified about child development that may help the sceptical practitioner to communicate better with younger people. I do find it hard to rule out entirely a linear model for understanding development, since it seems self-evident that the vast majority of us learn to walk before we can run, and that children who are well fed thrive better than those who are not. Looking at tables of developmental milestones or growth charts can help us see how one child differs from others; it need not imply that we value a person less because their growth does not follow a typical pattern, but it may help us understand them better. I fully agree that we should not accept the findings of 'science' uncritically and that it is right to unpack and challenge hidden bias. Psychology does, however, provide a frame to help us understand child development and this frame can be used to help us achieve more effective communication.

In this chapter, then, I will consider what research can teach us about the most relevant aspects of child development – cognition, memory, language and attachment – before considering what we can learn from observing children's behaviour. I will then consider the evidence on the role of the interaction between worker and child in facilitating or hindering communication between them and the question of whether we can always believe what children say.

Cognition

Of all the 20th-century psychologists, Piaget has been most influential in developing our understanding of cognitive development in childhood. In the Piagetian view, learning is a process of adaptation to the environment in which experience is organized through mental activities. Thought becomes increasingly abstract and internalized as the child approaches adolescence. Piaget postulates a number of cognitive stages through which each young person passes on the road to intellectual maturity. These stages are not necessarily closely tied to chronological age, since children develop at different speeds. However, there is in Piaget's view a strict progression: no young person can reach the final stage without passing through all the intermediate ones in order.

Piaget describes the baby or pre-verbal toddler as at the 'sensory-motor' stage: cognition is entirely concrete, based on feelings and actions, there being no language to represent ideas. Once the child begins to learn language, representational thought becomes possible. However, the pre-school child is still 'pre-conceptual': thinking is distorted to the child's own point of view. A young child who has a problem to solve seeks an answer by trial and error, using practical experimentation rather than logical thought. By the time a child is at primary school he or she is entering the stage of 'concrete operations'; that is to say, he or she has some understanding of categories but explanations tend still to be based on something practical. It is not until secondary school age that Piaget found youngsters could deal with logical abstractions without needing practical examples to illustrate them. Problem-solving could now be achieved through testing mental hypotheses and deduction: the stage of 'formal operations'.

Piaget developed and refined his theories from observation of young children at play, and from simple experiments. Since all were white middle-class Swiss children he has been accused of cultural bias (Burman 1994). The evidence for his theories has also been questioned. Piaget noted that 'conversations' between the children tended to lack logical flow, because they were not really listening to what the other said. From this he formulated his hypothesis of the egocentric thought processes of the young child: 'Each child, whether he is trying to explain his own thoughts, or to understand those of others, is shut up in his own point of view' (1959, p.99).

Young children, however, have had limited life experience, so any attempt to view the world from their perspective requires one to bear in mind that they may be making assumptions about the world around them that a more experienced person would not: 'The child's view is anarchic because without preconceptions. When you do not know what to expect of the world – when everything is astonishing – then anything is possible and acceptable' (Lively 1994, p.viii). However, a range of evidence demonstrates that they are: 'by no means locked in and unaware of others' (Cox 1991, p.155) and Piaget's experiments on children's egocentricity are now being called into question. Donaldson (1978) describes a reworking of one of these experiments, in which Piaget showed a child a three-dimensional model of mountain scenery. He then asked what the model 'explorer' on the opposite side of the 'mountains' could see. The children were baffled by the task, from which Piaget concluded that they were unable to imagine things from another person's perspective. In the reworked experiment, children were shown a model of a house. On the opposite side of the house was placed a toy policeman, who was said to be searching for a naughty boy. Children were given a doll to represent the naughty boy, and told to hide him somewhere in the house where he would be out of sight of the police-man. This time they had no difficulty completing the task, indicating that they could in fact imagine things from the policeman's perspective.

Donaldson concludes that the children in Piaget's experiment failed, not because of their egocentricity, but because the task made no sense to them: everyday life for a four-year-old does not contain mountains or explorers, and there was no apparent reason for the task of imagining the prospect before the explorer. Hide and seek, on the other hand, was a familiar and meaningful activity. She observes:

> All normal children can show skill as thinkers and language users to a degree which must compel our respect, so long as they are dealing with 'real-life', meaningful situations in which they have purposes and intentions and in which they can recognize and respond to similar purposes and intentions in others... These human intentions are the matrix in which the child's thinking is embedded. (Donaldson 1978, p.121)

Donaldson coins the phrase 'human-sense' to describe the characteristic of a situation that is meaningful and where a child can recognize its purpose.

A task may be abstract (see Practice Example 4.1), but a young child may still be able to master it if it makes 'human-sense'. Donaldson concludes that the adult's task is to help children make the step from understanding what is concrete to what is abstract by explaining it in terms that make 'human-sense'. In Parts 3 and 4, I will make suggestions for how the practitioner can communicate with younger children in practical and concrete ways, using explanations that will make sense to them.

PRACTICE EXAMPLE 4.1 EXPLAINING ABSTRACT CONCEPTS – LEILA

Leila was a seven-year-old child with limited English in a London primary school. Ruth, a teaching assistant, was working alongside her to help her understand a science lesson on freezing and melting when she realized that Leila had misunderstood. Ruth describes what she did next:

'I'd been doing work with Leila in a small group on making ice lollies and I knew that in class they'd done things like melting chocolate over a candle flame. I asked her to explain to me how she thought melting happened. She said that things melted in the sun, so I asked why, and she replied "Light". I thought maybe she hadn't understood the words, so I asked her to show me what she meant. She put some water in a dark cupboard to freeze it and took her ice lolly and put it next to the window to melt it. I presume that, whether or not she'd had ideas about freezing and melting before, she'd associated the candle flame as a source of light, and the significance of the freezer to her was that it was a dark box where you shut things up, so although both I and her class teacher had been careful to plan practical work that demonstrated in what we thought was a very clear way what caused freezing, what she had taken away from it was completely different. Only by creating the time to listen to what she thought and letting her express herself in a non-verbal way to confirm that we had communicated properly was I able to connect with her sufficiently for her to modify her ideas. I let her test her dark–light theory, and when that didn't seem to be working asked her to put her hand in the freezer and tell me how it felt and prompted her to remember that we had also used hot water to melt chocolate (and let her repeat that). By the end of the week she had much clearer ideas about what caused melting and freezing.'

The concept of 'human-sense' is thus closely tied in with what is a familiar experience for a given child, which itself will be rooted in the cultural context. The work of the Russian psychologist Vygotsky stresses the importance of the social context in which learning and communication take place, and from this perspective a further criticism made of Piaget's work is its failure to make sufficient allowances for the effect of the context on a child's understanding. (Wertsch 1985). Hundeide notes that a child asked by a teacher in the classroom why wood floats quoted Archimedes' Law. The same child, asked the same question by another adult out of school, replied 'Because it's light'. The questioner might wrongly have assumed the child was not aware of, or did not understand, Archimedes' Law: 'The correct logical procedure seems to have been embedded in a social episode involving a formal classroom setting with an authoritarian teacher posing the questions. It is a special game in a special setting' (Hundeide 1985, p.307).

This notion of interaction as a 'game' governed by rules is important if we are to understand why children do not always answer as we expect. Young children are often, for example, puzzled when adults ask them questions to which they (the adults) clearly already know the answers and their response in such a situation is often to say nothing. If children do not yet understand the cultural conventions governing speech, the onus is on the adult to see things from the child's point of view. Hundeide's argument is that Piaget often got locked into an adult's-eye view and so misinterpreted the child's position.

'You should be thinking what the child feels like. Put yourself in their shoes and imagine what you'd do in their situation.' (Kerry)

Piaget's work on children's cognition was groundbreaking, and for many years unassailable. The fact that some of his findings have been questioned does not invalidate the mass of his work, which contributed greatly to our understanding of the child's mind, rather it clarifies and adds depth to it. Basic requirements of communication with younger children remain that we hold our conversations with them in a familiar context, explain the reasons for our involvement, keep subject matter practical, avoiding abstractions as far as possible and link all explanations into the child's own experience.

Memory

If we are to understand children's needs, we may have to elicit information from them about past events and we must be able to judge the accuracy of what they tell us. This in turn depends, not only on their ability to understand and express themselves, but also on their ability to remember. Children's memory has received quite extensive research attention, due to the high political profile given to the issue of children as witnesses in legal proceedings. Many of the findings of this research have relevance for adults seeking to communicate well with children.

Young children were formerly thought to be very unreliable witnesses. An influential article written by a Belgian, Varendonck, in 1911 offered evidence that children were highly suggestible and argued that their testimony should therefore be dismissed: 'When are we going to give up, in all civilized nations, listening to children in courts of law?' (Varendonck [1911] 1984, p.27). This view held ascendancy through much of the 20th century and is one reason for the historical reluctance of courts to lend credence to a child's statement. However, Varendonck's arguments can now be seen to be seriously flawed. His article criticizes the conviction in a celebrated case of rape and murder, which hung on the identification evidence of two young children. These children, it appears, were taken out of their beds at three in the morning, told who the suspect was, and then asked: 'You saw Monsieur M., didn't you?', to which they replied 'Yes'. Varendonck relates several 'experiments' he carried out with groups of children in which he asked leading questions and elicited inaccurate answers. He concludes that children will always give the answer that they think is wanted, and so evidence based on their statements is unsafe. What Varendonck failed to do was to make any comparison with adults, and it is now clear that adults too can give inaccurate answers in response to social pressures. Obviously the conviction in the case Varendonck describes was unsafe, but this is because the methods used to make an identification of the suspect were unacceptable, not because the witnesses were children.

Current knowledge on children and suggestibility proves to be quite complex. It is summarized in Jones (2003). Both children and adults are now known to be suggestible; young people of ten years and upwards are no more suggestible than adults, the evidence on whether younger children are more suggestible is conflicting and, furthermore, there are wide individual differences, with less confident children and those under stress being more inclined than others to 'go along with' suggestions made to them by adults. The role of the interviewer is crucial: children are more vulnerable to suggestion where an adult asks leading questions or communicates their own moral judgements. The implications are clear: anybody interviewing a child and needing accurate answers must strive to keep an open mind and school themselves never to suggest to the child what answer they are expecting.

There are nevertheless very real difficulties in establishing what is an acceptable way to question children to discover the truth about their experiences. Memory is not one skill, but a complex of related ones and sophistication in their use develops steadily with age. Young people of 12 years and over can be expected to have similar memory skills to adults, younger children may be less skilled, particularly at organizing their memories so that they can deliberately recall them on request (Garbarino and Stott 1992). The evidence from research into young children's free recall of real-life situations is that it is accurate, and that familiarity aids recall. Chess-playing children, for example, have a better memory for chess positions than non-chess-playing adults, so adults' apparently better memories may simply reflect their wider experience: more things are familiar to them (Johnson and Foley 1984). The emotional significance of events influences their recall: where the experience in question is 'salient', memories are likely to be vivid and accurate. There can be few experiences more significant for a child than witnessing the murder of a parent, and interviews with children following such an experience can elicit: 'indelible, highly accurate and detailed visual images' (Pynoos and Eth 1984, p.95).

Younger children, however, recall less detail spontaneously than do adults or adolescents. This is probably because they cannot so easily retrieve a specific memory at will. However, what information they do provide in spontaneous recall is likely to be as accurate as that provided by adults. This finding presents us with a dilemma. Analysis of normal speech of pre-school children shows that communication of a memory is almost always triggered by a discernible external cue, such as a place, person or object that reminds them of it (Cole and Loftus 1987). To assist little children to talk about their experiences we should therefore provide 'triggers' to promote recall: for example, a photo of the mother before discussing the child's feelings about her. However, the government's guidelines for interviewing child witnesses (Home Office *et al.* 2002) explicitly warn against the use of props as triggers, since for legal purposes these may be viewed as 'leading'.

A linked issue is that of younger children's reluctance to answer 'I don't know'. Children's ability to identify a person they have met before does not appear to be much worse than that of adults. However, when asked to pick out a known person from a group *not* containing that person, children under 12 are twice as likely as older people to give a false-positive identification: they seem to feel some answer is expected of them and find it difficult to admit they cannot provide one. Cole and Loftus's (1987) suggestion is to routinely make it explicit to a child that it is acceptable to give no answer, perhaps by first giving them a set of pictures of other people and asking them to say which is a picture of themselves. Such techniques could be useful whenever putting questions to a child: they must be made aware that if they do not know the answer it is all right to say so.

Language

Language, like cognition and memory, is a complex of skills that develops over time from the one-word utterance of the toddler to the subtle and complex word-play of the adolescent. When working with a very young child one often faces the difficulty that the child has limited language as well as limited understanding, which can compound their difficulty in self-expression. Indeed, cognitive development and linguistic development are closely linked. As Chomsky (1959) demonstrated, innate cognitive faculties play a significant part in language acquisition. However, learning to speak is not something the child achieves in isolation, but through interaction: Macnamara argues that understanding always precedes language: 'Infants learn their language by first determining, independent of language, the meaning which a speaker intends to convey to them and by then working out the relationship between the meaning and the language' (Macnamara 1972, p. 1). Language learning, he asserts, is achieved via an understanding of context, nothing is learnt independent of its meaning. This clarifies why concrete explanations and a comprehensible context are necessary preconditions for a young child's understanding of an utterance and why figurative language can lead to confusion. Language should be kept literal and simple when talking with young children: long words and complicated concepts should be avoided.

This also explains why body language is such an important element of communication. Emotions are often communicated (sometimes unconsciously) through demeanour. Younger children are sensitive to body language and confused when the emotion expressed in words is at variance with that communicated by tone or posture (Jones 2003), so awareness of body language is important for good interviewing. However, misunderstanding can work both ways: an adult can fail to grasp a child's meaning, as well as vice versa. At its most basic level, this may be because of a young child's imperfect articulation, making their speech hard to follow. Melton and Thompson (1978) quote research suggesting that even familiar teachers misinterpret 10 per cent of what young children say. With unknown adults this proportion is likely to be much higher. It is advisable therefore when talking with pre-school children to have a familiar adult present, both to help the child relax and to act as an 'interpreter'.

'Adults should talk in your language, not like you're a baby. Like, when they see I'm my age and they say things like "bunny-rabbit". Or things that are too complicated like "the chairperson of this review is required to..."' (Patrick)

Another cause of misunderstanding can be when children use words in unexpected ways. An example from my own practice will illustrate. A four-year-old saying 'Me and Billy was shagging' led to a social worker being called in to investigate possible sexual abuse. However, when asked what the word meant the child explained that 'shagging' meant holding hands and jumping up and down! All conversations with children require circumspection: practitioners must always check out what children mean by the terms they use, not assume the meaning is self-evident; when working with children from a different social, cultural or linguistic background this will be particularly important. Since children may be unaware that they have not made themselves clear, or that they have failed to understand, the onus is on the adult to check out constantly that both parties to the communication have understood each other. Language can be treacherous, nevertheless we cannot function without it. Many terms we use routinely ('care' for example, or 'need') are culturally loaded (Woodhead 1990), but we do have to speak to carry out our jobs. What practitioners must do is to take care with language, explore the meaning of the words used with and by service-users and ruthlessly examine their own thoughts for unconscious bias.

Attachment

The theory of attachment, developed from the work of Bowlby (1969, 1973, 1980), examines the role of the relationship between the infant and parent or carer in shaping the child's subsequent development. Attachment behaviour (crying, clinging, following), activated by stress, is seen as an innate adaptive response that ensures the infant's survival through keeping the caregiver close and thus more able to protect. A securely attached child has the confidence to leave the caregiver when no danger threatens and explore the environment, and an inner representation of the attachment figure is thought to help in self-regulation and conscience development as the child matures. Different patterns of attachment and behaviour develop in children who have been parented in different ways, depending in particular on whether the parent/carer is warm and accepting or cold and rejecting and on how consistent their responses are. Consistency in parenting promotes the child's cognitive development, while warmth promotes emotional development. A balance between the two is linked to secure attachment and healthy all-round development. An interesting and accessible explanation of this theory can be found in Howe *et al* (1999).

This theory might not at first sight appear to have a direct bearing on communication. However, its proponents argue that attachment impacts on all human behaviour: 'More than just another approach to children's social and emotional development, it is the theory that subsumes and integrates all others. It is a relationship-based theory of personality development and our psycho-social progress through life' (Howe *et al.* 1999, p.10). Crittenden (1997) asserts that differential patterns of attachment affect the way individuals learn, remember, think and communicate, so that an understanding of attachment is essential for any adult working with children (or indeed with adults). Among other differences, she argues that the child who has been inconsistently handled is likely to talk more but less logically, to express more emotion and to demand attention, whereas the child who has been rejected may withdraw from human relationships, deny and suppress emotions and communicate as little as possible. Crittenden's view is that the way individuals process information affects the way they speak and that the analysis of their speech, paying attention to such issues as how much they say, how emotionally 'true' it appears and the way certain information is omitted or distorted, gives clues to their history and psychological well-being.

'My mum always says I "take umbrage" when things don't go my way. I don't say anything, but the dog hides.'
(Patrick)

Attachment theory has been very influential in the development of child-care practice and its impact will be considered further in Chapter 6 and in Parts 3 and 4.

Observing children

Communication is not just about words. Children express themselves, sometimes without being aware they are doing it, in a range of ways, only one of which is language. To make a reliable assessment of a child's view it is rarely enough just to ask them, and the younger the child, the truer this is. To get the full picture one should look at the whole child in all contexts: study her life history, take note of her health and growth rate and whether she has reached developmental milestones, consider her emotional well-being, attachments, educational progress, leisure activities and self-care skills (Department of Health 2003). Clues can be picked up by the astute observer from the child's behaviour and demeanour: adequate ascertainment of wishes and feelings requires sensitivity to all the ways in which a young person may be communicating his view (see Practice Example 4.2).

PRACTICE EXAMPLE 4.2 ASCERTAINING WISHES AND FEELINGS – ELLA

I was once asked for an opinion on whether Ella, an eight-year-old girl in foster care, should be placed for adoption together with her younger brother. Normally I would be opposed to the separation of siblings but the circumstances here were unusual. The two children had been living apart for some time and there was a history of marked rejection of the girl by the mother, dating back to birth and even before. The son, on the other hand, had been favoured by the mother, who had only recently given up on the attempt to care for him. When I asked Ella what she wanted she told me she loved her brother and wanted to be with him. Her behaviour, however, told me otherwise. When I saw them together they competed with more than normal sibling rivalry: they attacked and fought each other with a ferocity that made me fear for the little boy's safety. In one of my sessions with Ella I initiated a game with two rag dolls, who I said were a big sister and a little brother, and I asked her to make up a story about them. Her story involved the two dolls fighting, the girl doll winning, and then Ella physically jumping up and down on the boy doll and throwing it away. If I had relied just on what this child told me about her feelings for her brother I do not think I could have achieved an accurate assessment of the situation.

Observing a child's play, particularly fantasy play, can be seen to provide particularly rich insights into a child's inner world. Interpretation must, however, be made with care since the functions of play are complex and not fully understood (Millar 1968). It would be unwise to jump to conclusions about what a child is communicating through it. Scenes a child acts out may give us clues about their past experiences, or their wishes for the future; these scenes may represent what has actually happened, what they wish would happen, or a confusion of events and feelings that they are struggling to make sense of. Observation is thus a valuable tool, but one that should always be employed with caution.

Yarrow and Wexler (1979, p.32) survey evidence on observation and conclude that, though the human observer can be sensitive and flexible, giving us a subtle, in-depth account of what they have seen, he or she is also: 'a poor scientific instrument: non-standard, not readily calibrated and often inconsistent and unreliable'. For example, they found that, when two observers watched and categorized the behaviour of children in a school playground, there were wide variations in categorization, particularly where value judgements were involved: there was 77 per cent agreement on when a child cried, but only 9 per cent agreement on what constituted a 'threatening gesture'. Cultural bias can affect an observer's judgement. For example, teachers asked to code their own interactions with a class were found more reliably to code the incidence of punishment of attention-seeking behaviour when it was towards boys and that of displays of warmth and comfort when towards girls, irrespective of the frequency of such behaviours. Different methods of collecting data were also found to affect results: there was a low correlation between assessments of a mother–child relationship when this was conducted by observing them interacting, by asking the mother to complete a questionnaire on how she handled the child's behaviour and by interviewing the mother. A fourth perspective might also be obtained if one asked the child! These findings are important for any professional to bear in mind when conducting an assessment of child and family: Yarrow and Wexler conclude that an effective observer must have good concentration, must not easily be confused, must attend to details, be aware of her/his own biases and have an analytic approach. Even more important, perhaps, is the need to treat any uncorroborated observation evidence with caution.

Communication as interaction

For the adult to have a good understanding of child development and to observe a child's behaviour closely may be necessary for effective adult–child communication, but it is not sufficient. The child's interaction with the environment is crucial, but so is his or her interaction with the interviewing adult.

All effective communication is, of course, a two-way process. As Rich points out in his illuminating analysis of interviewing children and adolescents (1968), any interview consists of: 'Two people talking to and affecting each other…[so that] it is merely a convenience to describe only one of them as the "interviewer"' (p.3). What distinguishes an 'interview' from other types of conversation, however, is that control of the interaction is not equally divided between the two speakers; in the case of an interview between an adult and a child, the power base lies with the adult, and however careful the interviewer, this is likely to skew the outcome.

Power relations are built into every conversation: adults use different forms of speech towards children than towards other adults; young people adapt the language they use towards adults: there is an expectation that they will use more deferential forms, that they will not swear. Burman (1994) argues that an understanding of power relations is essential to understanding children's utterances. The listener must consider such issues as 'the speaker's right to talk, and the opportunities available for taking the conversational floor' (p.141). She quotes evidence that children address males and females, children and adults differently, and that girls and boys respond differently to requests. Girls, it appears, are less likely to refuse a request, but much more likely to ignore it!

Rich describes the difficulties caused by the unequal power base of adult and child when they interact: 'If the child simply answers the questions that are put to him and does not feel free enough and secure enough to explain the points the adult did not think of asking about, the truth will never become apparent' (Rich 1968, p.6). He distinguishes between a 'fact-finding' interview, where the adult takes control and assumes responsibility for discovering the truth, and a 'fact-giving' interview, where responsibility is passed to the child to tell the adult what he or she knows:

> If we abandon our adult arrogance and our assumption that the adult is always the interviewer, we can recognize that the child may be prevented from carrying out a fact-giving interview because the adult insists on carrying out an irrelevant fact-finding interview. (Rich 1968, p.10)

Empowering the child requires taking time for development of trust, offering choices, giving explanations and permission to express views and keeping an open mind. There has been some interesting research into the sort of language that reflects an open attitude in a questioner, and the influence such language has on children's responses. Allerton (1993) describes a piece of research in which he analysed interactions between teachers and children in an infant classroom, classifying them by question type and response type. Teacher questions were defined as 'closed' (those in which the answer is limited and predefined by the question, for example, 'What's the time?') or 'open' (permitting a range of appropriate answers, for example, 'What did you do at the weekend?'). He found that although closed questions led to more relevant answers, the responses were shorter and limited largely to information-giving. The open questions on the other hand yielded longer answers, more new information, a much greater variety of response types and more evidence of thought from the child.

'If they treat you like a kid you resent telling them something, but if you're tret like an equal then you want to share things.' (Robert)

Two interactions, both taken from conversations about birthdays, illustrate. The first is from the 'closed' question group:

Teacher: What else will you put on your cake?

Child: Candles.

Teacher: How many candles will you put on your cake?

Child: One.

Teacher: One? Only one? How old are you going to be?

Child: Five.

Teacher: Five, so how many candles should you put on?

(No response.) (Allerton 1993, p.47)

Allerton comments: 'This interaction sounds like a guessing game in which the adult knows the answers and the child has to guess the right one' (Allerton 1993, p. 47). The adult controls the interaction and the child 'has to adapt her responses to the adult's perception' (Allerton 1993, p. 47).

In the next extract the questioner attempts not to direct the child's responses but merely to reflect back what she has already said. It follows a question about presents:

Child: I'm going to buy him a…my Dad hasn't got a purse.

Teacher: He hasn't got a purse, has he?

Child: (Shakes head). He hasn't. I'm gonna buy him a book, a book for big people. And I bought that for my Mum's birthday. My Mum's birthday was a tomorrow from yesterday.

Teacher: Was it?

Child: And it was next…it was last week.

Teacher: So you're going to buy him a writing book for big people?

Child: (Nods). It's in the sweet shop. (Allerton 1993, p.46)

This time the adult listens and the child 'thinks on her feet' and so is enabled to exercise cognitive skills: 'to question, hypothesize, reflect, wonder, project' (Allerton 1993, p.47). Allerton's argument is that open questioning is more educational. It could also be seen as more likely to elicit useful information. It is salutary, however, to bear in mind Wittmer and Honig's (1991) finding that 88 per cent of questions asked by staff of young children in day care were closed ones.

Any interaction is a complex process and the child's expectations too can influence the outcome of the interaction. Great potential for misunderstanding exists where child and adult come from different cultural backgrounds (see Reflective Exercise 4.1), since the process of information-giving is governed by rules, and these rules are embedded in cultural systems. For example, in white British culture, avoidance of eye-contact is generally seen as shifty or impudent, whereas in the Caribbean it is a sign of respect for authority. As a result, the black child who lowers his eyes out of deference may be thought by the adult to be lying or giving cheek. Unless the worker takes the trouble to find out about the cultural background of the child, possibilities for misinterpretation are legion.

Reflective Exercise 4.1

Think about your own childhood, life history and cultural background. What influences from your past experience or current identity might affect the way you approach work with a child?

Imagine you are working with a child of a different gender or sexual orientation to you, or one from another ethnic, linguistic or religious group or social class. What assumptions might they make about you? How might this affect the way they communicate with you?

Lies and 'truth'

Effective communication can also be blocked because a child deliberately chooses to say something that is not true. Varendonck ([1911] 1984) represents the view that a child's word can never be trusted. Few modern writers would take so extreme a stance, but the sexual abuse allegation is one area where children's reliability continues to be questioned. Freud set the stage for this scepticism when he based his construct of the Oedipus complex on the assumption that his women patients were fantasizing when they told him of sexual encounters with their fathers. Masson (1992), however, argues convincingly these experiences were fact, not fantasy, and so demolishes the whole basis of the claim that children habitually fantasize (see Reflective Exercise 4.2) about seduction and hence that their allegations of sexual abuse are largely false. With the 'discovery' of sexual abuse in the 1970s and 1980s, some writers took the view that children never lie about abuse; the reaction to this view came with the Cleveland Report's argument that children should be taken seriously but not necessarily believed (Secretary of State for Social Services 1988). A balanced view would seem to be one that does not dismiss the child's account, but accepts that young people, like older ones, do lie sometimes, and seeks to clarify when and why they may choose to say something that is not true.

The adult's stance clearly affects what they make of a child's story, and so is important: Garbarino and Stott (1992) quote research evidence that social workers who believed that children often made false allegations of abuse were much more likely to judge a given 'disclosure' as a fabrication than were those who thought children rarely lied about such subjects (p.118). They collect evidence on lying in situations of suspected abuse and conclude that children are much more likely to deny abuse that they have experienced or accuse the wrong person than to say they have been abused when they have not.

Jones (2003, p.37) identifies five reasons why children may deliberately lie: to avoid negative consequences; to obtain a reward; to protect their self-esteem; to maintain relationships or to conform to norms and conventions. Younger children, he says, are more likely to lie for the earlier reasons, older children for the later ones. Lying, rather than being aberrant, 'plays a positive role in normal development' (Garbarino and Stott 1992, p.121). Parents are frequently economical with the truth: they weave fantasies of Father Christmas, they thank Granny effusively for the vase that the child knows has gone to the school bric-a-brac stall, and they encourage their offspring to do likewise. If we were all completely honest all of the time, the world might be quite an uncomfortable place. Children take the cue from their parents and practise saying things that are untrue from an early age. When young children learn that they can lie without detection it gives them satisfaction because it confirms their autonomy. It can also be a useful skill if it helps them avoid punishment. Among older children and adolescents, bragging and fantasy are common means of impressing the peer group. As such, untruths can be seen to be part of the normal currency of childhood. Extreme, habitual lying, however, is another matter. Where a child appears unable to tell the truth about anything this can fairly be described as pathological and is frequently evidence of an abusive upbringing: children who have lived under a long-standing requirement to lie about their experience and circumstances can develop a habit of being untruthful even when there is nothing apparently to be gained from it. Such young people may indeed have difficulty distinguishing fantasy and reality.

It will not always be possible for interviewers to distinguish truthful from inaccurate information, but bearing in mind these points may form a basis for judgements.

Reflective Exercise 4.2

Where do you stand on children and fantasy?

Think of a colleague or neighbour you know well and respect. Imagine a child told you that this person had bullied them, or hit them, or sexually abused them.

How would you feel? What would you think? What would you do?

Even when a child's information about the situation has been reliably elicited, however, it may still be best to be cautious, owing to the eternally slippery nature of 'truth'. Children may communicate what they see as the truth, but there may be limits to their understanding. They may believe something to be true when it is not, they may wish it to be true, or they may believe it is what the interviewer wants to hear. Indeed, post-modernist sociologists would go so far as to claim that absolute truth does not exist: 'People have no direct access to external reality. What we know is always what we have created through our own ideas and constructions of the world. Everything that is observed is dependent on the observer' (Pocock 1995 p.155). The implication of this view is that what the child and the adult believe about a matter may be quite different without either of them being wrong. The contribution of sociology to our understanding of children and communication is further considered in the next chapter.

'My social worker, he starts demanding things from me and that. Like, "You **will** be leaving care in the next three months!" He said, like, "I don't care what you think but I'm doing your leaving care form for you."' (Alistair)

'I don't want him to move out yet, I don't think he's grown up enough. His foster carers have said he can stay at least till he's 18. I don't think he'll ever stay till he's 18, but I want to try and keep him there at least another year.' (Alistair's social worker)

Chapter 5

The Child as Social Actor

The question of how our understandings of experience are constructed, and whose view of 'truth' is accepted brings us to another major theoretical discourse that can inform our practice in listening to children: sociology. Its insights may push us in quite a different direction from those of psychologists and others who may believe that we can discover truths about human beings through objective scientific experiment.

The sociology of childhood

'You wouldn't believe the looks I get when I walk past any of them houses. They stare at me like I've got a TV on my head. It's awful. I mean, we're just a bunch of kids that don't have anywhere to live, so we live in a kids' home. What is the problem? We've not hurt them or anything.' (Tammy)

Over the last two decades, sociologists of childhood have drawn attention to the disparate views of 'children' and 'childhood' underlying different approaches to child-care research, policy and practice. As Cairns and Brannen (2005) and Begg (2004) illustrate, media portrayals of children and young people in Britain and elsewhere in Europe promote a polarized public perception of them as either 'victims' who need to be rescued and protected or 'villains' who must be controlled and punished.

The possibility that a 'villain' might simultaneously be a 'victim' is rarely entertained. Still less is it considered that these victims and villains might be unique human beings with expertise gleaned from their own experiences who are active in shaping their own lives and might have better proposals than either protection or control for resolving the predicaments in which they find themselves.

Winter (2006) locates the failure to recognize children's capacity for self-determination in an 'ages and stages' model of child development against which outcomes can be measured. This 'deficit' model views children as 'adults in the making' and the focus of services is on what they cannot do rather than on what they can. They are thus rendered passive recipients of services benevolently aimed at improving their life chances and are not credited with the ability to shape their own destiny. Te One (2006, p.19) asserts that it is this view of children 'as "becoming" that feeds an enduring obsession with the child in the future... This concept can cloud understanding about children's rights because it presents them as "not there yet"'. These attitudes are reflected in the way social research is often conducted. Qvortrup (1990), for example, illustrates how children are largely invisible in national statistics, which tend to be predicated on an adult view of the world, and that children and their perspectives and interests can be overlooked: 'a population group which at a societal level is mute and is being kept mute by adults, the dominant group' (p.95). A model of the child as an 'active agent' on the other hand starts from the assumption that even the youngest people influence the social worlds they inhabit, have a capacity for self-determination and have the right to exercise autonomy within the limits of safety.

In a key text *Constructing and Reconstructing Childhood* (James and Prout 1990) the editors identified an 'emerging paradigm', a new sociology of childhood, which breaks away from the view of a child as 'human becoming' and is characterized by the belief that childhood is socially constructed and is experienced differently by different children, since the category of 'childhood' interacts with gender, class, ethnicity and so on to make each child's experience unique. Children are worthy of study in their own right, not just as dependants of adults; they should be viewed as active in the construction of their own social realities, not just as passive recipients of culture as handed down to them by adults. These writers believe that qualitative and participatory approaches to research are more appropriate for researching childhood than quantitative ones, being both more ethical and more valid, and that research can play an active role in 'reconstructing' childhood, enabling children to be viewed differently within society.

This set of beliefs underlies an approach to sociological research that is conducted 'with' rather than 'on' children (Christensen and James 2000). Practitioners who wish to listen to children can learn from this research in a number of ways, quite apart from the intrinsic interest of any of its findings. First, its essentially positive approach (focusing on children's competencies, rather than highlighting their deficiencies) chimes with an approach to practice that builds on strengths. Second, because of the attention researchers give to the ethical dimension of engaging with children. Third, because of the imaginative tools researchers have developed for identifying young people's perspectives. So although scepticism has been expressed that the new sociology of children as social actors in their own right has had much impact outside a narrow academic circle (Mayall 2005), it is well worth practitioners' while to take the trouble of coming to grips with it. As Mayall argues, while the 20th century can be described as the century of the child-care professional, if practitioners can learn a truly respectful and empowering approach to working with children, perhaps the 21st century could be the century of the child.

'The hundred languages of childhood'

Very young, even pre-verbal, children are regarded by these sociologists as having a perspective to share that it is incumbent on adults to discover: an adult's assumption that a child cannot communicate their views becomes a self-fulfilling prophecy. 'Listening to young children requires of adults some revaluing and relearning of the hundred languages of childhood' (Moss, Clark and Kjørholt 2005, p.5), in other words a range of communication techniques, of which speech is only one. The positive approach of this school of sociology is demonstrated by the way it seeks to acknowledge the capacities even of those traditionally regarded as having the most limited of abilities. Davis, Watson and Cunningham-Barley (2000), for example, describe an ethnographic research project in a special school for children with profound disabilities. The researchers worked alongside the children, observing their interactions with staff, some of whom clearly underestimated the children's capabilities. They observed how the young people responded differently to different staff and in different settings and so managed the environment to get their needs met, despite their difficulties with communication.

Eide and Winger (2005) illustrate the ethical complexities of research with children in relation to Norwegian government guidance on taking children's views into account when delivering services. They argue that to do this 'in a respectful and serious way' (p.74) requires us not just to rethink our services but also our basic attitudes towards children, which so often involve adults defining what is in children's best interests for them without seeking their view. However, this is not a straightforward endeavour, since simultaneously the adults should be asking themselves: 'What gives us the right as grown-ups to search for the

'I sort of have a habit of keeping problems to myself. I don't want to tell everything, you know.' (Patrick)

child's point of view?' (Eide and Winger 2005, p.75) The imperative to explore the child's perspective has to be balanced against respect for the child's right to refuse to participate.

Using research to inform practice

In contemporary social work, as in health care and education, there is sustained pressure for practice to become more evidence-based (Nutley, Walter and Davies 2002). This is emphasized over and over again in government documents and guidance (Department for Education and Skills 2005; Department of Health 1995, 2000, 2003; HMSO 1995), and is reflected in a proliferation of websites on 'what works' aiming to make research findings more accessible to practitioners (e.g., www.rip.org.uk; www.scie.org.uk; www.whatworksforchildren.org.uk). It would be perverse to decry this movement too strongly, since this whole chapter of the book concerns the lessons for practitioners that can be learnt from studying the findings of research. However, it is important that all research is viewed critically rather than taken at face value.

There is a tendency for those who advocate evidence-based practice to favour quantitative over qualitative methods, and positivist as opposed to interpretivist approaches to research: 'a focus on rigorous experiments evaluating replicable programs and practices is essential to build confidence in educational research among policymakers and educators' (Slavin 2002, p.15). The weakness of the type of social research that attempts to achieve scientific respectability through 'rigour' and 'replicability', however, is that it flattens into unhelpful generalizations the nuanced nature of human experience. It has been argued that qualitative methods and interpretivist approaches to research have a better 'fit' with social care situations (Everitt *et al.* 1992), and that since no two sets of circumstances are alike, research findings can never be more than a guide to practice: 'to apply or base practice on any sort of evidence without moral or ethical sensitivity, a wider assessment of the context, individual circumstances and situational requirements or a risk assessment of possible implications...is unacceptable' (Brown and Rutter 2006, p.39). Further criticisms levelled at the 'evidence-based practice' lobby are that the research findings it disseminates tend to be predicated on a model of the child as a passive recipient of services rather than an autonomous social actor (see, in contrast, Practice Example 5.1), that children's own perspective is missing (Winter 2006) and that the very real difficulties of how abstract research findings can be translated into practice are underestimated (Taylor 2004).

Clearly, insights distilled from research need to be adopted in a discriminating manner. However, that does not mean they are never useful, and there is a wealth of learning from the qualitative and collaborative work of sociological researchers on listening to children that deserves integration into child-care practice, every bit as much as does the quantitative information on outcomes that we are urged by policy-makers, inspectors and funders to take into account.

The relationship between research and practice is a complex one: it is not merely linear or unidirectional; each learns from the other. O'Kane (2000) acknowledges that some of her ideas for activities to use in her research came from the practice of direct social work with children. There is evidence that, in contemporary practice, social workers' skills in direct work and action techniques may be becoming devalued and are at risk of being lost (Gilligan 2000; Morris and Shepherd 2000). Perhaps the time has come for practice to borrow its skill base back from research. The new sociology of childhood has informed the thinking of policy-makers and practitioners in a range of disciplines across the world and has the potential to provoke new ways of looking at children and innovative approaches to practice.

PRACTICE EXAMPLE 5.1 REGGIO EMILIA

In the Northern Italian town of Reggio Emilia a pioneering approach towards early years education has been developed in which the child is seen as the leader and the teacher as the guide. Learning is viewed as a process of interaction between the child and his or her experience and is investigative and collaborative rather than didactic; teachers have to have a broad-based education so they can help the child explore the areas of their own curiosity rather than following a predetermined curriculum. Learning is project-based, crosses subject boundaries and is often done in groups rather than individually. Rather than children learning from teachers, children are expected to learn from each other and teachers to learn from children. This has significant implications for the role of the teacher, who is no longer seen as the expert, but as the 'scaffolding' for children's learning: 'We need teachers who feel they truly belong to and participate in this process as teachers, but most of all as people' (Rinaldi 2005, p.27). The role of the school changes also, to 'a place that plays an active role in the child's search for meaning' (Rinaldi 2006, p.19). What is remarkable about the Reggio Emilia experience is that, unlike most experiments in progressive education, it has been going for 40 years and is located in the state rather than the private sector.

Can listening be dangerous?

As we saw in Part 1, there are limits to how far we can take the notion of the child as an autonomous actor whose views deserve to be taken equally seriously as those of adults. The writers whose contributions to the debate I have summarized above do, themselves, balance their call for more power to children with a recognition that children have dependency needs too; that there is a point where those with more knowledge and capabilities may have to step in and protect them or speak for them. Fattore and Turnbull (2005), for example, while criticizing a model of child protection that sees the child as helplessly dependent on adult interventions, still accept the need for child safeguarding services and recognize that adults sometimes have to represent children's views for them. They urge, however, that the adults listen to and involve the children so far as possible, and attempt to advocate for them with 'sincerity'. The new sociologists do not reject all the findings of research into child development either, but urge that it is viewed critically (Taylor 2004) and applied selectively, taking into account the circumstances of the individual child (Eide and Winger 2005).

Moss *et al.* (2005) indeed argue that there are risks and contradictions inherent in notions of children as social actors, since relationships are never value-free but always imbued with inequalities. While they advocate seeking children's views and using these to develop more appropriate child-care services they warn that it will tend to be the more privileged child whose view is likely to predominate; adults will generally define the terms of the consultation – for example, asking the children how they would like their day-care service to be run rather than finding out whether they wish to be in day-care; observing children carefully may make it easier to control them. As such, consultation may support rather than subvert existing power structures. The encouragement to become a certain sort of ideal, autonomous, self-actualizing consumer may itself run counter to the culture a child identifies with. In sum, the risk is that adults will try 'to control the future through children, and that listening will become part of a technology intended to achieve this end' (Moss *et al.* 2005, p.12).

Kjørholt (2005) takes this line of reasoning a stage further, arguing that the expectation on children to be autonomous can in itself be oppressive: responsibility for decision-making can be a burden rather than a liberation. She locates promotion of autonomy in a cult of the individual that characterizes Western capitalism: 'Contemporary discourses...place human beings in positions that promote new forms of subjection: in this context individualism is an imperative, not a choice' (p.166). 'Freedom' and 'individualism' according to Kjørholt's analysis, are a new kind of tyranny through which governments get subjects to govern themselves, but the freedom is an illusion since the choices they are permitted to make have already been decided by someone in power. Other values, such as respect for others, community and interdependency, should be placed above the value of self-determination.

'I had a choice of whether I wanted to come here. But it wasn't much of a choice really, it was here or nothing.' (Kerry)

It is interesting to find the notion of autonomy being attacked because it is too individualistic. One of the objections the proponents of the new sociology of childhood make against developmental psychology is that it is too individualistic, examining its subjects in laboratory conditions divorced from their social context: 'by adopting psychological insights as underpinning knowledge for social work we are de facto approaching social problems in a particular way that is focused on changing individuals rather than engaging with structures and systems' (Taylor 2004, p.229). But the new sociology of childhood also stresses the uniqueness of each child as an individual, their agency in constructing their own social worlds, and the importance of research methods that empower. Empowerment is at least in part about promotion of individual autonomy. There is thus an element of overlap here between psychological and sociological ways of looking at children and childhood, which might suggest that their positions are not as polarized as some claim. I would suggest that the key difference in their approach to research is that the researcher who honestly tries to identify the child's perspective and collaborates with the child in the conduct of the research is more respectful, more empowering and therefore more ethical than the one who conducts research on a child without their informed consent. It is from this aspect of the new sociology of childhood that child-care professionals may learn most.

Chapter 6

Theories of Intervention

Social work theory and communication with children

A third perspective from which we may be able to learn about adult–child communication is that of child-care social work. If sociology uses a less hard-nosed scientific approach to enquiry than psychology, then social work is even further out on the continuum of 'soft' disciplines. Much of the theoretical writing in the field is not based on controlled experiment or rigorous analysis but on generalization from individual practice experience. This does not invalidate its insights, but it must always be borne in mind that these may be based on idiosyncratic views and small samples.

The early development of social work with children (Holgate 1972; Winnicott 1964) was heavily influenced by psychodynamic theory. Child psychoanalysts adapted the theories of Freud on psychosexual development of the personality to the treatment of children, substituting free play sessions for the free association in the psychoanalytic consultation, since through play the child was seen as 'acting out' bad experiences in order to gain relief from inner conflicts (Klein 1969). The therapist reflected back to the child the meaning of the play, thus enabling the child to gain insight and resolve the conflicts. The risk of this approach is that: 'if an interpretation does not correspond to the child's subjective experience, it is likely to be a misinterpretation and the child, consciously or unconsciously, will feel mis-understood' (Garbarino and Stott 1992, p.263). This is a question of pro-fessional power: the worker has a monopoly of the knowledge required for charting the subject's subconscious processes and this presents obstacles to either respecting or empowering the client. Simmonds (1988) argues against using psychodynamic approaches with children on the grounds that it is unacceptable to use techniques originally developed with consenting adults, to which children cannot give informed consent, and also because there is very little evidence that psychoanalysis of children actually helps them.

Despite these objections, the importance of psychodynamic theory in the development of social work with children should not be underestimated. It is widely accepted now that there are verifiable unconscious processes influencing behaviour (Garbarino and Stott 1992; Herbert 1981; Howe *et al.* 1999) and that early experience plays a crucial role in emotional development (Buchanan and Ritchie 2004; Lansdown, Burnell and Allen 2007). Both these ideas derive originally from psychodynamic theory. The influence of Freud contributed directly or indirectly to a range of therapies still used with children. Play therapy is one of these. In play therapy the child is allowed to play freely, and the therapist is 'alert to recognizing the *feelings* the child is expressing and reflects these feelings back to him in such a manner that he gains insight into his behaviour' (Axline 1969, p.93, original emphasis). Play therapy has been criticized for its weak empirical base and for its 'blinkered and silly' pursuit of insight as an end in itself while neglecting the practical pressures on children that may contribute to their problem behaviour (Rutter 1975, p.311). Nevertheless, play therapy has been a significant influence on some aspects of child-care social work (Bray 1991). Axline's approach to theory is eclectic: she takes elements from psychoanalysis and combines them with the Rogerian client-centred counselling approach (Rogers 1979). 'Warmth' and 'acceptance' are stressed; she talks about the 'powerful force' within each individual for 'self-realization' (Maslow 1970) and asserts that children have the ability to solve their own problems: 'a growth impulse that makes mature behaviour more satisfying than immature behaviour' (Axline 1969, p.15). It remains questionable whether the non-directive style is always the most effective one with children. Practitioners may also be faced with situations where they are obliged to put boundaries on children's behaviour or make decisions for young people that may go against their wishes. Client-centred counselling methods, developed for adults voluntarily seeking therapy, are thus not relevant to all work with young people.

Another school that developed out of psychodynamic theory, has been influenced by client-centred counselling and has had a significant impact on social work with children is Gestalt. Like followers of Freud, Gestalt uses psychoanalysis; like Rogerian counselling it aims to help clients achieve their potential and asserts that the body has a natural striving towards health; to these beliefs it adds the social theory of phenomenology: that events have a social meaning and that 'the central human activity is the need to give *meaning* to [one's] perceptions' (Clarkson 1989, p.5 – original emphasis). A major achievement of this school has been the wide range of imaginative approaches to communicating with children that it has inspired. Adherents of Gestalt theory have produced some excellent guides to direct work with children (Cipolla, McGown and Yanulis 1992; Oaklander 1988). These writers impart an infectious enthusiasm for working with troubled children, and they show great respect for young people as individuals. In addition they provide a particularly rich fund of practical ideas for how to engage children and how to tap into their wishes and feelings. Simmonds describes this method as 'an education in the emotions' (1988, p.15), but questions whether it is helpful to see expression of feelings as an end in itself when these may have been suppressed as part of a functional defence mechanism. Buchanan and Ritchie (2004) disregard all of the above approaches, given their lack of empirical evidence base.

A rather different, though equally important influence on work with children is learning theory. Unlike any of the psychotherapies, it is based on rigorous empirical research into animal and human behaviour and rejects anything that cannot be demonstrated in practice: behavioural methods developed from the classical research into conditioning have proven effectiveness in influencing children's behaviour and extinguishing undesired responses (Buchanan and Ritchie 2004). One text that explains how to apply learning theory to managing children's problem behaviour is Herbert (1981). However, it is the adults rather than the child who define the problem here and one has to search the book to find any reference at all to the child's view, any acknowledgement that the child has a part to play in defining the objectives of treatment, or indeed that she or he might prefer *not* to have his or her behaviour changed. Communication with the child does not merit a mention. The relevance of learning theory to those who want to develop skills in communicating with children is therefore limited.

Family therapy differs from the models examined so far in taking what Simmonds (1988) describes as an 'ecological' model of the child in its social context. Looking to systems theory to explain the processes underlying family interactions, a central aspect of family therapy is that it values each family member's view of what is going on, including that of the child. Another of its strengths is the attention it pays to communication: 'Problems are defined, shaped and influenced through language and interaction... The child is inextricably linked in a cradle of communication with significant others in his life' (Wilson 1998, pp.1, 5). Relationships are viewed in terms of information exchange, with feedback from each interaction capable of modifying the way either party to the exchange relates to the other. Families coming for therapy are viewed as having dysfunctional communication and belief patterns which must be addressed if individual family members' symptomatology is to recede. Particular attention is paid to the distinction between the overt content of a message and the hidden agenda that may be communicated non-verbally through gesture, tone, body language or facial expression (Walrond-Skinner 1977).

There is some evidence for family therapy's efficacy in addressing children's problems, though this is limited (Buchanan and Ritchie 2004). Its techniques do, however, merit study. Family therapy and other therapies which have developed from it, such as solution-focused brief therapy (O'Connell 2001), pay particular attention to the type of question the practitioner poses and how these assist clients to express themselves or resolve their difficulties. Among these are the scaling question ('How are you feeling today on a scale of one to ten?'), the miracle question ('If you woke up tomorrow and found your problem was miraculously solved, what would you notice that was different?'), the circular or reflexive question ('If I were to ask your mum how well you have behaved this week, what do you think she would tell me?'), and the use of the third person ('If another young person were here who was in the same situation, what advice would you give them?'). These techniques that have evolved in clinical practice can be successfully adapted to other settings, including the classroom (Ingram and Simm 2006). Advice on questioning children and also on how adults can modify their language to help children understand complex concepts can be found in the useful handbook on family therapy with children: *Child-focused Practice* (Wilson 1998).

Family therapy can be criticized in the same way as the psychotherapies, in that it was not developed from an empirical base. Not so attachment theory, which is grounded in research on animal behaviour, child development and experimental psychology. An influential school of child-care social work is based on attachment theory and since this is founded largely on research with children, rather than being an adaptation of a model developed for use with adults, arguably it can be seen as a more appropriate base for work with young people. While the work of Bowlby and his successors on attachment has come under attack both on methodological grounds (Barrett 2006) and for political bias (Burman 1994), there is no denying the important contribution it has made to our understanding of the emotional problems of young people, particularly those who have suffered separation and loss in early childhood. Writers on child-care social work who adopt an attachment theory perspective include Fahlberg (1994), Jewett (1984) and Romaine, Turley and Tuckey (2007): see Practice Example 6.1). The value of their approach lies in their carefully worked out application of research findings to the practical tasks of social work with children.

PRACTICE EXAMPLE 6.1 EXPLAINING ADOPTION

Romaine *et al.* (2007, p.70) give a lovely example of how to explain an abstract concept in terms that make sense to a young child. Four-year-old Polly was to be placed for adoption, but her social worker, Karen, was not sure she really understood what it meant, so she introduced a teddy, 'Molly Bear', to illustrate. Molly Bear, she said, lived in her office and came out with her sometimes on visits to children. Karen told Polly that it took a lot of work to care for Molly Bear properly and, although she loved her, it was hard to find the time. She was therefore looking for someone to be a new mother to Molly who could keep her forever and would look after her well. Polly eagerly offered to be the teddy bear's new mother, and after initial feigned reluctance Karen allowed herself to be persuaded that Polly really would take good care of her. She arranged a series of 'visits' when the teddy came to stay briefly before moving in, and Karen then called a few times to check how she was getting on, before arranging a 'ceremony' to say that Molly Bear would stay forever, with a certificate for Polly as her new mother. This whole process took five weeks, was planned to lead up to Polly's own introduction to adoptive parents and helped her to make the transition to their care from that of her foster carers more easily.

Helping Children Cope with Separation and Loss (Jewett 1984) is a particularly relevant text, since Jewett's theme is the application of the theory to the task of communicating with troubled children. Her contention is that:

> If you are working with a child who has suffered a loss or separation, one important task is to provide him with enough accurate information in an understandable manner that he can answer 'how' and 'why' in a way that makes sense. Such information relieves the child of blame, re-establishes his accurate self-perception, leaves his cause and effect reasoning unimpaired, allows him to progress in developmental tasks and lets him go on to have good relationships with others. (Jewett 1984, pp.85–6)

The book, which is discussed in more detail in Parts 3 and 4, is a manual of how to do this. Relating the text closely to Bowlby's findings on the grief process, as well as to Piaget's developmental stages, Jewett advises on how to help children make sense of confusing lives. The concept of 'human-sense' (Donaldson 1978) is clearly implicit. In Jewett's writing, however, as in much traditional child-care theory, the child is a rather passive presence, a subject to whom therapy is done. More recently, under the influence of the new sociology of childhood, one sees emerging in the writings of adherents of attachment theory the concept of the child as agent of his or her own destiny: 'The child must be seen as an actor in his or her own life, rather than just a passive recipient of parenting and other experiences' (Brandon, Schofield and Trinder 1998, p.37).

The view I reach after examining the contribution to child-care of all these schools of social work theory is that no one theoretical framework is beyond criticism, yet each approach has something useful to contribute to the range of techniques available. I have given more attention to the psychotherapies in this account than to some mainstream social work models, not because they are more important to social work as a whole, but because they devote more thought to the issue of communication with children. Only social learning theory and attachment theory have been developed specifically with children in mind, and of these only attachment theory gives weight to the question of communication.

Some of the most impressive contributions to practice do not, however, belong to any one theory, but adopt an eclectic approach. An excellent booklet produced by a cancer charity, for example (Cancerlink 1993), gives advice on explaining to children when a close relative has cancer. It advises in simple, common-sense terms how and when to tell the child, what to say to children of different ages and how to cope with their responses. Although no explicit reference is made to any theory one can see the influence of Rogerian counselling, of attachment theory, of Piagetian psychology and of Gestalt in the advice given, which seems to synthesize the best of what is known about sharing difficult information with young people. Combining ideas from all these schools of theory could lead us to a composite model of the skills that make up 'listening'.

A listening attitude

A strong belief in listening as a force for healing emerges from a review of this literature: 'Being listened to is itself of therapeutic value, and not being listened to or consulted can lead to feelings of rejection' (O'Quigley 2000, p.2). Almost all the writers discussed above who pay attention to the issue of communication with children stress the importance of listening. For Axline (1969), listening is the key to child-centred practice, as it implies 'a respect for the child's ability to be a thinking, independent, constructive being' (p.20). This view is shared by writers as diverse as the psychoanalyst Fraiberg and the transactional analyst Crompton. Fraiberg (1972) advocates letting the child set the agenda while the worker watches and listens and does not attempt to control: 'For diagnostic study and observation we need little more than our educated eyes and ears' (p.61). Crompton (1980) takes the argument a stage further, asserting that unless we listen 'with true respect' to children's points of view we cannot expect them to 'respond and behave in a sensitive and sensible way [or] take responsibility for their own way of life and learning' (p.20).

'A good social worker will take time out to come and see me and take you out and talk to you really down to earth. And when you're in a bad mood they cheer you up and that and if you're upset they'll comfort you – all the ordinary things that you'd tell a good friend from a bad friend.' (Kerry)

The evidence, as we saw in Part 1, nevertheless suggests that we are not good at listening: in schools and hospitals, in day-care and in social work interviews it seems to be the adults who do most of the talking, who set the agenda and who seek to limit and control the contributions children make to any dialogue (Barnes 1969; Butler and Williamson 1994; LeFrancois 2007; Wittmer and Honig 1991). A fundamental reason for adults' failure to listen to children may be that it involves allowing children to set their own agenda, and hence requires adults to relinquish some power. We all fear, to a greater or lesser extent, loss of control. To quote an article on listening to disabled children: 'Good communication, which allows for disagreement but maintains mutual respect, will foster an independent spirit. Unfortunately this is not a characteristic which all adults welcome in children, disabled or otherwise' (NSPCC 1993, p.5). Listening, the article argues, should be a skill taught in professional training. As Luckock et al. (2006) have established, however, there is no guarantee that professional training will currently cover communicating with children. The next part of this book therefore sets out to distill the insights of psychology, sociology and social work theory into a set of guidelines for how to listen to children in practice.

Part 3: Opening up a Dialogue with a Child

Children can feel, but they cannot analyse their feelings, and if the analysis is partially effected in thought, they know not how to express the result of the process in words.

From **Jane Eyre** by Charlotte Brontë [1816–54]
(Brontë [1847] 1996, p.30)

Chapter 7

Being Prepared

The silent child

Nicky was not keen to talk. He was in big trouble with his foster carers. He knew he'd pushed them to the limit and they wanted him out. He had probably heard them on the phone to me going on about how he had ill-treated the dog, attacked other children at school, deliberately smashed the greenhouse. Nicky was expecting me to tell him off too. However, I wasn't there to tell him off: I accepted relationships had broken down irreparably in this foster home and I had come to tell him I had found another place for him to live. This was not, sadly, the adoptive family I had been seeking for him, nor was it another foster home – none were available that would take him – it was a small children's home that I believed could contain and work with his very disturbed behaviour until he was more ready for living in a family. I wanted to know how Nicky felt about moving on to another set of strangers, to a group living environment, a new school.

Nicky remained resolutely silent. I could sense his tension but couldn't interpret his emotions: was he angry, upset, scared? I needed to know if I was to help him make the move. I got out paper and pens and asked him to draw me a picture of what he was feeling. Still saying nothing, Nicky carefully drew for me a plane flying towards a mountain peak and below it a stick figure suspended from a parachute. I asked Nicky to explain the picture to me and finally he broke his silence: 'That's the plane I was on', he said. 'It's flying towards that mountain. It's about to crash and all the people on board are going to be killed. But I've got a parachute and I just managed to jump out in time.'

So – relief for Nicky, and relief too for me, since if he felt positive about the proposed placement he was more likely to settle and do well there: research evidence has demonstrated this for 30 years (Bush, Gordon and Le Bailly 1977). And indeed, the move did prove a good one for Nicky in the long term, even though I would not normally have chosen to place someone so young (he was ten at the time) in residential care. The reason I tell Nicky's story is to illustrate how a simple technique like asking a child to draw a picture can break the log-jam of non-communication. Nicky was not an articulate child. He was not generally in touch with his own feelings or those of others, and putting names to emotions was not something he was skilled at: he may not even have known the word 'relief'. However, that did not mean he did not feel anything, and given the tools of pen and paper he was enabled to express eloquently the feelings he was unable to put into words.

In this part of the book I am going to look at the practical approaches and tools adults can use to promote communication with individual children they are working with or caring for. Some tools are as everyday as drawing materials, others are more technical. Information will be presented in the following chapters: this one looks at what preparation a worker needs to undertake before first meeting a child, the next addresses how to build rapport from that first encounter on. This is followed by a chapter on finding out the child's views. Next I discuss the need for an interviewer to be aware of how power dynamics between adult and child can affect the dialogue between them, and make some suggestions for working with young people who are disaffected and may be reluctant to engage, and finally there is a chapter on bringing work with a child to a close. More detailed information about techniques and approaches to use when an interview has a special purpose can be found in Part 4.

Tuning in to children

Many adults, if they are honest, are rather alarmed by the prospect of working with children: they find them anarchic and unpredictable and hence threatening. Will the youngster make a fool of them by misbehaving? Will other adults think they are not really working if they are down on the floor, playing? As Crompton (1980) observes: 'One of the greatest influences on adult behaviour with children is the fear of looking silly' (p.14). There is nothing to beat experience to prepare you for work with children: before you start a job where you will have to interact with young people, spend as much time as you can with and around children so you are attuned to them and can be relaxed and comfortable in their presence. It does not matter whether this is as a parent with your own children, through baby-sitting or playing with friends' children, as an observer in a school or volunteer helper in a local football team. Any relevant experience can be used to develop your confidence and skills and at the same time to reassure you that effective work with children may involve play and that there is no loss of dignity entailed in getting down to a child's level.

Every adult has an advantage over each child they meet in that we have all been children, whereas no child has ever been an adult. It should be easier, therefore, for us to understand their thoughts and feelings than for children to make sense of ours. The sensitive practitioner will be trying to see things from the child's point of view; recalling and reflecting on one's own childhood experiences can help us to do this (see Reflective Exercise 7.1).

Reflective Exercise 7.1

Think of an occasion during your own childhood when you lost something you valued or were separated from someone you loved.

What happened? How did you feel? What helped you cope? How might this experience help or hinder your work with children who have suffered loss and separation?

Professionals will not have shared the range of experiences faced by all the children they work with, so remembering your own childhood will only take you so far, however. Literature (including books written for children) may help you further develop empathy for other lives. *When Hitler Stole Pink Rabbit* (Kerr 1994), for example, describes the experience of a child refugee; *The Story of Tracy Beaker* (Wilson 1992) that of a teenager in a children's home, while *The Curious Incident of the Dog in the Night-time* (Haddon 2004) gives a fascinating insight into the mind of an adolescent with Asperger's syndrome. *Oleander, Jacaranda* (Lively 1994), a very different book, but equally thought-provoking, explores through a memoir of childhood the universal issue of how children perceive their worlds. These are only some of the very many works of literature that may illuminate different perspectives on childhood. These may help the practitioner to appreciate the child's point of view, and so are well worth dipping into, alongside academic texts such as those discussed elsewhere in this book.

Going equipped

There is a more practical way to prepare for going out to start talking with children though, and that is to equip yourself with some props. I was dubbed 'the bag lady' by one little boy I worked with, because I always took with me a bag of toys when I went to see him. I worked with him before he was placed for adoption. Sadly, his adoption did not work out and I came to see him again after a gap of over a year to help him make sense of what had happened. As soon as he saw me he dived into my bag and pulled out the same toys he had played with the last time he saw me – nearly one-third of his lifetime earlier. Such is the power of play: I very much doubt he would have remembered the words I had used.

In my bag I always carry paper and drawing materials whatever the age of the young person I am working with. I also have a range of small toys – cuddly, functional or grotesque: play figures, toy cars, jigsaws, glove puppets, a telephone, a snake (even though I hate them myself!), monsters. There is that indispensable social work tool, a magic wand, and I also have a number of children's books. I will choose which playthings and books to take on a given occasion, depending on the child's age and what I know of their interests, and I may add other items such as modelling materials as appropriate. Sometimes I give a child an item they have become attached to and then I have to find a way of replacing it. The reason I take these 'props' is that they can make the process of communicating with a child or young person so much easier: Nicky's story above illustrates that point. Practitioners may feel it will cost them too much or be impractical to be carrying boxes of play materials around in the boots of their cars. However, none of the items I use are expensive, and neither are they bulky: they fit into a medium-sized shoulder bag. Each worker can find out by trial and error which materials they find most helpful and feel most comfortable with and develop their own toolkit.

Finding out about this child

The final way in which a practitioner can prepare for an encounter is by finding out as much as they can in advance about the child they are going to see. What information is contained in the referral? Does your agency already have a file on this child or on her family? Reading this before you meet may prevent you from asking questions the child or their parent has already answered a hundred times. Forewarned is also forearmed: was the last worker who visited that house savaged by the family's Rottweiler? Speaking to someone who knows the child first is a good idea, if it can be done without breaching confidentiality: it is essential to know, for example, whether a child who has a disability uses particular techniques to communicate. It may assist you to carry out your intervention effectively and in a culturally sensitive way too if you have taken the trouble to establish whether the family belongs to a particular linguistic, ethnic or religious group, so that you can make sure an interpreter is present if needed, or to avoid causing offence by, for example, offering refreshments to a Muslim during Ramadan. This information will contribute to the way in which the interview or programme of work with the child is planned:

> Planning is important for a number of reasons, not least to ensure that the assessment is as fruitful as possible. It allows practitioners to find the least disruptive or distressing ways of approaching and interviewing the child and reduces the potential for repetition or duplication by different professionals and agencies. (Jones 2003, p.120)

More than this, thorough preparation and careful planning is essential to the process of listening to the child with true respect.

Chapter 8

Getting to Know Each Other

Building rapport

Starting any new relationship can be challenging, even for adults. How much more so for a child who may already be under stress, and who may have only a hazy idea of the purpose of the encounter. Before any child can be expected to converse with a strange adult there is therefore a need to build up a trusting relationship in which the young person can feel safe enough to speak of matters that may be sensitive. Fear of strangers is an in-built response in young children (Ainsworth *et al.* 1978). Rapport-building is thus a necessary stage both in individual interviews and in a whole programme of work.

'Most young people treat their social worker like a bit of dog-muck, like something you'd walk in and wipe off your feet on the mat. And all the social workers reply with "Don't talk to me like that!" But it's probably because they're in the office, or in a kids' home or in a meeting or something like that. If they took them out to a café or they just walked round town or sat in the park it might relax the kid more. Like, they've got to find out about the child. Get to know them. Ask about their friends and what music they like and make sure you understand them so you know what questions to ask without upsetting them.'
(Tammy)

Side by side with the need to develop trust is the critical importance of making sure the child is as clear as they can be about why you are meeting. The practitioner's purpose and aims in meeting with the child must be spelt out in simple terms that the child can make sense of and any unfounded fears dispelled: 'I'm the health visitor' may leave the child none the wiser and without further explanation of what health visitors do may raise a child's anxieties. The respectful health visitor will explain why they are doing a hearing test before they do it, if only because the child who understands what is going on and is reassured that it is nothing to be alarmed about is more likely to cooperate. It is most important that any 'ground rules', particularly regarding the limits of confidentiality, are spelt out early in the encounter, as children need to know the consequences of actions before they take them. A young person can feel bitterly betrayed if the disclosure they make in good faith to a supportive adult, believing it to be in confidence, is passed on to others. Following such a betrayal, trust may be impossible to re-establish.

Developing trust may be a lengthy process. Taking the long view of rapport-building, the psychotherapist Klein (1969) let a child play with toy cars for hours without speaking in order to develop a relationship before she embarked on therapy. Prestage (1972) tolerated a boy coming to her clinic, climbing a tree and staying there in silence for 14 successive weeks before he finally came down and started working with her! Such a leisured approach belongs nowadays – perhaps has only ever belonged – to the realm of private practice. Nevertheless, rapport-building is vital for effective communication and deserves more attention than it is often accorded (Davies and Westcott 1999).

With teenagers as well as with young children neglecting to build rapport can scupper one's best efforts at communication. The ethnographers Tammivaara and Enwright (1986) recommend engaging in activities while talking with adolescents, so as to give them something to do, avoiding 'the terrifying vacuum-like quality of strangers first meeting' (p.232). One cannot assume that even an articulate adolescent is at ease in an eyeball-to-eyeball encounter with an unfamiliar adult. The one-to-one interview can be 'alarmingly direct...a threat from which he will either withdraw or defend himself' (Winnicott 1964, p.40). This means that the practitioner has to improvise situations where the young person will feel more relaxed. I find car journeys fruitful times for conversation – perhaps because of the absence of eye contact. The essential is to avoid 'rushing' the child into premature intrusion into sensitive areas. You need to spend time first getting to know them and letting them find out that you are someone who will treat them fairly and respectfully. It is worth finding out the child's particular interests so that if possible you can engage in an unthreatening activity that will give you shared pleasure.

Activities for getting started on work with a child

Taking a child out is an appropriate way of getting to know them in many situations: teenagers will often appreciate being taken to a café where you can chat over a cup of coffee without being overheard. Younger children may prefer a ball game in the park or a runaround on the beach, and as they relax they may naturally become conversational. Often, though, the professional does not have the option of going outside, or the child might be alarmed by leaving familiar territory, so indoor activities need to be devised. The following games should not be too threatening and allow the child control over how much information about themselves they share. They do not all require lengthy periods of time, either, and could be employed by those workers who only have time for a brief intervention.

'My important things' board game

I find this a particularly good introductory activity with older children and teenagers. Worker and child each take a sheet of paper, divide it into six squares and number each square. Each draws one person or thing that is important to them in each square. They then take turns to throw dice. When the dice turns up number three, they ask the other to talk about what they have drawn in square number three and so on, continuing to throw the dice until each has asked the other about all six squares on their paper. One of the advantages of this activity is that it is reciprocal: the worker tells something about themself too; it is not just the child who is expected to reveal themself. The other advantage is that each is free to share as little or as much as they choose.

'They should tell the kid a bit about themself. Like, whether they're married, if they've got kids. When they were a child whether they had a hard time with their mum and dad. What they watch, what music they like – just general things, nothing really really private.' (Tammy)

Sentence completion

Prepare a list of open-ended unfinished sentences for a child to complete. This can give them opportunities to write about their likes and dislikes, feelings and relationships, and can lead into discussion. The openness of the 'questions' enables unexpected themes to be introduced by the young person. Again, however, they retain control over how much they give away. Here are some possible sentence starters; you can make up others:

1. My name is…

2. I…

3. What I like doing best is…

4. I hate it when…

5. My mum…

6. My best friend can…

7. I'm scared of…

This is an activity only suitable for those who can read and write quite well: make sure you check out the child's literacy level before you give them this task to do.

Picture completion

This is something like a visual version of the above. You ask the child to draw a picture of something or someone and then use this as a basis for discussion. It could be their family, or their ideal holiday, or their worst nightmare. There are resources available with sets of partially drawn pictures for the child to complete. *Talking Pictures* (King and Chaplin 1989) is a particularly useful one. You may wish to choose which pictures to give the child to complete, or you may let them choose. Some are more challenging than others: 'Where I would go on my magic carpet'; 'Look through the keyhole and see my biggest secret'.

'I desperately wanted to go and live with my dad and I used to draw pictures because I couldn't really speak my mind. I used to draw pictures of me with my dad and they'd ask me who it was and I'd explain it that way.' (Kerry)

Story-building

Start off a story, for example: 'Once upon a time there was a…' Stop mid-sentence, and ask the child to carry on. They too have to break off after a bit and then you pick the story up and you make it up as you go along. This activity again can be more or less challenging. It is possible to direct it more towards feelings, for example, or towards issues that you know to be salient for the child: 'The boy felt terribly afraid, because…', or 'She couldn't find her father anywhere so…'

Family talk

You may wish to bring the conversation around to talking about the young person's home life. Toys can be used to introduce the topic naturally. I have a simple jigsaw of a house, with lift-out windows and doors, through which one can see members of a family at work and at play in the different rooms. This is a useful lead in, with young children, to questions such as 'Who lives in your house?' A doll's house can be used in the same way. Another versatile tool is a button box: children enjoy rooting around in the box and you can ask them to pick one button for each family member, and tell you something about each of them. Any small objects will do for this – it could be toy cars or animals, pebbles, beans or shells.

Books

Reading a story to a child can be one of the shared enjoyable experiences you are seeking. It can also encourage them to talk about what is important in their lives, or what is troubling them. I always take books with me when seeing a child and choose with some care those that are not just attractive, worth reading and aimed at the right age group, but that may also have some relevance for the child's circumstances: for example, a story about a house move for a child who will shortly be moving. Children's librarians can be very helpful when it comes to tracking down stories on a particular theme. Some children are not interested in books, but others love having stories read to them and will want the same ones over and over. The key in the early stages of work with a child is to give them choices so they do not feel under pressure: if you have books in your bag they can ask you to read them, or they may choose another activity. If you read them a story it may prompt them to start talking about a similar experience they have had, but if they don't feel like talking they don't have to.

Chapter 9

Hearing the Child's View

Wishes and feelings

Finding out what a child's views are is central to the whole activity of listening to children. In a wide range of situations (court proceedings, children in need, children in care) there is a legal obligation on practitioners to find out what children think. There are, in addition, many other situations where it could be argued that it would be ethical to identify and consider the child's perspective, even if it is not a legal requirement: parents moving house, councillors cutting the grant to the local play-bus or teachers transferring children to a different class, to give just a few examples. There are many things, however, that may hinder clear communication: the intimidated child may be afraid to say what he thinks; the confused child may be unable to put her feelings into words; insecure children may be in the habit of saying what they think adults want to hear; a child embroiled in family conflict may be deeply ambivalent about his situation. Kenney (1999) cites a nine-year-old who expressed seven different wishes about where he should live to different people. Finding out what a child really thinks or feels is thus not always straightforward.

'I don't like saying anything, really. It feels like they're doing enough work for you as it is and you don't want to cause them any more.'
(Karen)

Good practice guide

I will give here a series of tips for discovering children's views (summarized in Checklist 9.1). Although they are in this chapter, they are so central to what it is to really listen to a child that they apply equally to all the other situations addressed in other parts of the book. Eliciting wishes and feelings is not a discrete activity: the listening practitioner has their ears open for the child's wishes and feelings whatever the focus of the piece of work they are undertaking.

Checklist 9.1 Ten top tips for finding out children's views

1. Stop, look and listen.

2. Keep an open mind.

3. Give the child some control.

4. Start from where the child is.

5. Give permission to talk.

6. Avoid direct questions.

7. Offer prompts and triggers.

8. Provide information and explanations.

9. Encourage questions.

10. Check out understanding.

Stop, look and listen

The adult who wants to listen needs to learn to keep their mouth shut and their eyes and ears open. We have to relearn the value of silence: listening 'involves a readiness to wait for the child to speak and to tolerate silent periods, as well as the ability to avoid making interruptions, or at least to restrain them' (Jones 2003, p.65). It also involves observation of the child's moods, gestures and body language: 'Communication…may or may not include language, but it will certainly include movement, behaviour and silence. We have to learn how to listen to the silence and how to hear the behaviour' (Argent 2006, p.10). Behaviour is not always easy to interpret, but it should be noted and can be added to other evidence to build up a picture of what the child is trying to communicate (see, for instance, Catriona's story in Practice Example 9.1).

'I hated it there so I behaved very badly with them and that's why I was moved. That's just an obvious way to react if you don't like it somewhere. You behave badly.'
(Robert)

PRACTICE EXAMPLE 9.1 CATRIONA

It is not just very young children or those with language difficulties who do not put their feelings into words. Even the most articulate adolescents may choose not to speak their thoughts, but may communicate them in other ways. Catriona was an intelligent and sensitive teenager who had been diagnosed with a terminal illness. The decision of the adults around her – her parents and the doctors – was not to share the prognosis with her, as they felt she was too young to cope with the knowledge that she had not long to live. She was artistic, and among the pictures she painted was one of a silhouetted figure with an earring in the form of a crucifix hanging from one ear. The figure gazed at a gravestone, which was casting a long shadow towards her.

Now who was protecting whom by not speaking about this young woman's impending death?

Keep an open mind

'My dad…didn't want to listen. And when he'd heard what *he* wanted to hear he changed the subject. He didn't want to listen to what *I* wanted to say' (Boy, 13, quoted in Butler and Williamson 1999, p.10).

Adults frequently impose their own agenda on a conversation with a child and in doing so miss what the child really wanted to tell them. One of the reasons for allowing silences, for not jumping in and suggesting answers to your own questions, for letting the child tell you what is troubling them rather than starting a conversation about what you think may be troubling them is that you may have got it completely wrong. It is important that you do not make assumptions or jump to conclusions. Once you do this the child may feel you do not want to hear about their real concerns and so they will keep them to themselves. The trick, however sure you are that you know what the problem is, is to suspend judgement until you have gathered all the evidence you can, or you may find you have reached a false conclusion. See Chapters 4 and 12 for further discussion of this important issue.

Give the child some control

Many of the difficulties for adults in finding out what children really think arise from the differences in power between them. Children are very sensitive to what has been called the 'valence' of an utterance, that is to say the relative power and status of the speaker relative to the listener, and the speaker's degree of dominance within the conversation (Garbarino and Stott 1992). Since adults are habitually in a position of authority over children it is hard for children to understand that their communications may have purposes other than control:

Even the most innocent of informational questions ('Do you go to school here?') or rhetorical questions ('Nice day, isn't it?') can be perceived by [children] as falling into the 'control' mode because of the inherent power/authority position that adults typically hold over children. (Tammivaara and Enwright 1986, p.229)

These writers suggest attempting to empower children by letting them take the initiative, by avoiding filling in pauses and hesitations with what we thought they were about to say, by avoiding asking questions where we already know the answers since these are particularly controlling, and by acting stupid: 'Once the [adult] is established as a "dummy" in need of guidance (a lasting one-down status) the child...will often provide explanations and information voluntarily' (Tammivaara and Enwright 1986, p.231).

There is a practical way, too, in which a worker can attempt to reduce the power imbalance in the interview situation, and that is by giving the child choice. Where it is feasible, offer the child a choice of venue and of timing for the meeting. I remember one boy whose reluctance to engage in conversation with me turned out to relate to me coming to see him just when his favourite TV programme was coming on: it was an easy matter to plan subsequent visits at a different time. It may be possible to offer a choice of activities, books or drawing materials, to check whether the child needs refreshment or wants to go to the toilet. You should let them know that they don't have to answer your questions if they don't want to: you could arrange in advance a sign the child can make if they don't want to talk about a certain subject, or if they are getting upset. Each of these small concessions to the child's autonomy assist in giving the message that the child has some control over the process of communication.

Start from where the child is

You may need to get down on the floor so you don't tower over the child. Starting from where the child is covers more than the way you occupy physical space, however. Early on in your interaction you must pick up clues about the child's cognitive level and the way she uses language so that you can understand each other: what names does she use for members of her family, for example if she mentions 'Dad' does this mean father or step-father?

Starting from where the child is requires you to find out what their preferred modes of communication are: with small children this is likely to be through play. Nicky, who I introduced in Chapter 7, found it easier to draw pictures than to express himself verbally, and he found it much easier to express himself verbally than to put his thoughts in writing. Louise, on the other hand, who attended a support group for teenagers whose parents misused drugs, found the best way to express her feelings was to write poems about them: talking about them was too painful. Lees (1999) observes that our culture tends to regard the spoken word as 'the pinnacle of human achievement' (p.77), and responds to those who do not or cannot communicate verbally by 'assuming that all people with communication difficulties are unable to express themselves in any way; failing to listen to such people; failing to take sufficient time to interact with them; and regarding them as less than human' (Lees 1999, p.78). She points out how vulnerable this can make disabled children to abuse, and stresses that every child communicates in some way. It is incumbent on professionals, Lees argues, to take the time and where necessary seek expert assistance to establish effective channels of communication with disabled children, so that their views too can be heard.

Even where young people are well able to talk, they may still prefer other media for communication. Coleman and Rowe (2005) advocate using the media that young people themselves use. Teenagers are at home with IT and the internet and so, they argue, adults who wish to engage with young people should develop their own IT literacy and communicate with them online. Teenagers also habitually communicate with each other by text message, so professionals could make more use of mobile phones in developing conversations with young people reluctant to engage face to face.

Give permission to talk

Some young people may continue to be uncommunicative and need to be given more explicit permission to speak. Roe (1994) describes a project to help withdrawn children in an infant school, who were relating neither to their teacher nor to other children. Her belief was that: 'The main problem was not lack of language but lack of confidence in themselves and their ability to relate to others…inside every "quiet" child is a "loud" child trying to get out' (p.62). Her solution was to take small groups out of the classroom to a relaxed environment where she got down on the floor with them, initiated play and encouraged them to be noisy. The sessions progressed from games involving eye contact but few words, to body contact games, music-making, rhymes, word games, storytelling, acting, and finally, to loud and lively physical activities. After this the children became more willing to speak in classroom situations.

It can be a strange experience for some children to be asked their views by an adult. They may have been brought up in a family where children are expected to be 'seen and not heard', or where those who express an opinion at variance with those of the adults around them suffer painful consequences. The worker therefore needs to make it explicit that they don't know the answers to the questions they are asking and that it is the child's views they are seeking, not any sort of predetermined right answers. This can be achieved as a part of describing why you are there. Bray (1991) wears a badge saying 'I listen to children'. I have a rug, which I call my 'talking' rug, which I say is for children to sit on when they tell me what they think about things. (The rug has the secondary very functional purpose of saving carpets from felt-tip pen stains!) Another ploy is to ask some questions to which you cannot possibly know the answers – what they had for lunch, what their favourite TV programme is – to establish that you are looking for information that only the child has.

Avoid direct questions

It will already be clear that the sort of questions the adult asks will profoundly affect the answers they get. Because of the risk of children perceiving any question as being controlling it may be best to avoid questions altogether however, and stick to statements that give a broad invitation to the child to talk on a given subject ('I'd like you to tell me as much as you can remember about what happened last night' 'I wonder what you think about going to live with your grandad').

> 'Adults who want to listen to children should be just sitting down with them and not filling them with questions but just letting them talk, rather than having a question you've got to answer.' (Robert)

There is research evidence demonstrating that children provide more information, and more varied information if direct questions are kept to a minimum. There should be encouragement to the child to keep talking by being attentive, making 'listening' noises like 'Mm' and 'Uhuh', and when they pause by repeating their last word or phrase, with a gently lifting intonation: '…and then we came home.' 'You came home?' Probing questions are experienced as intimidating and should only be used as a last resort.

Offer prompts and triggers

The difficulty about taking the non-directive approach to its logical conclusion is that if the adult never asks the questions they are itching to ask, the child may have no idea what they want to know. Open invitations to speak freely may lead to the articulate and confident older child simply telling you what they think, but many children, of course, do not fall into this category: 'It is ironic that the children in the most turmoil and distress are the ones who are most often asked their wishes and feelings' (Brandon 1999, p.70). So more may be required than a simple invitation to express views, and this is where the 'prompts and triggers' – the contents of the toy bag – come in.

As adults we know how a place, a smell or an object can trigger a memory. Research evidence demonstrates that for children, physical triggers are even more important to enable them to talk about the past or about people who are not present. This is both because of 'concrete thinking' and because they may not yet have developed the cognitive processes that will allow them to retrieve memories at will. So if you want to explore a young child's feelings around home or family when they are away from home, you need first to prompt them to start thinking about their home and family. Ways of assisting them to focus their thoughts on the topic might be to provide a family photograph album or to ask them to draw pictures of family members (see Rachel's story in Practice Examples 9.2 and 9.3).

PRACTICE EXAMPLE 9.2 RACHEL

Storybooks can also trigger feelings and memories and children will identify with the parts of stories that chime with their own lives. I worked with a four-year-old girl who was to be adopted, and for whom the story of *Paddington Bear* (Bond 1972) held a special significance: she worried about what would become of Paddington's aunty, now she hadn't got Paddington to look after her. I reassured Rachel that the aunt was well cared for in the rest home for retired bears, and that it wasn't Paddington's job to look after his aunty. He was only a young bear who needed to be looked after himself. Paddington's story had become for Rachel a metaphor for her own, and her underlying anxiety was for her mother, who was mentally ill. She might not have been able to put her worries into words, but her response to this story made it clear that anxiety for her mother's welfare was creating some ambivalence for her concerning the proposed adoption. My own daughter was four at the same time and she liked the story too but identified with quite different parts of it: she showed no interest in Paddington's aunt at all; she was more excited by the fact that the Brown family had a green front door, like ours. Each child will take something different from the prompts and triggers you offer them, but you can learn a lot about their preoccupations from they ways in which they respond.

Provide information and explanations

When we ask children about their wishes and their views this presupposes that they have some understanding of the options that are open to them. However, they may need more explanation first before they can make an informed choice. This was put very clearly by Anna. Describing her review meeting she said:

> I think because of my age, and because I'm quite, er, articulate, I understood what the review was about, mostly... If I'd been someone who had problems with understanding what it meant, then I don't think it would have been very helpful... Being sat down, and sort of told 'This is your review, and what's your view of the last six months, what's happened, and what would you like to happen in the next six months?' Well, what do they mean: 'What would you like to happen?' You might say: 'I'd like to win the lottery, please, and go on a desert island.' What I could influence and what I couldn't influence wasn't explained to me. You know – I could possibly influence my placement, possibly influence the rules, could maybe have changed my social worker.

Her point is clear: it is impossible to participate in decision-making if someone else lays down ground rules for the decisions that can be made but does not share them with you.

The same considerations about needing to know what choices are available apply whenever a child is asked their views. For example, the practitioner may want to establish where the child wants to live. If staying where he is is not an option, for example because his foster carers only take short-term crisis placements and do not wish to offer any child a permanent home, the child needs to understand this before stating a view. He will feel let down if

> 'When I first came into care I was given a leaflet about living in a children's home. It was very sort of "This is your right" rather than "This is how to go about getting things done". I would have liked to have something on things in Social Services and how they work rather than the legal stuff.
> I think it would have been useful to have been given a pack with leaflets in and maybe a sort of list of who's who: the director of social work and the name of your social worker.'
> (Anna)

asked his views only to be told they will be discounted. In some cases further explanations are necessary before the child can make sense of why certain options are or are not available. There is more about providing explanations in Part 4.

PRACTICE EXAMPLE 9.3 RACHEL (CONTINUED)

Rachel, the little girl who engaged so strongly with the story of Paddington Bear, had had many moves in and out of care and was completely confused about why they had happened. Before she could settle in her adoptive placement she had to understand something about the nature of her birth mother's illness, and why it had made her unable to look after a child. She also had to make some sense out of her own confused and confusing history. Acting out her moves using toy cars, ambulances, houses and play figures made her history visible for her and for the first time comprehensible. It was like a light coming on when the ambulance took the figure of her mother off to hospital leaving the figure that represented herself alone at home. 'Oh!!! Who's going to look after the baby?' she cried, and eagerly brought the social worker figure in his car to the rescue to take her to a foster home.

Encourage questions

As there are children who have been discouraged from expressing opinions, so there are some – often the same ones – who have learnt never to ask questions. This may be because their curiosity has been punished in the past, or it may be because their questions have been ignored, and after long experience of never getting answers they give up trying to ask. We need them to ask questions, however, since otherwise we may not discover what it is they do not know. Practitioners should always ask if children and young people have any questions they want to ask, but simply inviting questions may not be sufficient. Modelling the asking of questions may give children a clearer message that this is permitted: where there are two workers they can ask each other for explanations and clarifications; where there is only one worker an alternative idea is to have a rather dozy puppet, who repeatedly gets things wrong, misunderstands and can ask for explanations. This introduces an element of humour, and allows children to be in a one-up position, able to show the puppet how knowledgeable they are, at the same time as clarifying that it's OK to say if you don't understand.

Check out understanding

Misunderstandings are very common when working with someone whose use of language may be less competent than, or just different from your own, yet the consequences of undetected misunderstandings could be serious. It is important always to be checking both that you have understood what the child has said, and that they have understood you. Just saying: 'Do you understand?' is not helpful: the child will probably answer: 'Yes' to such a question, whether they think they understand or not – and even if they think they *do* understand they may be mistaken. The dim puppet who was used to model asking questions can come in useful again here: it can tap the practitioner and ask for an explanation; the practitioner can then suggest to the puppet that it asks the child to explain. The child may explain more readily to the puppet than to the adult and that way it is possible to see whether she or he has understood. Alternatively, you could ask: 'If you decided to tell a friend about this, how would you explain it to him/her?' Another way is to check out what the child knows or remembers through a game. Nicky, introduced in Chapter 7, enjoyed board games, so I devised a board game based on the story of his life (he, like many children in the care system, had moved numerous times). We threw dice and moved counters, and when we landed on a square representing one of his many homes he had to turn over a card and answer a question. Who lived in that house? What was the cat called? Why did Nicky leave? How did Nicky feel when he left? In the cases of questions like the last one, I would turn to Nicky, if it was my counter that had landed on the square, saying that only he could answer that question.

The information we give to children who have had troubled lives can often be quite complex as well as potentially distressing, so it is in any case not reasonable to expect a child to take it in the first time it is explained. Returning to the same topic several times and presenting the same information in different ways may be the best way of ensuring that it is taken in. Finding out wishes and feelings, as I hope this chapter has demonstrated, can be a complex activity, requiring skills and sensitivity on the part of the worker. Among the skills that are key to effective communication are self-awareness and sensitivity to the child's unspoken messages. These unspoken messages deserve a chapter to themselves.

Chapter 10

The Power Dynamic in the Interview

Under the surface

The effective communicator does not just listen to the spoken words but is alert to what is going on under the surface of an encounter. This can be crucial when a child or young person gets into conversation with an adult who is, or seems to be, in a position of authority, which is the case in many, if not most, adult–child relationships: parent/child, teacher/pupil, social worker/client, doctor/patient, researcher/subject, to name but a few. There is often more going on in an interaction than meets the eye – coercion, submission, jockeying for position, currying favour, deception – so that setting up constructive communication channels with young people is rarely straightforward. What the practitioner needs to do is to develop a heightened awareness of these hidden agendas: understanding the power-plays that go on in relationships can be challenging, but it is essential if we are to truly hear what people younger than us have to say.

In Bell's (2002) research on children involved in child protection investigations, she found that though children were offered limited choices, they managed to 'exercise choice in more subtle ways, [using] a range of strategies to avoid engagement, such as non-communication and diversionary tactics' (p.4). When I analysed the tapes of my interviews with looked-after children and young people in the 'Listening but not Hearing' study (McLeod 2001) it became apparent that all the young people I interviewed used such strategies: their tactics varied in subtlety but all could be seen as bids to take control of the interaction.

Several young people were approached but declined to take part in the research; one agreed but then never turned up for the appointment; one ran riot, throwing things around the room and all my efforts to engage him were in vain. Steven was more cooperative than this child, but many of his responses were openly hostile: teachers were sods, the police were shits, social workers should fuck off. Other young people subverted my agenda in more covert ways. Karen claimed to be happy to talk with me but I found it difficult to draw her out to say anything at all. She volunteered nothing in response to prompts and answered questions with monosyllables. One way of interpreting this behaviour would be to see Karen as keeping some control over the exchange by giving nothing away. Silence can be an effective defence.

A range of different tactics enabled young people to keep one jump ahead (see Reflective Exercise 10.1). Patrick changed the subject when he did not like my line of questioning. Kerry talked so much and so fast that I couldn't get a word in. Choosing to be economical with the truth is another means of maintaining some control over the communication: Kerry and Steven both claimed not to know things that I suspected they did know; Tammy exaggerated to get her points across; much of what Alistair said was far-fetched. For example, he said he had been assaulted by a member of staff:

> Alistair: And he still comes over and threatens me. Because of him I'm having to waste 30 quid a month now.
>
> AM: Why?
>
> Alistair: I'm having to get someone to watch me 24 hours a day. Cos he carries a knife with him. So any time these people that's watching me sees him, I always get a black car coming up beside me and I just jump straight into it.

This left me guessing as to which parts of the information Alistair gave me could be relied upon. As we saw in Chapter 4 lying can be both normal behaviour and experienced positively by young people. The practitioner working with adolescents must expect them at times to be less than open and honest, and sometimes to fabricate. The challenge is to work out when!

What is interesting about the interviews is that when I interviewed the young people's social workers, they reported unprompted, similar behaviours. Steven's social worker complained that all she got from him was abuse. Karen's social worker told me what a struggle it was to get Karen to say what she really wanted. Patrick's social worker said that he changed the subject when she broached sensitive issues with him and would not discuss them. Kerry's social worker described how Kerry talked and talked and would never listen, while Alistair's described him fantasizing. Thus, it would seem that the strategies I identified in the interviews may have been habitually used by the young people to manage interactions with adults (McLeod 2007b).

Reflective Exercise 10.1

Imagine you are being quizzed by someone in authority – your boss, your tutor – and you don't really want to answer their questions. What tactics would *you* use to avoid giving them the answers they are looking for?

As Rich (1968) points out, there is always an imbalance of power when an adult interviews a child and withholding information or side-stepping the adult's agenda can be used by the child as techniques for increasing her/his power base:

> The child will communicate only if on balance it is worth his while to do so. He must recognise that the interview is relevant to his problems and that…the interviewer [is] somebody who can do something about them. (p.25)

Dilemmas of interpretation and management in interviews (whether children are telling the truth, how directively to question) are thus essentially questions about the use of power. If we truly want to hear young people's voices we have to find out what is on their agenda rather than to impose our own, otherwise 'listening' will not empower them but will merely be 'serving and legitimising adults' agendas' (Spicer and Evans 2006 p.178). The more closely predetermined the answers we seek, the less likely it is that we will find out what the child really wants to say.

Building a more constructive interaction

It is easy to highlight what can go wrong in an interview, harder perhaps to make the most out of our efforts to communicate. Here are a few pointers for how to get the best out of conversations with young people when power issues threaten to get in the way.

PRACTICE REFLECTIVELY

If becoming sensitive to the power-plays in an interaction is a step towards better communication skills, the first requisite for developing that sensitivity is to become more self-aware. Schön (1983) has described a process of 'reflective practice', which involves the practitioner reflecting on an experience, connecting with the feelings it aroused, evaluating what occurred, learning from it and going forward with an adapted set of responses so as to be able to practise better in future. This cycle can be applied to any professional endeavour in teaching, social work, health or research, and is indeed a practice that can be applied to everyday life and relationships too. Thus, though our practice is never perfect we can be in a continuous loop of improving it. This process helps us to see every imperfect interaction in a positive light, since it can show us the way to do it better next time.

'They've really got to look at themselves and say: "Am I really a good social worker, or am I being rubbish at the job I'm supposed to be doing?"' (Kerry)

ADDRESS POWER ISSUES

In every situation, even the least promising (for example, visiting a young person in custody or setting up communication with a young person who has profound disabilities), there will be opportunities to give the child choices so that it is not simply a case of the adult imposing a completely pre-determined agenda. The sensitive professional will exploit these opportunities. Morris (1998), for example, when seeking views of disabled young people constantly re-established consent as the interview went on: 'Is it all right to ask you about...?' She found use of language was important: 'We realised how using the word "interview" could act as a barrier...because it set up expectations that we would gather information by asking questions and writing down answers' (p.11). Instead she adopted the word 'visit' to describe her meetings with the young people. She asked how the young people preferred to communicate and where they had to speak through a facilitator she gave them a choice of facilitator where possible.

RESPECT THE CHILD'S RIGHT NOT TO COMMUNICATE

Kohli (2006b) talks of how unaccompanied asylum-seeking children are often extremely guarded, so getting them to talk about themselves is like pulling teeth. He describes them as enigmatic 'closed book' children who 'present as compliant, polite, yet troubled individuals who worry about safely talking to others' (p.708), and explains that they may keep silent for a range of reasons: fear of having their asylum applications turned down if they say the wrong thing; fear that their families at home may be victimized if they let slip their true identity; a numbing of their own emotions against the pain of trauma and loss; a mistrust, born of bitter experience, of all in authority; the normal reticence of adolescence; a cultural inhibition against drawing attention to oneself or expressing feelings; plain confusion about what to say. He concluded that silence was a complex issue for these children, as perhaps it is for all vulnerable children in uncertain circumstances. In his study of social workers supporting unaccompanied asylum-seeking children he found that the social workers had gained an understanding of why these children were so unforthcoming, did not pressurize them to talk more, and where they succeeded in communicating this understanding were able to build up some trust: 'They appeared to know the language of silence and to respond well to the spoken and unspoken worlds that the children carried with them' (Kohli 2006b, p.720). The key to building more effective relationships with these very defended individuals lay in a combination of empathy for the child's situation and respect for his or her defences.

> 'Like everyone, I've got certain barriers against people. It takes time to drop your barriers because I've been hurt so many times. They seem to forget you've been hurt and they just go on about it.'
> (Kerry)

TAKE YOUR TIME

A third issue that is critical to gaining the trust of an individual who does not want to engage in a dialogue, is time. The social workers in Kohli's study (see above) had a long-term relationship with the children in which the worker could demonstrate reliability. Building trusting relationships with disaffected adolescents and other troubled children is rarely something that can be done overnight, yet it is central to hearing what they have to say: reaching an understanding of the viewpoint of a marginalized young person can be a time-consuming business. This has implications for the structure of services as well as for individual workers: 'Children's well-being is closely linked to their relationships and emotions. This implies that services should not only focus more on these, but also enable staff to use relationships positively, rather than concentrating on behavioural or organisational outcomes' (Jordan 2006, p.48). Unfortunately practitioner time is a scarce commodity, and interventions are often perforce brief; performance indicators are more often quantitative than qualitative, since these are easier to measure and compare, and organizations inevitably prioritize those aspects of the service against which they are to be judged. Quality of relationships between practitioners and service-users is unlikely to be high on the priority list. The traditional notion of 'case-work' (Searing 2003), with its emphasis on continuity of relationship and in-depth understanding of family and child may have to be rediscovered if children are to be heard.

CHALLENGE WHERE NECESSARY

Good channels of communication can be blocked where an individual feels disempowered, so it is normally incumbent on the adult to try to empower the child. There are occasions, however, where it may be necessary for the adult to take control of the situation. There is a time for being sensitive and empathetic, but there is also a time for being robust and challenging the unacceptable (Wilson 1998). Violence or the threat of violence are never acceptable; racism and homophobia may be thought to be condoned if they are not confronted; lies and fantasies can escalate if they go unchecked. Steven's social worker felt she could not accept the foul language and abuse he hurled at her: 'I'm constantly saying to him that that sort of behaviour is not appropriate... I don't get beyond that, so quite often I have to break away because we're just not getting anywhere.' Like me, Alistair's social worker felt that a lot of what the boy said was pure fantasy: 'He's a bit of a Walter Mitty is Alistair with his mad ideas...' and he was not prepared to accept it. He took a no-nonsense approach to confronting Alistair's fantasies and misdemeanours: 'I suppose I've been very directive with him. There was so many things going wrong you had to make him look at the consequences. I mean, I try not to go along with his airy-fairy Walter Mitty stuff. It's a case of got to tell him where it's at.' This can be a difficult balance to get right: Alistair's social worker appeared to have succeeded in building a constructive relationship with Alistair but Steven's social worker was still struggling to establish any dialogue with Steven at all. There is evidence, though, that young people do prefer practitioners to be straight-talking, even where this is uncomfortable. One of the young people I interviewed, Kerry, said a good social worker should be like a friend. Asked what that meant she said: 'My dad listens to me. He's like a friend. Like, when you've got a friend who listens to you and tells you when you look horrible in a skirt or something. He's like that. He's honest.' This confirms findings from Butler and Williamson (1994) to the effect that young people trust adults who are 'straight' with them, even though this may mean being at the receiving end of uncomfortable home truths.

Adults who are new to working with youth may lack confidence in their right to lay down boundaries: reflection, or discussion with a colleague or supervisor can help you decide where the line is that you are not prepared to let the young person cross. Direct confrontation can make matters escalate: sometimes humour can deflect aggression more effectively. I remember a lovely story of a residential worker threatened with assault by a young man. She seized his hands as he ran towards her with his fists flailing, said: 'Yes, I love ballroom dancing too!' and waltzed around the room with him. This completely took the wind out of his sails, and they both ended up helpless with laughter. Certainly, understanding where children are coming from, so that the worker appreciates *why* they may be swearing or fantasizing, bragging or lying, may make it easier to lay down boundaries in a way that the young person finds more acceptable. It is important to direct any criticism at the behaviour, rather than at the child, and to acknowledge the feelings underlying the behaviour. A combination of recognizing the child's feelings while keeping one's own feelings under wraps can be a powerful one. Nicky, who we met in Chapter 7, once seized a toy sword during one of our sessions and made as if to hit me with it. It was only plastic, but it would have hurt. In his moment of hesitation before he brought down the sword I managed to keep the alarm out of my voice and said: 'I can see you're feeling angry. Try hitting the sofa with that sword – it might make you feel better.' He did, and that was another occasion when I felt relief (and Nicky did too, I suspect).

Chapter 11

Endings

Bringing the dialogue to a close

It is a characteristic of relationships between a practitioner and a child that they are time-limited. Unlike family relationships and some friendships, which will continue as long as both parties are alive, relationships between a professional and a service-user are almost always temporary: the nurse never sees the child again after he is discharged from hospital; the child moves to another class and gets a new teacher; the social worker closes the case or changes her job. For a child who has suffered unresolved losses, each further loss, however small, can bring back the feelings associated with the previous one, so that something that another child accomplishes with ease, such as the move to a higher class, can be an ordeal. Vulnerable children can find all transitions difficult, and the end of a relationship with a professional they have come to trust is no exception.

Bell found that continuity of relationships was very important for abused children and that 'children felt bereft, forgotten and confused' (2002, p.4) when their social workers left. Looked-after children, as a group, have suffered more moves, more trauma, separation and loss than most, and my findings on looked-after children reflected Bell's: much of the hostility Steven directed at his social worker, for example, appeared to stem from his feeling that he had been let down by his last social worker leaving. The current social worker told me: 'His previous social worker he'd had for a long time, and constantly I've had that "I want my old social worker back!" and I'm still trying to get round it.' When I met Steven what he said confirmed this: 'My old social worker was quite good. I had her for eight years. She's just left… But my social worker who I have now never comes round… She's pathetic.' It may have been the sense of betrayal he felt at this desertion that made him so resistant to any dialogue with the replacement worker (who had in fact been working for him for six months – the previous worker had not 'just left' even though it might have seemed that way to Steven). The difficulty for professional staff is that they may be unable to deliver the long-term relationship that the child would prefer, yet they do not want to leave the child feeling let down when they leave. Whether interventions are short or long, how can endings be managed?

Our endings are in our beginnings

The key to negotiating the end of a piece of work is to bear it in mind and bring the child's attention to it from the beginning. This applies to each interview, and also to a whole programme of work. The school year is broken into terms and the day into fixed periods, so children know exactly how long a lesson will last. This gives a structure and predictability that children by and large find reassuring. At the start of a meeting with a child, the practitioner can draw the child's attention to the time, and explain when she expects the meeting to finish. Referring at intervals to how much time is left helps to prepare the child for the meeting's end. If you stick to the plan this also helps to reassure the child that you are a reliable person whose word can be trusted. In the case of a group-work programme, facilitators can share with group members a timetable of sessions, so they know from the outset what to expect. A mid-programme review session helps keep the approaching end in mind and then the end of the series can be marked by a celebration – all of the group sharing a cake, for example, or going out together for a meal – or by a session that is a little different from those that went before: there could be an 'award ceremony' in which certificates of achievement are handed out, perhaps.

Many encounters between professionals or carers and children are not pre-planned to the extent that it is possible to predict how long sessions will last, how often they will meet, or how long the child will stay in the carer's home. Nevertheless, except where you expect the relationship to be a lifelong one (for example, if you are adopting a child), you should make explicit the temporary nature of your involvement from when you first meet. It may seem brutal to the foster carer to be telling the child who has newly arrived that she will only be staying until the social worker can find a home where she can stay for good, but it is not nearly as brutal as having to tell the child once she has settled in and wants to stay that it is time to be moving on. Practitioners, too, should make it clear that they are not there as a friend but because it is part of their job to see the child and that sooner or later it will stop being part of

'I had my special teacher with me then. I went to her house once and I was getting conkers off the tree and she helped me and I stayed for tea. She used to help me, but then she left because she didn't think she was needed any more.' (Patrick)

their job. Then once they know when it is they have to move on they can start to count down ('I'm coming twice more'... 'I'm coming once more'... 'Today's my last visit').

Jewett (1984) recommends decreasing the frequency or length of meetings before terminating them, and dressing this up as a reward to the child for having worked so hard. 'You must be sure that the child does not harbour any suspicion that the termination is due to any wrong he has committed: he must understand that it truly results from his success in overcoming his difficulties' (p.140). She is speaking of a planned end to therapy sessions; in other cases the termination may be unconnected with the child's achievements, but the importance of ensuring the child does not feel it is their fault that the worker is leaving applies in all cases.

Finishing the intervention with some sort of celebration may be appropriate where the relationship has been a long or important one, or it may be in order to give the child a small gift. Jewett advises asking the child how they want to say goodbye, and says that they often choose to give the worker a hug. However the parting is managed, it is important to say goodbyes formally and directly to the child, rather than just disappearing from their life without warning. Poorly managed termination of contact reinforces for a child the view that no adult can be trusted, that they are worth little and should expect abandonment, and that telling your story to another person only ends in increased distress. Managing endings positively is thus important for children in the long term as well as the short. This is particularly important when dealing with children who have suffered serious trauma and loss. In the next part of the book we look at interventions with such children and some of the special skills that can enhance communication with them.

Part 4: Particular Conversations – Interviews for Specific Purposes

Seldom, very seldom does complete truth belong to any human disclosure, seldom can it happen that something is not a little disguised, or a little mistaken.

From **Emma** by Jane Austen (Austen [1816] 1966, p.418)

Chapter 12

Finding Out What Has Happened to a Child

The previous part of the book gave general guidance on promoting communication with children in any circumstances. This part is focused on skills needed for interviews that have specific functions. Each chapter considers a specialist task on which an interaction with a young person may focus: this first chapter addresses looking into allegations of ill-treatment. The subsequent chapters cover sharing sensitive information with children and helping them to recover from the effects of distressing experiences.

Investigative interviewing

The investigative interview is a rather special sort of conversation with a child. It has received a great deal of research attention, particularly in the United States, because in a forensic context the way a witness statement is obtained can make or break a prosecution. Where the witness is a child who is young, traumatized, disabled, or for any other reason has difficulties with communication, obtaining a statement that will be regarded as reliable by a court of law is challenging. Yet there are some crimes (notably child sexual abuse) where there are no other witnesses and there may be no corroborating evidence, so a conviction rests on the child's word against that of the adult. It is not only in order to obtain evidence for legal proceedings that an adult may need to know what has happened to a child, however. There are many more everyday situations where we want to ask children about their experiences, from the teacher needing to sort out playground bullying, to the casualty officer enquiring how a child came by an injury, to the parent curious to discover whether their child is really enjoying going to day care. In each of these situations the principles of good practice underlying investigative interviewing in a forensic situation, selectively applied, may help us to find out what actually happened, rather than what the child thinks we want to hear.

Reflective Exercise 12.1

Consider your feelings about parents who neglect, over-chastise or sexually abuse their children. How might these feelings affect the way you respond if a child says something to you that suggests they may have been ill-treated in any of these ways?

The characteristic of an investigative interview that sets it out from other types of interaction is that its purpose is to try to discover the answer to a specific question: did or did not an alleged incident take place? What exactly happened? The adult has a very definite agenda that may exclude anything that is on the child's agenda. At the same time, however, the interviewer must avoid suggesting an answer to the child for fear of contaminating the evidence and this can get in the way of being open about exactly what the agenda is. The combination of an imposed agenda that may also be covert gives this type of interaction an innate tendency to be oppressive. Child protection enquiries also carry the risk that, due to the stigma attached to child abuse in the public perception, to be accused of ill-treating a child is deeply threatening and can carry far-reaching social consequences. Therefore, a 'narrow concentration on the alleged incident' of abuse, leaving the needs of child and family unmet, can make matters worse for them rather than better (Department of Health 1995, p.55).

The rationale underlying the protocols for investigative interviews is that they may provide the best or only way of protecting a child from significant harm and as such the end justifies the means. However, to minimize the risk of negative consequences for child and family the interviewer must take particular care explaining the limits of confidentiality; pay attention to the child's needs for support; view the alleged abuse in the context of a holistic assessment of all the care the child is receiving; and as far as possible ensure that the family as a whole receives appropriate services to meet any unmet identified needs.

Official guidance

The British government has brought out two documents of guidance on interviewing vulnerable witnesses, including children, in situations where a criminal prosecution may be brought. The first was the *Memorandum of Good Practice* (Home Office 1992) and a revised and expanded version, *Achieving*

Best Evidence (Home Office *et al.* 2002) was brought out ten years later. *Communicating with Vulnerable Children* (Jones 2003) was commissioned by the Department of Health at about the same time as the latter document and complements it. Despite its general-sounding title, this book does not concern itself with other scenarios in which adults may communicate with children. Its focus is on investigative interviewing of child witnesses and it provides much more detailed and useful advice than that found in either of the official guidance documents.

The *Memorandum* filled an important vacuum when it was published. The Cleveland Report (Secretary of State for Social Services 1988) had highlighted poor quality of practice in interviewing children where sexual abuse was suspected and recommended that more guidance and training be provided for practitioners carrying out this difficult task. It was also clear that successful prosecutions of those who sexually abused children were rare, in part because the traumatic effect on children of cross-examination meant that their evidence rarely stood up in court. The *Memorandum* laid down a framework for the forensic interview based on five stages, popularly known as the 'step-wise' interview, and practitioners welcomed this approach. It became clear in time, however, that the *Memorandum*'s guidance was limited and rigid, it militated against offering children adequate emotional support and paid insufficient attention to the particular requirements of interviewing young, disabled or ethnic minority children (Davies and Westcott 1999).

Achieving Best Evidence attempts to rectify these shortcomings. It is much longer and more detailed than the *Memorandum*, applying to vulnerable adult witnesses as well as children. It covers in more detail the legal requirements, particularly the new provisions brought in for interviewing vulnerable and intimidated witnesses by the Youth Justice and Criminal Evidence Act 1999. Issues of preparation and support before, during and after any criminal hearing as well as planning and support before and during interviews are given attention. Its recommendations for how to conduct interviews are more flexible as regards timing, duration and frequency and there is guidance on interviewing very young children, disabled children and those from ethnic minorities. Indeed, it states on the first page that: 'Each witness is unique and the manner in which they are interviewed must be tailored to their particular needs and circumstances' (Home Office *et al.* 2002 p.1). Specific examples are given of the sorts of questions that will be acceptable at each stage of an interview. It is thus a document that is likely to be of more use to practitioners than the *Memorandum*. Essentially, though, *Achieving Best Evidence* maintains the same central emphasis on the 'step-wise' or staged interview, which ten years of practice had established as a broadly helpful framework.

The 'step-wise' interview

Achieving Best Evidence has four stages to its interview, as against the *Memorandum*'s five, but the progression from less directive to more directive questioning is the same, and is a principle that can be adopted whenever an adult wants to discover something from a child.

Stage one

This is the introductory stage of the interview, and one of its main functions is to build rapport. We have already discussed the issue of getting to know a child before addressing potentially sensitive issues with them. However, in the context of a forensic interview there may be particular difficulties establishing rapport since this will often have to be achieved during a brief initial phase of the first (and often only) interview, not over the extended period that might be available in a long-term intervention. One cannot but feel sceptical about how much trust can be developed between a child and an adult who is possibly a complete stranger through a few minutes' chat about school or hobbies before plunging into an enquiry about whether a child has been abused. Nevertheless, it is important that the interviewer does what they can in adverse circumstances to make the child feel relaxed.

'My old social worker was very nice and used to take you out places where you could relax and then you'd talk. Situations like meetings – all adults and just one child – you're very isolated and you feel out of place.' (Robert)

The first stage in an initial interview is important, even if it is brief. One of its functions is to assist with assessment: the interviewer will need to keep eyes and ears open in order to gauge the child's cognitive and linguistic level, enabling them to pitch questions at a level the child can comprehend. Another function is to set ground rules. This is about preparing the child for what to expect in the course of the interview. Asking open questions in the rapport stage will make it clear that the interview is not to be an interrogation. It is also advisable to make sure that the child does not believe that they have to answer every question whether they know the answer or not, or that the adult already knows what happened and is somehow testing the child out by asking them.

The focus here is on clarifying the basis of the encounter for the child to ensure that the most accurate statement possible is elicited. Where an interpreter is present (because a child does not speak English, or has communication difficulties), the role of the interpreter in the interaction must be made clear for all participants. Another issue that will need clarifying from the child's point of view is the question of the interview's confidentiality – or rather lack of it. The ethical practitioner will explain the roles of any other persons present, show the child the camera and video/DVD equipment, and if there is a one-way mirror will take them behind it. They will explain in age-appropriate terms that the benefit of being filmed is that the child will not have to repeat their story so many times or stand up in court to give evidence, and they will also tell the child who else will be able to see the recording once it is made. *Achieving Best Evidence* does not cover the consent issue as part of ground-rule-setting – it assumes consent will have been given before the camera starts rolling – but whenever it takes place it is a crucial part of the process. Being fully informed might make some young witnesses reluctant to speak at all in front of a camera, but to film them without their informed consent would be neither open nor honest, is potentially abusive and would constitute a breach of their human rights. Even where consent has been established in advance it should be re-established before starting to question the child.

So a lot may be going on in stage one of the interview and handling it well may make all the difference to its overall success. Research studies, however, have found that rapport-building is not always well-handled: closed rather than open questions are the norm, ground-rule-setting may be omitted, the alleged offence is often mentioned prematurely, questions can be mechanical and responses lukewarm: 'interviewers seemed to regard rapport-building as a formality that must be observed, before getting down to the real business of talking about abuse' (Wood, quoted in Jones 2003, p.125). It will be time well-spent if interviewers take care, when planning their approach before meeting the child, to pay attention to the initial stage.

Stage two

This is the 'free narrative' stage: the point at which the child is asked to tell their story without any prompting or questioning from the adult. This is 'the core of the interview and the most reliable source of accurate information' (Home Office *et al.* 2002, p.41), nevertheless it seems the hardest for practitioners to get right. A statement made completely freely is more valid as evidence since it is less likely to have been affected by interviewer bias; it also allows the child to say what is on their agenda rather than simply to respond to that of the adult, so it gives the child more control over the process and is less oppressive. But research evidence indicates that in nearly a third of interviews conducted under the *Memorandum*, stage two was completely absent (Davies *et al.* 1995, p.2).

Why should free narrative be so difficult to elicit? Practitioners carrying out such interviews should all have been specially trained. The answer seems to be in part that adults find it very hard to stop acting as though they are in charge when children are around. Even with training, it is hard for us to shed our preconceptions and assumptions, go into an interview situation with a genuinely open mind and let the child tell the story their way: we feel compelled to take over and direct the process.

A second reason for the absence of a stage two in interviews is that it may be very difficult to get a free narrative account out of a child without more direct questioning: if they do not understand what is required, they are shy, anxious, intimidated or inarticulate, they may decide that keeping quiet is the best policy and then the adult is driven into questioning, perhaps in desperation. *Achieving Best Evidence* therefore gives detailed advice on how to establish that the child understands why they are there and can get started on talking about what has happened to them. It recommends a whole series of ways of inviting the child to speak without putting ideas into their heads, to be attempted in turn, in the hope that one of them will prompt the young witness to start talking:

Tell me why you are here today.

(*If no response*):

If there is something troubling you it is important for me to understand.

(*If no response*):

I heard you said something to your mum/teacher/friend yesterday. Tell me what you talked about.

(*If no allegation*):

I heard something may have been bothering you. Tell me everything you can about that.

(*If no response*):

As I told you, my job is to talk to children about things which may be troubling them. It is very important I understand what may be troubling you. Tell me why you think (carer) may have brought you here today.

(*If no response*):

I heard that someone may have done something that wasn't right. Tell me everything you know about that. Everything you can remember. (Home Office *et al.* 2002, p.40)

The prompts start very general, only moving towards the more specific if the child does not respond. The alleged incident is not mentioned at all. These invitations need to be spoken in a tone of gentle enquiry, with long pauses between each if the interviewer's persistence is not to be experienced by the child as interrogation.

'When they ask me all these questions and that, sometimes I go all shy and I don't know what to say, so I just go: "I dunno."' (Karen)

While this set of opening gambits is designed with a forensic context in mind the same principles can be applied to other enquiries. Jones (2003) gives the example of a psychiatrist interviewing a teenager who has self-harmed. Again the prompts start very general and move to the more specific if there is no response:

Do you know why that happened?... Have any things been upsetting you?... How are things at home/at school/with your friends? ... Sometimes young people hurt themselves when there is something very upsetting they have seen, or has happened to them, and they don't know how to talk about it. (Pause) Has anything like that happened to you? (p.135)

The intention is that in response to very unspecific prompts the child will launch into a full and detailed account of their experiences. Once they have started to tell their story it is still necessary for the adult to hold back from questions or requests to clarify, as these may interrupt the child's flow and deflect them from what they had been meaning to say. Inconsistencies or things that are not clear will have to be returned to later: 'The interviewer's role is that of a facilitator, not an interrogator' (Home Office *et al.* 2002, p.41). The adult must continue to appear interested, however, and can demonstrate this by body language: attention, nods and affirming sounds ('Mm', 'Uhuh'), or by reflecting back what the child has said: 'Child: "So we went round to his house..." (Pause) Interviewer: "I see, you went round to his house..."' (Home Office *et al.* 2002, p. 41). The guidance goes on to suggest methods for encouraging children to give more detailed information if their free narrative account is faltering. The interviewer can say: 'I can see this is difficult for you. Is there anything I can do to help?' They can ask whether the child has been told to keep something secret and what they fear will happen if they tell. They can offer the option of writing something down, telling a puppet or speaking into a telephone: 'Pretending to talk on the telephone may act as a vehicle for talking with the interviewer and may also help the child feel some sense of control over the interview, since he can stop the conversation at any time by hanging up' (Garbarino and Stott 1992, p.191). The aim is to give the child as many opportunities as possible to tell their story their way without adult interference.

Jones (2003) suggests that if the child has provided only limited information at this point, rather than moving on to the questioning phase of the interview it is better to return to the rapport-building stage and try to find a new lead in. For example, where suspicions focus on a particular family member, a child could be asked to draw their home or a family tree in the hope that this may spontaneously trigger the child to talk about the issue of concern. While in the earlier guidance, use of any such props was frowned upon, the more recent guidance recognizes that vulnerable witnesses such as children need special allowances to be made if they are to make statements that can be used in court.

Alternatively, Jones suggests taking a break and returning to the interview room after refreshments to see if this helps the child to feel more relaxed. The interviewer should only start asking questions once all efforts to encourage the interviewee to describe freely what has happened have been exhausted.

Stage three

Stage three, which should be put off as long as possible, is where the interviewer does start questioning the child. This is the time to clarify inconsistencies and parts of the story that the interviewer has not understood, or that the child has failed to mention. The interviewer may need certain details, such as what clothes an offender was wearing on the day in question, to flesh out the account and provide useful evidence later. To a child such details would not be significant so they are unlikely to mention them unless they are asked directly. It is still essential that the adult takes care over the way questions are asked. I remember viewing a videotaped interview in which the interviewing police officer asked: 'And what happened next? Did your dad put his hand down your pants?' This illustrates exactly the sort of question that must be avoided. While her first question ('What happened next?') made the possibly unwarranted assumption that something *did* happen next, and directed the child to focus on a particular place and time, and so can be described as a 'specific' question, it did at least leave open to the child the possibility of a wide range of answers, from 'Nothing' to 'A flying saucer landed right in front of me', and so can be described as 'open-ended', which is what we should strive for questions to be wherever possible. However, she did not give the child a chance to answer this first question, instead she launched straight into the second one: 'Did your dad put his hand down your pants?' This is the worst kind of question, since not only is it 'closed' (the interviewee has very limited opportunities for response, in this case only 'yes' or 'no') but it is also 'leading', in that it suggests to the witness that a certain person did a specific thing before they have had a chance to say it unprompted. Responses to 'leading' questions are in most cases inadmissible as evidence under British law, so this video-tape could not have been used in court. Poor interviewing technique in this case could thus have led to waste of police and social work time and failure to prosecute an offender. It could also have led to a child being left unprotected when she needed safeguarding.

Achieving Best Evidence's stage three combines the *Memorandum*'s stages three and four: 'open questioning' and 'closed questioning'. The *Memorandum*'s logic for separating questioning into two stages was that closed questioning should only be attempted once open questioning was exhausted. *Achieving Best Evidence* recognizes that while it is always preferable to start with open-ended questions, these are not discrete phases: in practice the practitioner may move backwards and forwards between the two types of question, closing down the focus with a specific query and then opening it up again with a more general prompt that allows the interviewee to expand, for example: 'Did you go into the living-room?' (closed question), followed by 'Tell me everything that happened there' (open prompt). Lamb, Sternberg and Esplin (1998) call this technique 'paired questioning' and it is one that is well worth practising.

Davies and Westcott (1999) cite research evidence demonstrating that open-ended questions elicit longer and more detailed responses containing more accurate information, particularly in the case of younger children. However, research has found that interviewers are not good at keeping their questions open: Davies and his co-researchers found that in one in three of interviews they analysed, the free narrative phase was not followed up with an open question, and 'spontaneous information from the child was further curtailed by an excessive number of closed as opposed to open-ended questions' (Davies *et al.* 1995, p.2). A constant risk is that the interviewer will come with preconceptions that cloud their judgement so that they fail to 'hear' things they are not expecting to hear:

> Interviewers need to be aware that the common human frailty
> of ignoring information contrary to one's own view may be
> even more likely to affect their interviews with vulnerable

people whom they are having difficulty understanding, or may believe to be less competent than other people. (Home Office *et al.* 2002, p.79)

Keeping an open mind is never more important: closed questions can be the outward sign of a closed mind.

Part of the problem is that 'interviewing is an adult means of obtaining information' (Garbarino and Stott 1992, p.202) which has to be adapted to the communicative competence of the child, and sometimes opportunities for free narrative and open questioning do not elicit an adequate response. In such situations more specific or closed questioning may be the only option. There may be occasions when an interviewer is pushed by the child's reticence into making a 'permission-giving' statement that could be viewed as suggestive. Jones gives the following example: 'I talk to a lot of children, and sometimes to children who have been touched on private parts of their bodies. It can help to talk about something like that. Has anything like that ever happened to you?' (Jones 2003, p.138). The key, again, if this tack produces a response, is to return to open-ended questions, so that the child is freed up to generate new material not contained within the suggestive prompt. This will demonstrate that they are not merely responding to the suggestion contained in the adult's question, but are accessing genuine memories of their own. In rare cases, for example a child with a disability who communicates using an aid that only allows for yes/no answers, the child's responses may perforce be restricted to 'yes' and 'no'. In this case the interviewer will require great ingenuity to ensure all avenues have been explored and that their own assumptions have not limited the child's options for reply. Morris (1998) quotes an example of a disabled girl who had been taught to smile to indicate 'yes'. This system was fine for 'Yes, I want a drink' but rather less appropriate for 'Yes, I have been abused'. Morris comments: 'Such a situation in itself speaks volumes about the barriers to the young woman making a complaint about her experience' (p.36).

Achieving Best Evidence does acknowledge that it may be impossible to avoid leading questions completely as some witnesses, such as those with learning disabilities, may simply not understand that they are being asked to make a statement without a very broad hint. However, it cautions that:

the interviewer should never be the first to suggest to the witness that a particular offence was committed or that a particular person was responsible. Once such a step has been taken it will be extremely difficult to counter the argument that the interviewer put the idea into the witness's head and that her/his account is therefore tainted. (Home Office *et al.* 2002, p.77)

Research gives further pointers for techniques we should use and those we should avoid. Questions to avoid include ones that force a child to choose one out of two options: 'Did this happen on Saturday, or was it Sunday?' (when the child might have wanted to say 'Friday night'); portmanteau questions: 'Did you say anything and how were you feeling?' (The child doesn't know which bit to answer); double negatives: 'You didn't say he wasn't there, did you?' (confusion! if the response is 'yes' – or for that matter 'no' – what are we to understand by it?); long and complex sentences and jargon (Lamb *et al.* 1998). Recommended techniques, on the other hand, include feigning confusion: 'You say you were in Mr B's bed. I'm confused. How did that happen?' (Lamb *et al.* 1998); rephrasing rather than repeating questions the child has not understood; leaving pauses; using names rather than pronouns – 'he' might not refer to the person you think it does (Garbarino and Stott 1992); or pairing a negative question with a positive one to get a balanced response: 'What was the worst thing about it?... And what was the best thing about it?' (Jones 2003).

If after opportunities for both free narrative and questioning the interviewer still feels there is more the witness has to tell that they have not said, *Achieving Best Evidence* suggests moving on to a broader discussion of possibly related issues: secrets, for example, or 'good' and 'bad' people, or what the child would like changed in his or her life. The final piece of advice, however, comes from Jones (2003), who recognizes that many investigative interviews fail, despite the interviewer's best efforts, to elicit a statement that will clarify for the concerned professionals or worried parents what has really happened to the child: 'These situations can be professionally frustrating, but it is preferable to close the session without having pressurized the child than to be drawn through anxiety into a hectoring or coercive stance' (Jones 2003, p.139). This stage of the interview is, after all, for questioning, not for interrogation. We should remember Bell's (2002) finding from her interviews with children who had been subject to child protection investigations: 'The most common criticism was of questioning experienced as invasive or threatening' (p.4).

'Social workers just jump in and bombard you with questions and pry really.' (Tammy)

Stage four

This is the final stage of the interview, when the interviewer brings it to a close and ties off loose ends. There is much less written about how to finish an interview than there is about what adults clearly see as the meat of the interaction: how to extract critical information from a possibly reluctant witness. Nevertheless, the way the meeting ends is important, for the child if not for the interviewer. If the adult gives up the attempt in evident frustration, a child may feel that she has somehow failed, when in reality she may have seen nothing and have had nothing to tell. This might lead her to feel that if she wants to please adults in future she had better make something up. Alternatively, if a young witness has found the experience of sharing his secret traumatic and he is now afraid for the consequences, he may feel doubly abused if the person to whom he has bared his soul abandons him without a word of support or reassurance as soon as the prized disclosure is safely on the tape.

Again, sadly, the evidence suggests that professionals can neglect to complete interviews with children in a properly respectful manner: studies indicate that 'closure is often brief to the point of abruptness and key elements are omitted' (Davies and Westcott 1999, p.23). Indeed, the official guidance accords this stage of the interview a marked lack of priority: of its 173 pages, *Achieving Best Evidence* devotes less than a page to how to end an interview. Jones (2003) gives more detailed advice about this part of the interview and pays more attention to the child's support needs. He says the interviewer should show concern, acknowledge any distress and 'vindicate' the child's story by recognizing that serious matters have been discussed. However, he advises against telling the child they have done well, lest this be interpreted as a 'reward' for sharing their story. He lays stress on offering the child the opportunity to say anything else: 'Is there anything else you think I should know? Are there any other questions I should have asked?' (p.143). Children should also be encouraged to ask questions. He recognizes that the child may need information to allay their anxiety and advises the practitioner to answer all questions honestly and as openly as possible, though without making any promises that can't be kept. The child will need to know what comes next in terms of further interviews, treatment or placement, and questions about what will become of the tape of the interview are likely to surface again, though the adult will be unable to say at this stage whether the matter will come before a court. The practitioner should also avoid discussing what might happen to the alleged abuser or expressing personal opinions on the legality or morality of what has been described. There are thus numerous caveats as to what information may or may not be provided.

Jones also directs the interviewer to think ahead: contact details should be provided in case the child has more to add to their statement but also in case they need help. The practitioner will simultaneously be assessing the child's current emotional state in the context of their overall needs: what support might they require after the interview? In some cases a social worker's next responsibility may be to take steps to remove the child from an environment in which they have been ill-treated: there will be legal interventions and complex arrangements to be made. Thought must be given in every case to what information to provide for the child's parents, carers and school and consideration given to provision of therapy for the child, though if any is provided before a court case this must comply with official guidance (Home Office, Crown Prosecution Service and Department of Health 2001) if it is not to prejudice criminal proceedings. Thus, any thought for the child's needs for support has to be tempered with attention to how this might affect the likelihood of a successful prosecution. It is a dilemma for the practitioner who will want to put the child's needs first, but who also has to recognize that the child's efforts in providing a statement will be wasted if their evidence is rejected as unsatisfactory by the court, as may so easily happen.

Despite the best efforts of the authorities to make allowances for the special vulnerabilities of child witnesses, one cannot help feeling that in all the guidance on investigative interviewing, the imperatives of the criminal justice system take first place, well before the needs of the abused child. Wrongful conviction of an innocent person is a terrible injustice, and it is proper that the system should protect the rights of the accused. However, this stacks the odds against the right to protection of the maltreated child, whose voice courts can seem reluctant to hear.

Chapter 13

Making Sense of Mysteries

Explaining things a child does not understand

The role of an adult is often to help a child understand things that are confusing: parents do it every day; teachers earn their living that way. In the context of listening to children's views, explanations can be crucial since young people may not be able to express a view on a question that they do not understand, nor can they make a choice between options if they are unaware what options are available.

> 'Then my dad gave me the choice of going into care or going back to my mum. I couldn't understand why I had to make that choice and I didn't really know what care was, so I chose to go and live with my mum.' (Patrick)

Health and social care practitioners frequently find themselves having to explain complex and emotionally charged matters that many adults might assume were beyond the comprehension of children (see, for instance, David's story in Practice Example 13.1). Information may need to be shared of a type that most children in our society are protected from and that adults themselves may find inexplicable or distressing. How do you explain to a four-year-old that his mother has died, or to a 13-year-old that the reason she was adopted was because she was conceived when her birth father raped her birth mother, who was his own 13-year-old daughter? How do you find out which of his warring parents a seven-year-old would really prefer to live with, or help a teenager make sense of her mother's heroin addiction? These tasks are of a different order of difficulty from those that adults usually find themselves explaining to children.

The worker who is skilled at helping a child understand sensitive issues will have a better chance of finding out what the child really thinks and of empowering them to make constructive choices. The explanations may themselves be in a sense therapeutic as they may help the child to survive adversity and so to cope better with life: Jewett (1984) speaks of the bereaved as having:

> a driving need to make sense of what has happened and to understand the hows and whys that led to the loss. This comes partially from a need to restore order and meaning to chaotic feelings and partially…so that further losses might be prevented. (p.78)

This chapter gives advice on explaining issues that may be distressing as well as complex and on sharing unwelcome information with children (summarized in Checklist 13.1).

Checklist 13.1 Nine top tips for explaining difficult information (I couldn't think of a tenth one!)

1. Plan your approach.

2. Decide what the child needs to know when.

3. Sort out your own feelings first.

4. Be ready to support the child.

5. Put yourself in the child's shoes.

6. Relate explanations to the child's experience.

7. Address issues of blame and responsibility.

8. Encourage controlled expression of feelings.

9. Give permission to mourn and move on.

PRACTICE EXAMPLE 13.1 DAVID

David was seven when his mother died suddenly and he was the one who found her body. There were no other members of his family willing and able to take care of him, so he came into foster care. His social worker talks about how she tried to help him understand what had happened and how challenging this process was for her personally:

'He was asking a lot of questions that were really hard to answer, about death. He wanted to know why his mother died and he was very much wanting open and honest answers. He was asking really direct questions that as adults we would avoid, like "Why were her eyes open?" and "Where is her body now?" and "What else is in the coffin?" Questions like that that were hard to answer. It made me really question how you explain to a child about death because everyone has their beliefs and I didn't want to put my beliefs on him. Like he said "Do you believe in God?" and I said "It's not what I believe, what do you believe?" I had to do a lot of thinking about that and for me it was a really difficult time because it was raising a lot of things for me that I hadn't thought about death really.'

Guidelines for sharing difficult information
Plan your approach

Sometimes an adult does not have the luxury of planning how to make an explanation. The child puts them on the spot by asking a difficult question, the adult feels compelled to answer straightaway rather than prevaricate, and they have to think on their feet. In many situations, however, it is possible to work out tactics in advance. When a parent is terminally ill, for example, the other parent will often have some prior warning and so have time to think through how they will prepare the child for the bereavement, support them afterwards and explain what has happened. The prepared adult is likely to be in a better position to handle the explaining well than is the one who has not thought the issue through.

'Nobody explained what was going on. I didn't know what was happening. It was horrible.' (Ben)

Decide what the child needs to know when

It is tempting to think children are too young for whatever the knowledge is in order to avoid the pain of facing up to the issue oneself. However, it has been demonstrated that even pre-school children can have a mature understanding of an abstract concept such as death if it is relevant to their experience and they have had it sensitively explained to them (Elsegood 1996). There is an opposite risk, however, that the adult feels they must tell the child everything there is to know about the matter, when in fact he is too young to take it all in (see Reflective Exercise 13.1). For example, the four-year-old will need to be told that his mother has died. He will have to be helped to understand that that means she can no longer see or hear or walk or talk or feel and also that he will not see her again, ever, except in photos and memories he has of her in his head. It may be appropriate to tell him that her body has been put in the ground or (if that is what the adult honestly believes) that she is in heaven. However, he does not need to know at this stage that his mother died from inhaling her own vomit after excessive alcohol consumption. The time for that will come later.

Reflective Exercise 13.1

How should we explain sex to children?

If you are a parent, and have already faced questions from your child about sex, consider how it made you feel. How well do you think you handled it? With the benefit of hindsight, do you think you might have answered differently?

If this is a scenario you have not yet had to face, think about how a parent might go about it. What information should be provided, at what ages, and using which words?

Brodzinsky (Brodzinsky and Schechter 1994) has made a particular study of how the adopted child needs to learn about adoption, and argues that at certain developmental stages they need different questions answered and that information should be provided incrementally. Brodzinsky suggests that toddlers should be made aware that they are 'adopted' before they are ready to understand what the word means, and should take in from the way it is spoken that this is a good thing to be. At the pre-school stage, when they start to ask where babies come from they should be told like other children that they come from mummies' tummies, and then be given the additional information that they were born to different parents but could not live with them and so came to live with their adopters. By school age they will want to know why, and should be given simple age-appropriate explanations that are truthful, but that do not necessarily tell the whole story if it is a difficult one. Adolescents will be curious to know more about their story and may need to face up to painful and difficult information about the past that has not up to now been shared with them. They may require support in doing this. The overall aim of this childhood-long process is that adopted adults will fully understand what adoption means and why they were adopted and will be at ease with the knowledge. A similar phased approach can be taken to sharing other information that may be sensitive.

Sort out your own feelings first

Children can be remarkably sensitive to body language and unspoken cues and know when an adult is uncomfortable with a topic. Adults who want to talk about difficult issues with children must therefore resolve their own feelings first, otherwise they risk transmitting them to the children in unhelpful ways. For example, infertility leads many childless couples to seek parenthood through adoption and when adopters find it difficult to talk about adoption it can be because it arouses feelings in them around their infertility that are still unresolved. Adopted children, sensing their parents' discomfort, can come to think it is a dreadful thing to be adopted and some-thing they must not mention. In the same way any adult talking with a child about a matter that they find painful or embarrassing – sex, death, abuse – needs to manage the way they present themselves.

A particular challenge for adults working with distressed children is that if they truly come close and empathize with how the child is feeling the pain may be disabling. It is important, therefore, that staff working with traumatized children have access to good support systems themselves, both in and out of work, since it goes without saying that such work can be intensely demanding and stressful.

Be ready to support the child

If the adult needs support, so too does the child. Before sharing sensitive information the practitioner should prepare a support plan for the child, in case they become upset. Ideally, the child should be in a secure, nurturing and familiar environment and it may be best for all those who need to know the information to be told together. It will help if it is timed so that the child is able to give full attention and does not have too many stressors to handle at once. We cannot always manipulate circumstances to be ideal, but we may be able to think ahead, provide paper handkerchiefs, offer the child the choice of having someone with them for support, find out how they would like the adult to respond should they get upset, respond to their emotions with sympathetic understanding, and manage the interview with the child so it does not end abruptly after the discussion of the sensitive issue but the child has time to wind down afterwards. Practitioners should also ensure that the child does not have to go home alone while upset and that parents or carers are forewarned of the possibility of distress later.

Put yourself in the child's shoes

It is important to try and get an insight into the child's perspective so that you can put things in terms they will understand (see, for instance, David in Practice Example 13.2). Elsegood (1996), writing about the particularly poignant circumstance of having to tell a child that they are terminally ill, uses the concept of 'aligning' yourself with the child. This means taking the process step by step at the child's pace. First you establish what the child already knows and find out what more they would like to know; then in response to these wishes you give factual information about what has happened and what is likely to happen next. After this you 'align' yourself with the child again by checking what they understand (see Chapter 8) and whether there is anything else they want to know. This gives the child some control over how much information they are presented with at once, while helping them to be prepared for the future.

> 'My social worker's tried really hard to explain things to me but it's gone in one ear and out the other. I can't focus on it. I ignore her. I just blank it out.'
> (Tammy)

PRACTICE EXAMPLE 13.2 DAVID (CONTINUED)

Children do not always communicate their feelings directly and workers need to tune into the ways they try to get them across. In the case of David (see Practice Example 13.1) he chose to speak through his pet guinea pig, Fred. When his social worker started to talk about the adoptive family she had found for him at first he did not want to know. He was scared to move away from his foster carers and resisted accepting that he could not stay with them. However, when his social worker brought pictures of the new family to show him he said: 'Fred wants to know what their house is like. Tell Fred whether they've got any animals. Fred would like to meet them…'

Relate explanations to the child's experience

Jewett (1984) recommends when sharing difficult information to start by referring to something the child already knows or has experienced: 'You know that your mom and dad have not been getting along too well lately' (p.5). The reason for doing this is that it ties an abstract concept such as divorce into the practicalities of life, making it easier for the child to grasp. It also validates the child's own observations, which leads her 'to sense: "I am the sort of person who can figure things out"'(Jewett 1984, p.6). This will promote feelings of self-efficacy, which itself is linked to resilience – the ability to recover from adversity (Gilligan 1997), and gives support to Jewett's argument that 'this lays an essential foundation for the work of healthy mourning' (1984, p.6). Once the explanation is rooted in known information you can take the next step into providing new information, what Jewett calls the adult reality: 'You and your mom and dad have all tried hard to be a family to each other but it just isn't working' (Jewett 1984, p. 6). This may come as less of a shock and will be more comprehensible if it is linked in the child's mind with 'evidence' from her own experience.

Speaking figuratively is liable to confuse children: '"We lost Grandpa" is all too easily absorbed as literal information: "Where did you lose him?"' (Jewett 1984, p.9). It is best, therefore, to avoid metaphor when giving information to younger children, or to those with learning disabilities, including those with autistic spectrum disorders, who may find the figurative particularly hard to grasp. Concrete illustrations can help to clarify abstract concepts. Jewett suggests using a candle flame, because of its warmth and brightness, to represent love. She gives the example of a child who is reluctant to show affection towards his stepfather from a feeling that it would be disloyal to his father: the helper can light a candle to represent the child's love for his father, and then another to show he can love his stepfather too: '"The important thing for you to remember is that the light of love you feel for your dad will not go out. Loving is not like soup that you dish up till it's all gone. You can love as many people as you can get close to. But no one can make you blow out any of your candles. You do not have to take the love you feel for your dad away to love Ted"' (Jewett 1984, p.18).

Explanations also need to make sense in terms of the child's current understanding of the world. When a child or young person asks 'Why did granddad die?' or 'Why did I come into care?' it may be impossible, because it was so long ago, to utilize the child's relevant memories to tie the explanation down to reality. The answer may involve something that is very hard for a child (or even an adult) to make sense of, such as suicide or drug misuse. Jewett considers how to explain such issues and recommends asking oneself: why would an adult do something like that and what similar experience has this child had in her own life? (Jewett 1984, p.87) For example, when a child's mother is in prison: 'The reason here is that the adult broke an adult rule and is being punished in a way used for adults. "What are some of the rules at your house?" you might ask the child. "Do you ever break any of them? Then what happens?"'(Jewett 1984, p.89).

Address issues of blame and responsibility

There are two further questions that Jewett advises the practitioner to consider before attempting to explain sensitive information: how can this information be conveyed in a way that places no blame, and is there anything that the child might misunderstand or feel responsible for, or any action by the parent that the child might feel compelled to repeat? (Jewett 1984, p.87)

Dealing with the issue of blame is a tricky one: children may assume they are responsible for things that were in reality beyond their control; this occurs frequently if adverse experiences occur while children are still young and do not fully understand cause and effect: they will think the last thing to happen before a disaster must have caused it to happen (see, for instance, Carly in Practice Example 13.3). The child who broke a window with his football the day his father died in a car accident may never want to play football again.

> 'It starts to take an effect on you after a while, because you start thinking: "Well, if nobody wants me and I've been left with a family that doesn't really like me, what does that say about me?" You know, you've been taken away from your mum, you didn't know why, so the obvious thing is to think that she didn't like you.' (Robert)

PRACTICE EXAMPLE 13.3 CARLY

I once did life-story work with Carly, a 13-year-old girl, who still believed that the reason she had been adopted was that she was a bad child and her mother had rejected her. The reality was that her mother, who had been sexually abused by her own father, a drug dealer, suffered from a mental disorder and was in a violent relationship with the child's father, who had served a prison sentence for drug-related offences. Carly had been physically and emotionally abused and neglected and had been removed from her parents' care when very young, much against their will. Care had to be taken, in consultation with the adoptive parents, to decide which parts of her birth family history this child was ready for, but the message that she was in no way to blame for what had happened had to be a central one.

An alternative risk is that children with difficult histories may place excessive blame on their parents. They may come to the conclusion that their parents must have been evil people to have behaved the way they did. While this may be an understandable response, it too can be unhelpful, as it can get in the way of any future reconciliation, and also because having a positive view of one's parents is important for building a positive sense of self.

> However difficult it is to find a balanced way of thinking about some birth relatives, it is essential not to demonise the child's birth family. A way of telling the story must be found that avoids the sense that any human being is bad beyond explanation or for-giveness, since the child themselves, their siblings and...carers, will do bad things sometimes and need to be understood and forgiven. (Schofield and Beek 2006, p.362)

Putting a positive slant on the behaviour of an abusive parent can sometimes tax the adult's ingenuity (see Practice Example 13.4). I find a useful approach can be to say that we are all good at some things and not so good at others: 'I used to be good at English when I was at school', I will tell the child, 'but I really struggled with maths. How about you?' Once it is estab-lished that the child, and others she knows, have some things they do better than others, you can make the analogy with their parents: 'That's how it was with your mum: she was great fun to be with/had a lovely singing voice/knew loads about motorbikes, but one thing she found really difficult was looking after little children.' Some discussion of all the tasks and responsibilities of parenthood may help to make the point that it is not an easy role to fulfil, and that failure to perform it well does not equate to wickedness.

PRACTICE EXAMPLE 13.4 CARLY (CONTINUED)

When telling a story like that of Carly (see Practice Example 13.3) there is a risk that the child will be crushed by the weight of all the negatives: Carly's self-image was poor already, I did not want to make it worse by making her birth family sound like a cast of monsters. One way of leavening the lump of bad news is to share it a bit at a time: Carly's adoptive parents were not easy with her knowing yet about her mother's history of sexual abuse or her father's offences, so this information was saved for later. There were still enough reasons in the history to explain why she could not live with them. I did not want Carly to judge her birth parents too harshly, either, so I tried to help her think about the reality of bringing up a small child when you are young, poor, isolated, unwell and unhappy. At the same time I did not want her to view them one-dimensionally as victims, so I was keen to find some positive information about them to build a more balanced picture. In this case I was able to find out from the old file that her father had been keen on the outdoors and interested in wild animals, and that he loved sport, as Carly did. I knew, because I had met her in the past, that her mother had been a good-looking woman and that Carly resembled her, and from a professional currently involved with her mother I learnt that she now lived in a beautifully decorated and immaculately kept flat full of photos of Carly as a baby. This information I hope will have created a more rounded picture of her background for this teenager.

Jewett (1984) gives an example of how to counter blame in the case of the parent who is in prison by again using an analogy that will make sense to the child: 'You may find the child thinking "My parent was a terrible person." Here you can say "You know what lots of kids, especially little kids, tell me about breaking rules? They say that sometimes they just want something badly enough that they hope they won't get caught. I guess your mom was a little like a little kid that way"' (p.89). In the case of the child who blames himself unreasonably she suggests using the absurd to demonstrate that the blame is wrongly placed: '"There you were, a tiny baby growing inside your first mom. You must have known that she really wanted to have a little girl. What made you decide to be born a boy?" The obvious unfairness of this line of thinking seems to help eradicate self-blame in the child' (p.92).

Sometimes it may seem to the adults that a child is at least in part responsible for her predicament, and this may make it hard to assure her that she is not to blame. For example, when the last foster placement broke down because of the child's behaviour it may seem inappropriate to tell her it was not her fault. How then can she learn from the experience? The adults need to examine their own logic to see that they are not unfairly blaming the child for acting in ways that, though counterproductive, seemed to the child like the best response to the situation she found herself in. They should attempt to reframe the way they are looking at the sequence of events. Could it be that the adults who placed the child with those carers in the first place were the ones who made the mistake, since the carers clearly did not have the skills to manage her behaviour?

Encourage controlled expression of feelings

Questions about feelings are a later stage in the process than questions about facts: it may be some time before traumatized children are ready to address the challenging area of emotions. They often spend much energy suppressing and denying feelings that are too painful to acknowledge, so talking about them does not come easily. However, it is important that children are helped to express the way they feel about information adults give them if they are to be able to resolve those feelings and integrate their new knowledge into a positive sense of who they are. How to do this is discussed further in Chapter 14.

Give permission to mourn and to move on

Mourning can be seen as a process of resolution of a loss (Hallam and Vine 1996). Grieving is healthy and functional. It is not helpful to expect a child to get over a bereavement, loss or other trauma too quickly. Adults who find children's grief painful to witness and so discourage it do not do them any favours. We need to understand also that it is possible for people to grieve for something they have never had:

> I think losing, you know, your birth family, your parents and your country and community and culture and everything, people don't think it's very relevant because you've never known it, and so I don't think people think you have a right to actually grieve any of that. (Inter-country adopted adult quoted in Argent 2006, p.25)

Giving children the message that it is OK to feel sad, and recognizing that sorrow for things that are lost may recur at intervals for many years, will enable them to come to a healthier adjustment.

It is possible, however, for a child to become 'stuck' in despair well past the point at which one might have hoped that they would be ready to leave it behind and get on with their life. They may, for example, feel that they are betraying a previous carer if they attach to the new one. Getting the first carer to give them a message that they want the child to be happy in their new environment can be very helpful: there is evidence, for example, that adoptions are more successful where the parent has given consent for the child to be adopted, and where previous carers cooperated in the transfer of the child to their new home. However, where the child continues to express grief or anger that is out of control and does not abate with time, it may be necessary to seek therapeutic help.

Chapter 14

Helping Children Cope with Trauma

Therapeutic listening

There is a long-established view in social work literature that listening to children is in itself therapeutic (see Chapter 6). Berry (1972), for example, in a book entitled *Social Work with Children* written a generation ago, asserted: 'Empathetic listening is treatment as it will help the child to come to some perspective on his life as a whole, to be more in touch with his feelings' (p.54). Indeed, it can be argued that every encounter between a practitioner and a child has the capacity to help or to hurt, to be therapeutic or, indeed, traumatic, whether its purpose is to elicit a child's views, to find out whether they have suffered harm, to give them information or to explain to them a matter they find puzzling. However, there is a particular sort of adult–child interaction whose main purpose is to assist the child to recover from a significant emotional trauma, and this deserves a chapter of its own. There are professionals with specialist training – psychiatrists and psychologists, therapists and counsellors – whose work is entirely focused on healing hurt minds, operating from a plethora of competing perspectives, sometimes at daggers drawn with each other. I make no attempt to introduce the reader to the technical skills of any of these approaches. This chapter is aimed rather at lay people or practitioners who are not specialists in mental health but find they are faced with a very distressed child who needs help now. With lengthy waiting lists for child and adolescent mental health services it can often be non-specialist staff or carers who find they have to undertake this most critical of tasks.

Building resilience

Gilligan (1997, 1999) has made a particular study of why it is that some young people do well despite coming from adverse backgrounds, while others go under. He provides research evidence demonstrating that a range of circumstances and activities can help a children survive trauma, and so that it is possible to create an environment that will promote their natural resilience. Since many of these are remarkable more for their ordinariness than for being high-tech solutions, he coined the phrase: 'the therapeutic potential of the everyday' (Gilligan 1999, p.195).

Key elements of the environment that helps the child to recover naturally are that it provides security and promotes the child's self-esteem, so we should strive to create settings where there is predictability, consistency, routines, trustworthy responses from the surrounding adults and a reliable support network. We should help young people to develop a positive identity by sharing enjoyable activities with them, helping them to be successful, praising them and giving them positive feedback on their achievements. Helping children to do well at school and to develop hobbies is constructive; they also need adult mentors to support their efforts. It is important that children themselves believe that they can be effective. To assist them to develop this self-belief we should offer choices, involve them in planning and take care not to set them up to fail, by setting small achievable objectives. Finally, young people who are to survive adverse experiences need to learn a range of problem-solving skills that will get them through life, and the adults around them can help them to do this. Velleman and Templeton (2007) argue that it is the responsibility of all practitioners to work holistically in ways that promote children's resilience and that this may have more impact than attempting to address the problems of their parents. There is much, therefore, that can be done that is constructive without specifically setting out to address the issues that may be troubling a child. However, sometimes, until these worries are addressed they seem unable to make progress.

> 'The past is still a part of me. I've got my nice memories and my horrible ones.' (Kerry)

Coming to terms with the past

The approach to therapy that is most closely associated with the idea of 'therapeutic listening', at least when applied to looked-after children, is life-story work, described by some as 'life-journey work' (Romaine *et al.* 2007). This process has been described as 'an attempt to give back some of their past to children separated from their family of origin' (Ryan and Walker 2007, p.3), 'a key focus for making sense of the events that have taken place in a child's life' (Schofield and Beek 2006, p.358) and a means of enabling them 'to feel more confident about moving into the future'

(Romaine *et al.* 2007, p.10). The term can be applied to any form of activity whose aim is to help a young person come to terms with painful events that have happened in the past, and although my focus here is mainly on children in public care and adopted children, the approach can be used with any child who is troubled by past experiences. We call it 'work' because it is not always easy for the child and is not done just for fun but has a serious therapeutic purpose.

It is important to distinguish between life-story *books* and life-story *work*. People often talk about the two as though they were synonymous. Making a book *with* a child about their life can often be one stage in doing life-story work with them. However, life-story books are often made by adults *for* children, and this is not the same thing. For example, foster carers may construct a scrapbook for a baby who is to be adopted, containing information about the child's stay in their home, for her to look at when she is older, and may call this a 'life-story book'. To have a repository of information about their early life may well be valuable for a child, but this is not the same as life-story *work* since the child has played no part in the book's production and its purpose is primarily informational rather than therapeutic.

'We started to prepare a book each week about what had happened in my past and drew pictures and things to put in. It just helps you to relax to know what happened and knowing that somebody else knows about it and it wasn't just you imagining everything.' (Robert)

The idea of life-story work is founded in a belief that making sense of an experience helps a person resolve the feelings it aroused and hence is a step in recovery from trauma. Schofield and Beek locate its justification in attachment theory: 'the child's need to have *information* that enables them to put together a *coherent story*, one that has *meaning* for the child…as elsewhere in attachment theory, the emphasis is on the crucial links between cognition and emotion' (Schofield and Beek 2006, p.358, original emphasis). Life-story work also has roots in the psychodynamic perspective that seeks insight into the past as a basis for coping better with the future (Winnicott 1964). This approach has been attacked on the grounds that we cannot prove a causal link between past experience and present difficulties, and that problems are more readily solved by looking to future possibilities than by dwelling on historical failures. I cannot argue with the view that: 'When driving a car it can be useful to look occasionally in the rear-view mirror, but it is advisable to spend most of the time looking through the front wind-screen' (O'Connell 2001, p.16). However, it also makes sense to me that self-esteem is an important element of resilience and promotes constructive coping strategies, and that it makes it easier for a child to build a positive sense of self if they have a coherent account of who they are and how they got to where they are now (Daniels, Wassell and Gilligan 1999).

The aims of life-story work are to:

- provide accurate information about the child's history

- explain it in terms the child can understand

- help the child to express their feelings about what has happened

- demonstrate that it was not their fault

- help them to feel better about themselves, and

- equip them to cope better with life in the future.

The process of the work reflects these aims.

Research the child's life carefully

Where children are confused about what has happened to them, have blanked it out, or had experiences when they were very young of which they have no conscious memory, the worker's first step will be to research their life history. Information can be obtained from a variety of sources: family members, former carers, professionals who know the child now or knew them when they were younger. You may have access to agency records; archives of a local paper might supply information on issues ranging from a house fire to a school production the child took part in; the hospital records department might be able to supply information the young person wants, such as the time of their birth. It is as well to do this research thoroughly: where possible, try to find out not just what happened, but why it happened. Seek for a balance between positive and negative information.

Work through the information with the child

With an able teenager this might largely be a process of explanation and discussion. Younger and less able children will need practical demonstrations, props and play to help them make sense of what you tell them (see Chapters 8, 9 and 13). This could involve collecting photos of people and places, re-enactment with play figures and toy houses, maps of the child's moves, pictorial flow charts to clarify a sequence of events, visits to former homes or carers, painting pictures or dramatic reconstructions to facilitate talk about what happened. The aim here is to clarify the factual information: what happened and when.

Explain the things that are confusing

This stage of the work is about helping the child to understand why things happened the way they did. It may also involve clarifying who else is aware of the information and whether they may believe a different interpretation of events. Chapter 13 gives detailed advice about how to explain sensitive and complex information and convey it in a way that frees the child from inappropriate blaming. Bell describes this process as 'positive reframing of the events that they have experienced' (2002, p.5). The 'reframing' is more challenging where information is very negative and the worker themself finds it hard to comprehend or present positively, for example in cases of multiple abuse. Schofield and Beek (2006) comment on how very difficult it can be for some young people to make sense of the complex and disturbing information that their life stories may bring up. Young children in particular may find it hard to grasp that people are not all good or all bad, but a mixture of the two. For this reason the same material may have to be reworked a number of times as the child matures: 'Life story work, often undertaken at critical points of change… can never be a one-off event, when [it] is actually life-long for all of us. Even in…old-age we review the meaning of our life' (p.358). The process is valuable, however, since it is 'an opportunity to draw on and build the child's capacity for empathy and perspective-taking' (Schofield and Beek 2006, p.361), which will in itself assist the child to form more positive relationships in the future.

> 'I did things like family trees and sort of the history of my life and we got in touch with people and we did like a snake diagram and had all the memories I had. At first I didn't really want to do it, some of the things I didn't want to talk about really because it upset me. But now I've thought about it for a while as in trying to accept problems and not fear any more and there's no point keeping it to yourself.' (Patrick)

Encourage controlled expression of emotions

Going back over painful memories is not easy. Many children will resist it, as indeed will adults. O'Connell argues that many adults who would benefit from counselling avoid it out of a belief that 'the primary purpose of therapy is to identify the roots of behaviour in one's personal or family history and that this may well prove to be a painful experience' (2001, p.23). Schofield and Beek (2006, p.360) point out that children will have evolved their own strategies for dealing with painful feelings and so will react differently to the process: suppressing and denying their feelings, refusing to discuss the painful issue, or splitting people into 'angels' or 'monsters', for example. Clearly, encouraging children to recall past trauma entails risks and must be done with care.

We should expect those who are confronted with a past that is uncomfortable to feel distress, anger or fear and part of the process of direct work is to assist the child to externalize those emotions. The theory underlying this approach is that expression of suppressed emotions has the psychological effect of lancing a boil: it lets out the poison so healing can begin:

> Like if I keep it all bottled myself, then one day it'll all just build up in myself and I'll just end up taking it out on the wrong person and start doing something. Like start fighting with them or something, but that's how you are better off just letting it all out and telling somebody. (Young person quoted in Corbett 2004, p.186)

Talking about the feelings is not, however, according to Jewett (1984), enough:

> Most people…also need a physical component to the release of feelings. This varies from crying to door-slamming, but is an integral part of working through the strong feelings following a separation or loss, particularly in children. (p.60)

There are a range of ways in which a practitioner can help a child express feelings safely: the child can run up and down stairs or round a playground to let off steam. You can give the child a rolled newspaper with which to bash a chair, a punch-bag or a football to kick against a wall. They can write poetry, paint pictures or make models of their feelings. Messages can be written on stones and thrown into the sea. They can picture an absent person sitting in an empty chair and then tell the chair what they think of it. I have even known a child relieving his feelings harmlessly but effectively by drawing the face of someone he was angry with on a ping-pong ball, floating it in the toilet and then trying to sink the ball (an exercise that works better for boys than for girls!). Oaklander (1988) and Cipolla *et al.* (1992) provide many more ideas on expression of feelings.

'You become more open about things. You don't just bottle everything up inside because she teaches you to let your anger out. I had this box that when I wanted to scream I had to scream into the box rather than out into the open.' (Robert)

An important point is that the child should be encouraged to see the emotions and behaviours as things that have a separate existence, rather than being an intrinsic part of themselves. There is a risk that a child will believe that, if they have bad thoughts or feelings or do bad things, then they must be a bad person. If they can 'externalize' a feeling or a behaviour – view it as something separate from themselves – they will find it easier to control it (Wilson 1998). So, for example, where a child has wild outbursts of anger they can be taught to visualize a 'tantrum monster', which they can learn to 'tame'.

Some children, particularly the severely maltreated, may find expression of emotion hard because they have coped with unbearable experiences by suppressing their feelings about them. This has become so ingrained a habit that they can no longer recognize and identify what they feel, or link it with how they behave. In such cases, work to help them identify, name and distinguish happy, sad, angry and scared feelings, through 'feelings faces' and other techniques, may be necessary before the child can move to being able to express them in a controlled way. It is essential in all this work to ensure that the child neither hurts themself, nor anyone else, nor damages precious things while thus giving vent to their emotions, and the worker will have to set clear boundaries to make sure all activities are undertaken safely.

Making a record of the work

Each of the stages in this process may in practice overlap or be undertaken simultaneously. However, the record that emerges of the work is logically the final stage. Traditionally this record is in the form of a book (hence the term 'life-story book') and this does give the child something concrete to take away. However, we should allow for creativity here and let the child dictate the form of the record: she may prefer to record a tape, create a wallchart or even, as in one case I heard of, sew a bedspread. Or she may not want to make a permanent record at all. The practitioner will in most cases need to keep some record of the work, by way of case-notes for agency purposes, but it may be advisable to keep a copy of what is produced as well if this is feasible, in case it needs to be replaced in future: children have been known to destroy all their photographs in a fit of anger and then bitterly regret it, and family members, too, sometimes dispose of evidence about a child's former life.

Whatever kind of record is made, it should so far as possible be the child's own work, and in their own words. If it is in a format to which the child can add in future, for example a loose-leaf folder, then so much the better: this gives the message that life goes on. In a book there should be pictures (photos, drawings) and diagrams (family trees [see Reflective

Exercise 14.1], eco-maps) as well as words, and there should be both facts (places, names and dates) and explanations (the reasons for moves, losses and changes, expressed at an appropriate level for the child's age and understanding). All manner of documents could go in: birth certificate; press-cuttings; birthday cards; certificates for achievements; tickets from trips and holidays: it should be a celebration of the good things in the child's life as well as a repository for their distress and anger. There could be a dilemma for the worker if the child wants to leave the more distressing information out. However, it is the child's record, and if it is to reflect the child's voice rather than the adult's view of what the child should be thinking, then the child should be the arbiter of what is included. Provided you have had the conversations about the difficult issues, then the important work has been done. A life-story book, as we said at the beginning of this chapter, is not an end in itself, it is just one of the possible products of a piece of life-story work.

Reflective Exercise 14.1

Draw a family tree of your own family. (If you are not sure how to do it there are instructions for this and a number of other useful techniques for making a visual representation of personal and family information in Parker and Bradley 2007.)

Imagine you are telling a stranger something about each family member as you write their name on the paper.

Did this exercise arouse any particular feelings in you?

Remember that if you are to ask a child to draw their own family tree, particularly where there have been bereavements or conflictual relationships in the family, the simple activity of putting the family structure down on paper may be distressing.

Therapy, relationship and power

The relationship between the child and the adult facilitating the therapeutic work is clearly crucial if the work is to achieve its aim of helping the child to find a resolution to their distress, rather than exacerbating it. Kohli (2006a), writing about social work with young asylum-seekers, highlights how long it can take to build up a trusting relationship, but describes the trusted practitioner as 'acting as a lightening rod for the intensity of feelings that they sometimes encountered, allowing sadness to be earthed' (p.9). Schofield and Beek (2006) argue that the role of the practitioner carrying out the life-story work with the child is like that of an attachment figure, acting as a 'secure base' for the child to explore past, present and future.

The notion that skill in building and using relationships is central to the role of the helping adult is accepted by a wide range of academics and practitioners. Jordan (2006), for example, amasses evidence to demonstrate the impor-tance of positive relationships for chil-

'My social worker's been brilliant. I've been a proper, and I mean a really spoilt brat with her. I've put her through hell, and she's just been there all the time. I've told her I didn't want her, I didn't want her at all, I wanted a different social worker, but I didn't mean it – it was just my mood and she was there to take it out on. But she was dead calm about it. She's brilliant!' (Tammy)

dren's well-being and argues that children's services should 'give children and young people warm, supportive and consistent adults with whom to explore the world, and…help them to make sense of their experiences of growing up' (p.42). Morrison (2007), in an article about the importance of emotional intelligence for social work, asserts: 'the conversation between worker and user [is] at the heart of social work practice, and the essential tool for the formation of a relationship within which any movement or change can take place' (p.250). Both these writers claim that such relation-ship skills are undervalued by policy-makers. 'The place of relationships and emotion in social work is in danger of becoming increasingly marginal-ised' (Morrison 2007 p.260): they have been neglected in favour of more measurable performance indicators, according to Jordan (2006). Primary schools may:

> attempt to create communication in which children learn to relate to each other, to help each other and to understand the world outside. But they do not gain stars from Ofsted for doing so, nor does their success in this feature in league tables. (p.45)

Despite widespread agreement about the importance of the relationship between the helping adult and the child, the role of social worker as thera-pist is not universally accepted or welcomed, however. Gilligan's work supports the view that relationships are central to children's well-being, and relationship skills fundamental to the role of the social worker working with looked-after young people, but he argues that therapeutic help for children is often more effective and acceptable to them if it comes from informal community sources rather than from an 'expert' practitioner (Gilligan 2000). Kurzt and Street (2006) indicate that for black and ethnic minority young people a combination of stigma, language difficulties and lack of knowledge of services meant they were reluctant to talk about their worries with those they did not know well, therefore they were more likely to seek help for mental distress from family members than from health or social care professionals. The young people I interviewed in the course of the 'Listening but not Hearing' study (McLeod 2001) were quite resistant to the suggestion that the role of the social worker was therapeutic, or that part of their task was to explore the young people's feelings. Several of them complained that social workers were 'nosy' and that young people's feelings were none of their business. While they wanted social workers to listen to what they had to say, the young people felt they were entitled to set the agenda for their conversations themselves.

This is not to say that the young people I interviewed did not regard their social workers as important allies. The issue is rather one of control of the agenda and hence professional power. Schofield and Beek (2006) or Bell's (2002) description of the social worker as fulfilling a quasi-parental role, which is rooted in attachment theory, is disputed and would be unacceptable to many practitioners and indeed young people. It is an issue of expertise: if children are the real 'experts in their own lives' (Clark and Statham 2005), then the practitioner cannot simultaneously set themself up as an expert, taking the lead in a therapeutic process or knowing better than the child what is good for them. O'Connell (2001) argues that if 'the therapist adopts a "not-knowing" position in which she disowns the role of expert, "the keeper of the truth" in the client's life...negotiat[ing] jointly...will create the possibility of change for him' (p.15). The 'expert' model of helping, O'Connell implies, sets the stage for conflict between therapist and client, whereas treating the client as the expert on his own problem means 'the client can teach the therapist how to join with him effectively' (O'Connell 2001, p.24).

The question, therefore, of how far it is legitimate for the helping adult to take the lead in therapy with a hurt child is a contentious one, and hangs on views about the appropriate use of professional power. In the next part of the book I look further into the practice of listening to children and examine how far adults could or should go in taking a 'one-down', non-expert line and letting children, individually or collectively, make their own decisions on matters that affect them.

Part 5: Young People and Participation

The reason why we have two ears and only one mouth
is that we may listen the more and speak the less.

Quotation attributed to Zeno of Citium [333–246 BC],
from **Lives of Eminent Philosophers** by Diogenes Laertius
(Laertius, trans. 1925, Vol II, p.135)

Chapter 15

Consultation and Advocacy

In Part 5 we move on from the one-to-one dialogue between helping adult and child to considering how young people's voices can have influence on decision-making, both at individual and group levels. This chapter considers techniques for promoting young people's participation by consulting with them and advocating for them. In Chapter 16 there are guidelines for involving them in decision-making processes. Chapter 17 considers what we know about enabling young people to take part in wider community processes: education, local planning, policy development, research, politics. Practice in many of these areas is rudimentary, but it is fast developing. Much can be learnt from innovative, small-scale projects, even though they are the exception and not yet the rule, and even when research identifies poor practice, we can at least learn from this what *not* to do.

Consulting with groups of young people

There is an expectation now from government that public bodies will consult with service-users about their services, and that where services impact on children they will be among those consulted (Children and Young People's Unit 2001; Department for Education and Skills 2004a; Department of Health 2004). As a result, many consultation exercises are now carried out every year with many groups of young people. There is always, however, a risk of them being carried out in a perfunctory way without real commitment for purposes of manipulation or 'window-dressing'. A Social Care Institute for Excellence (SCIE) practice guide acknowledges that consultation exercises are a form of participation favoured by organizations because they are relatively cheap, quick and easy but they 'can reinforce the unequal power relationships between adults and children as adults often initiate, manage and control the outcome of the exercise' (Wright *et al.* 2006, p.37; see also Reflective Exercise 15.1). There is a risk, according to Moss *et al.* (2005, p.10) that consulting with children can support rather than subvert existing power structures: 'a means of reducing pressure by "letting off steam" and "getting things off your chest"' whose real aim is managerial effectiveness. There can be difficulties in making sense of children's responses; adults must recognize that they too are participants in the interaction, and that their interpretation of what they have been told is subjective and must be tentative; they cannot be confident that they are transmitting the child's authentic message. We should not give up on attempts to consult with children, they conclude, but should do it with humility, always conscious of power relations and 'thinking critically about the meaning, process and consequences of listening' (Moss *et al.* 2005, p.12).

Research has identified flaws in the process of consultation exercises even at the highest levels. Kelley (2006) makes a damning critique of the British government's consultation exercise on one of its new children's policy initiatives. The ISA (Information Sharing and Assessment, since renamed ContactPoint) is a database planned to enable agencies to share information about children. Kelley (2006, p.38) describes it as 'the flag-ship policy of the *Every Child Matters* agenda'. *Every Child Matters* (Department for Education and Skills 2004b) claims that children's views are a key driver for its policies. However, as Kelley points out, ISA departs significantly from children's views, being built on automatic sharing of children's personal information between agencies without the children's permission. In the Department for Education and Skills' own figures, 24 per cent of children and young people said adults should never share information about a child without that child's consent, a further 19 per cent said children should be involved in any information-sharing and 39 per cent said information should be shared only if there was risk of serious harm to the child. 'How much influence did these views have on the developing policy?' asks Kelley: 'the simple answer is none' (Kelley 2006, p.39). This is not just a question, she explains, of cynical adults seeking views and then ignoring them, it is rather embedded in the political process as: 'just an example of the way in which all policy-makers grapple with the idea of evidence-based and stake-holder influenced policy in a world dominated by short-term political imperatives' (Kelley 2006, p.39).

Kelley's second criticism of the ECM consultation exercise is that it was methodologically unsound: sampling, questionnaire construction and respondents' understanding of the issues were all questionable. 'These flaws make the data generated difficult to analyse or interpret in a useful way...a factor which renders the data far easier to dismiss or misrepresent' (Kelley 2006, p.42). Thus it was that the government was able to claim that children welcomed better information-sharing through the ISA, when in fact 'far from welcoming the proposal they appear to have said no to it' (Kelley 2006, p.42). This, she asserts, says a lot about the government's true attitude to children's views, which is at variance with their expressed policies.

The British government is not alone in carrying out flawed consultations. The evidence from research indicates that in consulting with children, practice remains unimpressive (Cavet and Sloper 2004; Worrall-Davies and Marino-Francis 2007). Nevertheless, there is now considerable agreement around the issue of what constitutes good practice. Sinclair, a long-standing and well-respected writer on children's rights and participation, was asked to write a summary of the research on the topic for wide distribution in support of the UK government's programme to improve children's services in the late 1990s, 'Quality Protects' (Department of Health 1998). Her pamphlet (Sinclair 2000) stresses that participation can never be a one-off event: 'Actively involving children is a continuous process, shaped by a participatory culture' (p.5). Consultation methods should be attractive and accessible, yet valid, and there must be clarity and honesty about how much influence the children's views will actually have. Consultation exercises demand careful planning with attention given to such issues as how child consultants are to be recruited and the logistics of transport and accommodation when events are organized. Special needs must be anticipated and catered for in advance. There must be respect for the child's own agenda (which may well differ from that of the adults) and this respect requires that the young participants are provided with follow-up information about how their views have influenced outcomes.

Reflective Exercise 15.1

Think back to your own childhood and recall an occasion when an adult made a decision that affected you without consulting you first. How did you feel about this at the time? In retrospect, do you think their behaviour was reasonable? If so, why? If not, how could and should they have handled the issue?

All this seems quite straightforward, and one might have thought, achievable. Why are so many consultation exercises unsatisfactory in that case? (For a successful exercise, see Practice Example 15.1, The Junction.) Kelley argues that political pressures get in the way and concludes that we need to get away from 'short-term, reactive and highly politicised forms of policy development' (2006, p.43) and protect children from exploitative pseudo-consultation exercises. They must always have an opportunity to influence outcomes, Kelley asserts, or they should not be asked to take part. 'Hard to reach' groups should be renamed 'easy to exclude': it requires money and time to reach the marginalized, but otherwise the whole endeavour is flawed. When children's views are sought on complex issues such as information-sharing, the exercise must include education about the topic first so that their opinion can be informed. A questionnaire without explanations is otherwise meaningless. The dissemination of findings as well as the conduct of the research should be ethical: participants should not be misrepresented.

PRACTICE EXAMPLE 15.1 THE JUNCTION

'The Junction' is an in-patient unit for adolescents with severe mental health problems in the town of Lancaster in Northwest England, joint-funded by Health and Children's Services. When it was first set up, senior managers decided they wanted to incorporate young people's views into its development and employed an external consultant to help them do this in a way that would be genuine and not tokenistic. A lead nurse for participation was also appointed internally. The consultant took staff through an initial programme of training and awareness-raising. Then a group of six young consultants was set up, consisting of teenagers who had pre-viously received in-patient psychiatric treatment, and the consultant led group work with them. The *Hear by Right* materials (National Youth Agency 2005) were used to map and plan the project and to evaluate its progress. Small groups of staff members and young con-sultants then worked together to develop plans for policies, daily structure, building and furnishings, education, care planning and advocacy, information materials and staff recruitment and training. To widen the consultation a day was held with other former service-users, their parents and carers. One burning issue to emerge from this was opposition to the plan for meals to be brought in ready-cooked and chilled, which was felt to be particularly inappro-priate for young people with eating disorders. Evidence was collected from units nationally and, with the full support of the management, plans were developed to change the kitchens and set up the appropriate systems and training for the nursing team. The young consultants participated in choosing a name for the unit and in planning and delivering an opening day, which the external con-sultant described as 'fantastic, with everyone working together on the same agenda'. They have remained involved since the unit opened, meeting with residents monthly and offering ongoing support to review and develop the service. They have also presented at a national conference. The plan is that over time the young consultants group will come to consist of former residents at the unit.

The actual techniques used to access young people's views are thus critical to obtaining reliable data, and the indications are that these may not be the same methods that would be best for consulting with adults. Kelley suggests 'open knowledge systems' (e.g., online discussion fora) as an egalitarian and young-person-friendly medium. Coleman and Rowe (2005) advocate the use of websites designed by young people and utilizing the young people's IT skills so that they can express their views creatively and unfettered by adult structures. Their teenage informants only wanted to engage with sites that were 'cool' so they conclude that when consulting with adolescents their peers must be involved in the planning and design stage of the exercise.

Not all writers agree that IT provides the best route to understanding the young, however. Hill (2006) carried out a large-scale piece of research in Scotland, in which he sought children and young people's own views on the best ways of consulting with them. Hill's clearest finding from this research is that there is no one right method: it all depends on the subject, the context, the age and gender, but also the personality, temperament and literacy level of the children concerned. Children can see the pros and cons of different methods. Young people typically disclose more on computer questionnaires than with pen and paper or in a face-to-face interview, but it tended to be boys and middle-class children who were most computer literate. Neither online nor written questionnaires were popular with young people overall though online questionnaires that other young people had helped construct were seen as preferable to those written entirely by adults. Some expressed a preference for writing answers to taped questions, and where the subject matter demanded privacy, questionnaires were seen as more confidential than other methods of gathering data. One-off events with activities, exercises such as role-play and group discussions were liked by children since they found the experience of being consulted to be fun. The downside of one-off events could be their expense and time taken to organize them. Focus groups were liked by some but not all: some children were more nervous in a group than one-to-one, others were

'The leaflet was obviously written by management in what they considered to be a young people's style. Which wasn't 100 per cent effective.' (Anna)

more confident; there were always some who said nothing in a group setting and sometimes dominant group members caused resentment. Generally, children were more relaxed if they could attend with friends. However, where the subject matter was sensitive, young people sometimes preferred not knowing other members of the group.

'I wouldn't tell any of my friends about being in care. I don't want anyone to know.' (Ben)

In individual interviews young people preferred to be given a choice of talking or other activity such as drawing, and they also liked to be interviewed by their peers rather than by adults. Time and venue were other issues considered. Generally, young people preferred not to have too much of their time taken up by acting as consultants:

> Children see their own time as a precious resource which needs protecting from adult time demands…their willingness to be consulted was not a gift they should be grateful for but more a right, and one that they need not exercise if they had better things to do. (Hill 2006, p.78)

The context could influence the findings: if interviewed at school, children tended to perceive the researcher as a teacher. If, on the other hand, children were seen at home they might be more reluctant to share some sensitive information.

It emerged clearly from this research that there are many means of accessing the views of children and young people, and different methods suit different purposes. For the young people themselves, however, the means was less important than the end: they were much more interested in whether their views would make a difference than on how their views were elicited.

Speaking up for children

All the research on consultation indicates that within the relatively powerless minority group of citizens under the age of 18 there are certain to be even more disadvantaged sub-groups whose voices are the least likely to be heard. These include younger children, children with disabilities, young people in public care and those who are from ethnic minorities or who do not speak the majority language of their community. 'A key difficulty arising from the need to listen to children and young people is finding ways for them to speak about their experiences in the first place, a problem that is particularly acute for disadvantaged young people' (Harnett 2004, p.131). One approach to ensuring that these groups are not silenced is to use advocates to speak for them. The concept of advocacy developed in the early 1970s within the disability rights movement when people with learning difficulties first began to voice their views in public with the aid of advocates (Harnett 2003). Its application to child-care settings came later. Among the drivers were shocking revelations about abuse of children within the care system (Waterhouse 2000) combined with the evidence that, although looked-after children had had a formal right to complain and to have their complaints investigated independently since the implementation of the Children Act 1989, few had the confidence to do so (Aiers and Kettle 1998).

'The complaints procedure? A waste of time and energy!' (Steven)

Aiers and Kettle found that less than half of young people in residential care were aware of complaints procedures, and the numbers were even lower among younger, disabled and non-English-speaking children, and that as a result: 'the groups making the least number of complaints are those likely to be the most vulnerable' (Aiers and Kettle 1998, p.21). They recommended providing advocates to support youngsters who had a grievance.

One might ask why social workers do not act as advocates for children in care. Advocacy is, after all, an essential part of the social work role – Key Role 3 for social workers in the English *National Occupational Standards for Social Work* is: 'Support individuals to represent their needs, views and circumstances' (Skills for Care 2005). There may, however, be conflicts of interest for employees of an organization when supporting someone to make a complaint against that organization, and research makes it clear that in such circumstances young people prefer an advocate who they can see as independent (Dalrymple 2005). It is against this backdrop that the Adoption and Children Act 2002 brought in an amendment to the Children Act 1989 requiring local authorities to provide independent advocacy services to assist children wishing to make a complaint about their services. This has led to a substantial increase in advocacy provision for young people in England and Wales in the last few years. As well as looked-after children, advocacy projects have been developed for users of mental health services for children and adolescents (Harnett 2004), for children whose parents are going through divorce (Mullin and Singleton 2006), for young unaccompanied asylum-seekers (Harnett 2004), for disabled children and for children involved in family group conferences (Dalrymple 2005). Interest is growing internationally: Standbu (2004) describes advocacy services for the last-mentioned group of children in Norway.

The advocate's role is a delicate and difficult one, sitting on the fence as it does, between two camps. The task of representing someone else's views is an exacting one: it is not always easy to be sure you have fully understood and properly expressed what they want you to say for them. There is a tension always present in the relationship between child and advocate because of the power imbalance in the relationship: is the advocate taking over, belittling the child's concerns or putting an adult spin on them? Dalrymple (2005) cites the example of an articulate looked-after young person who attended his review meeting together with his advocate and then left all the talking to her: 'Although…he was not critical of the advocate, her acceptance by the other adults involved was such that he was still effectively excluded from the decision-making process' (p.10).

An advocate faces a double jeopardy, however, since professional colleagues may feel he or she has gone too far in supporting the child. Aiers and Kettle (1998, p.32) found that: 'When complaints were made against staff by young people there was considerable resentment' and when adults support young people in making complaints they too can be the focus for resentment. 'By…stepping outside the all-powerful adult role and aligning themselves with young people, advocates confuse their peers and could almost be described as anarchic: posing a threat to the adult–child order' (Dalrymple 2005, p.12). The defensive response of staff, Dalrymple found (2003), was to dismiss advocates as naive or ill-informed. There can also be confusion about what they are actually there for:

> While Social Services staff could appreciate that there could be tension between their views of a child's best interests and the child's wishes and rights, they could not always appreciate that the advocate was there to help voice the child's wishes rather than moderate these wishes or mediate between parties. (Pithouse and Parry 2005, p.53)

All this led Dalrymple (2005) to sum up: 'Advocacy therefore is a skilled task requiring an ability to work alongside the young person who requires advocacy support, while at the same time working within systems which seek to exclude both the young person and their advocate' (Dalrymple 2003, p.1058)

This mistrust of the advocate's role may go beyond the individual practitioner to the whole organization. Pithouse and Parry identified a flaw in the thinking that made local authorities fund services whose staff would support service-users in criticizing those same local authorities: there was evidence that 'marketization' threatened the integrity of advocacy services. Local authorities would fund a service on a three-year contract but providers who challenged the local authority found they were threatened with having their funding cut. Changes in service provider led to loss of continuity for young people and falls in service quality. This led to 'a deeply felt and widely shared view by most providers that independent advocacy was a good idea whose time was yet to come' (Pithouse and Parry 2005, p.48).

Since this field is so new, though fast developing, there is relatively little evaluative research to tell us what is happening on the ground and what works best. Pithouse and Parry's study of all local-authority-funded advocacy schemes in Wales is one of the more substantial pieces of research. They found that most services were small and based on individual case-based advocacy undertaken by adults. Most were for looked-after children, some for those involved in child protection procedures and a few were for disabled children. Many were frustrated by their lack of independence from local authorities, their precarious funding and their vulnerability to hostile funders. Young people valued the services – measures of user satisfaction were high – however, it was difficult to measure their impact: numbers of cases said more about willingness of social workers to refer children to the services than about service quality. Few of the local authorities evaluated the quality of the services they were paying for and only a minority could identify benefits offered by the services: they were more likely to see them as offering no benefits or presenting challenges. The writers concluded that the current system could not help local authorities to achieve consistency in outcomes for young people: it would be better for the services to be provided by an independently funded organization at a regional or national level.

There are some indications in the literature as to what makes an advocacy service work. Harnett (2004) describes the difficulties of getting off the ground a group peer advocacy scheme for young unaccompanied asylum-seekers. The first difficulty was finding anyone willing to join the group. This was achieved through the use of an open access community facility offering services to asylum-seekers, and then by word of mouth. However, the group had a changing membership. Attendance was constantly in flux because of the instability in these young people's living arrangements so group organization had to be flexible. Supporting and encouraging group members to continue participating was an ongoing endeavour. This was achieved through a trusted key worker, who was a young person trained, supported and paid to act as facilitator and coordinator, and also through the use of a safe space with informal but clear ground rules. Giving the group ownership of the group process was essential, so that they could feel empowered to take control of its agenda, nevertheless it is clear that there was significant adult input behind the scenes enabling this group to function. As Jacobs (2006) comments, the more powerless the group, the more adult input is likely to be necessary if they are to find a voice.

There was a further challenge facing this group and the others Harnett describes, and that was getting policy-makers to take any notice of their views once they had been formulated. To get access to decision-makers he found it was necessary either to have official funding or to be championed by a well-known organization, such as a national charity. The young people also had to learn to speak in what he terms 'official language' if what they said was to be taken seriously. The difficulty here is that, once a group has received funding from an official body, pressure may be brought to bear, as it was on the advocacy services discussed above, to refrain from rocking the boat. Thus, all the evidence on this interesting emerging area of youth advocacy only serves to demonstrate how hard it is for small individuals to challenge vested power bases.

Chapter 16

Involving Children in Decision-making

As we saw in Part 1, children's involvement in decision-making in their everyday lives is rarely optimized, either within their own families or in formal processes for making decisions about children in need such as family group conferences, child protection procedures or care planning for looked-after children. However disappointing the research findings may be on what is happening in practice though, there is no shortage of good advice on how best to involve children and young people in ways that empower them, and the practitioner who wants to do better can learn from this. The following pointers for good practice in Checklist 16.1 have been distilled from the literature on participation.

Checklist 16.1 Ten top tips for involving children in decision-making

1. Involve children at an appropriate level.
2. Give choices.
3. Clarify the options.
4. Consider the roles of parents and carers.
5. Plan meetings with children, not for them.
6. Make meetings child-friendly.
7. Take children's views seriously.
8. Give the child a record of decisions made.
9. Decision-making is a process, not a one-off event.
10. Supporting children's involvement in decision-making has to be resourced.

Involve children at an appropriate level

Children can play a part in decision-making at a number of levels, and different levels of participation may be appropriate for different children faced with different decisions at different times in their lives (see Reflective Exercise 16.1 at the end of the chapter). In the case of a child too young to express a view, as Thoburn (2004) points out, the appropriate level of participation may be for adults to observe a child's behaviour, deduce her views, and take them into consideration when coming to a view as to the best way forward. As children grow, they should be progressively more fully involved. Playing a limited role in a decision can still be valid, and better than playing none at all. For example, a severely disabled young person may be able to communicate preferences about what food he would like to eat. For one young person this may be the limit of what he can achieve. For the next it could be a building block on the way to drawing up a list of his likes and dislikes and so influencing wider issues, such as his school routine (Franklin and Sloper 2006). Decision-making needs to be paced to what the individual child can handle and should accord with their sense of fairness. This does not mean that all children must be treated the same. In fact, children from the same family may need varying amounts of involvement with the same decision (Butler *et al.* 2002). There is a fine balance to be struck between overburdening children with responsibility for life-changing decisions that they are not mature enough to take (Thoburn 2004) and overprotecting them, which 'leads to serious questions about why children are being denied the right to make mistakes' (Leeson 2007, p.274).

Give choices

There will always be some situations where adults will overrule children's wishes and make decisions for them. A court, for example, may decide that it is not safe for a small child to return to the care of abusive parents despite the child's clearly expressed desire to return home. Thoburn (2004) argues that children's wishes should only be disregarded when there is clear evidence that this is necessary. In family situations there will always need to be some give and take when family members' wishes conflict: the child may have to accept that her mother has a right to a night out and so she cannot always have her own choice of evening activity: children's innate sense of fairness helps them to accept this sort of turn-taking. However, when adults exclude a child from contributing to a decision, or reject their contribution, they should always explain why, and when there are limits to what influence the child can have on the decision these should be made clear.

It may also be possible to allow for some choices in the way an unpopular decision is implemented. For example, adults may decide that a disabled child must go to a respite care placement, despite clear indications that he or she does not want to go, because the likely alternative, breakdown of the home situation for example,

'They should treat children as an equal, not just tell them off. Giving them boundaries, not letting them go past the boundaries, but making the boundaries quite far.'
(Robert)

would be even worse. 'Nevertheless, enabling [the child] to have choices within respite care, such as what they eat, which other children they stay with, can enhance their experiences and give them some sense of control' (Franklin and Sloper 2006, p.118). Another choice that children should be allowed is the right to opt out of making the decision when they feel it is too difficult for them: 'Children's reluctance to be drawn on what they "really" want is not only a reasonable response in many cases, but should be seen as an equally legitimate exercise of their participation rights – the right to choose not to participate' (Schofield 2005, p.40).

PRACTICE EXAMPLE 16.1 DAVID (CONTINUED)

We first met David in Practice Examples 13.1 and 13.2 in Chapter 13. His social worker went on to talk about how she had persuaded him to move to an adoptive family, despite his initial reluctance to leave his foster carers:

'So I explained to him and I said I had listened, but sometimes adults have to make decisions for children, the really big decisions, but any of the little decisions he could make. So we said yes, Fred the guinea pig could go too, and they would get another guinea pig to keep it company. And he could choose the hutch and decide which part of the garden it went in, which sound quite trivial, really, but to him they were major – things like "How do we make sure the cat doesn't eat it?" He had a choice of what colour to paint his bedroom, whether he wanted bunk beds, things like that. Day-to-day decisions we tried to give him as much choice as possible.'

Clarify the options

Children and young people cannot be expected to make informed choices if they do not understand the issues, nor can they participate meaningfully in decision-making fora, such as meetings or courts, if they do not understand the rules of engagement. Time has to be spent with them first, explaining in age-appropriate terms what has happened, what may happen next, what the options are and how the decision will be arrived at. It may help the young person to make sense of the process and their role in it if a meeting is role-played in advance, if they make up prompt cards to help them remember the points they want to make, or if a visit is paid to the court or conference room in advance so it is not totally unfamiliar and intimidating. Information should be presented in an accessible way using child-friendly materials, of which a range are available (Sinclair 2000). Direct work of this kind may be time-consuming, it may be intense and it requires particular skills (Romaine *et al.* 2007). See Chapter 13 for more on explaining complex information to children.

Consider the roles of parents and carers

In many cases it will be the parent who is primarily responsible for involving the child in a decision, but where it is a professional who is undertaking this work, they always need to bear in mind the rights and responsibilities of those with parental responsibility. The parents may need to give consent to the child's involvement in the decision, or to the making of the decision, and in any case their cooperation will assist the child's involvement. Difficulties arise when the parents' views or wishes are in conflict with those of the child. This is a complex area of law and the outcome is decided both on the basis of the child's age and of whether they have sufficient understanding and intelligence to understand fully what is being proposed (House of Lords ruling, *Gillick* v. *West Norfolk and Wisbech Health Authority,* 1986).

The Department of Health (2001) has issued a useful booklet of guidance for medical staff on consent for medical treatment; this advises on what to do when a child refuses treatment that the parent wants them to have, wants treatment that the parent opposes, or wants treatment without the parents' knowledge. While this refers specifically to medical interventions it could appropriately serve as a guide for other sorts of contested decisions as well. As Thoburn (2004) points out, the involvement of children in meetings such as family group conferences and child protection conferences will have to be negotiated with those who have parental responsibility, and the worker may have to tread carefully to uphold the child's rights while respecting the parents' views where the family's cultural expectation is that children will not take part in decision-making. Sensitive listening to the child's wishes in this situation is important, and flexible approaches to making sure the child's voice is heard will have to be adopted if the child is excluded from the meeting. Where children are looked after, the role of carers will also have to be considered: they are likely to be important supports for children (Romaine *et al.* 2007) and may also play a major part in explaining matters, providing information and advocating for the child (McLeod 2007a). Looked-after children may wish to attend review meetings but not to be confronted with their parents. Since both have a right to attend, ways must be found of separating them, through having two parts to the meeting, perhaps.

> 'I walked straight out. Meetings like that just wind me up. People talking about me as if I'm not there.' (Alistair)

Plan meetings with children, not for them

Where a child is the subject of a meeting, and if they are to have some sense of ownership of the process, it makes sense that they should have some say in the way the meeting is run. A looked-after child cannot choose not to have a review meeting – this is a statutory requirement – but they can at least have some input into its organization. If they have been asked who should be invited, and have perhaps designed and sent out invitations, and if their wishes have been considered before deciding when and where the meeting is to take place, and what refreshments might be provided, then they are more likely to feel positive about the whole experience (Kiely 2005). They can also be asked what topics they would like to put on the agenda, and in what order they would like them to be addressed. These are all small issues, but they build up to give the child some sense of control over an event that they may see as an unpleasant necessity. Children can be given the opportunity of thinking how they would like their views to be presented. Do they want to attend? Do they want to speak up for themselves? Or would they prefer to present their views in writing or through their parent, carer, social worker or an independent advocate? All of this requires flexibility in the adults who need to shift their thinking to see it as the child's meeting rather than their own.

> 'I just don't like saying things with people looking at me. And there's loads of people there and that.' (Karen)

Make meetings child-friendly

Meetings are an adult invention and they are often uncomfortable for children. A nine-year-old girl in foster care, explaining why she did not want to attend her review meeting, said: 'Two people came last time I didn't know. I felt a bit shy and a bit bored and like there was a lot of people looking at me' (McLeod 2007a). The best solution may be to avoid making the decision at a formal meeting at all. However, where the meeting must be held it will often be right and appropriate that the child should attend, and in that case it is the responsibility of the adults to adapt the meeting to fit the child, rather than to expect the child to be able to perform like a small adult. Thoburn (2004) says too much is often attempted in one meeting and that much could and should be negotiated and decided outside the meeting. Sinclair (2000) likewise suggests making meetings smaller and shorter, and simplifying the agenda, perhaps by holding a series of mini-meetings, rather than one big one. She also urges ensuring that any special needs the child has are catered for, including, where children are not confident English speakers, the provision of interpreters. Chand (2005) discusses the difficulties of using interpreters in meetings: interpreters must be acceptable to the child, understand the issues involved, and be engaged on an ongoing basis to translate for the child, not just for the meeting. Extra time must be allowed for meetings; chairpersons as well as interpreters will require training.

'They've all got pads they're scribbling on and you feel like they're writing about you. And all these questions they're giving you, you're so nervous. It feels like the whole world is staring at you and you can't move and you can't say anything. The only reason I go is so they don't chat behind my back.' (Kerry)

The role of the chairperson or facilitator is a crucial one if the meeting is to be accessible to the child. Seeing the child in advance and planning it together is one way of enabling the child to feel fully involved with the process. Kiely (2005) suggests that the chairperson/facilitator can set the tone of the meeting by avoiding formality, creating a flexible structure, halting the use of jargon and other obscure language, focusing the meeting on the child and giving the child space to talk. After the meeting they should meet with the child, preferably alone. This gives an opportunity for feedback, which allows the chairperson to learn to manage future meetings better. It is also a chance to check out what the child has taken from the meeting and that they understand what decisions have come out of it. These suggestions all aim to include and empower the child.

'Graham, he's brilliant. When he chairs my review it's so cool. You can talk to him and like, he and my social worker'll talk to me, and they'll talk to me as well, and it's, like, they'll include me in it.' (Tammy)

A more radical approach is for children to actually run meetings themselves (see Practice Example 3.1 in Chapter 3). They may require some training and support before they have the confidence to do so, but young people can successfully act as the chair-person of a formal meeting and there is no better way of making the point that it is their meeting and not the property of the professionals.

Take children's views seriously

It is easy, too easy, for adults to dismiss the views of children: because the views may be clumsily expressed, because the children are naive and lack awareness of the wider picture or long-term implications, because the adults are locked into a view of children as incompetent and in need of protection, or just because it is inconvenient that the child's wishes happen to conflict with those of the adult. Practitioners who want to practise in a respectful and anti-oppressive way, however, will regard a young person as the expert in their own life, and this means always taking their views about what happens to them seriously. The decision on how much weight to accord to a child's views when they wish to do something that adults believe to be against their best interests can be a very tricky one, requiring careful assess-ment of the individual circumstances, and in extreme cases needing to be settled by a court (Department of Health 2001; Thomas 2002). The pre-sumption should be in favour of respecting a child's wishes unless there are clear reasons against (Thoburn 2004) and, within reason, allowing children to make mistakes and so to learn from them (Leeson 2007; Munro 2001). Where a decision goes against a child's expressed views, it is most important to explain why, and this explanation may need to be revisited once the emotional temperature has had time to cool.

> 'They give me a lot of opportunity to talk. They ask the questions, most of them, directly to me. You can see them scribbling away on their pads as they get down what you're saying, and I think they really do listen.' (Patrick)

Give the child a record of decisions made

Another risk of the unequal power base between adults and children is that they will take away different understandings of an interaction and hence different views of what has been agreed. The adult will just assume that their interpretation is the correct one and the young person will later feel cheated when it turns out that what they thought had been agreed does not happen. One way of avoiding such misunderstandings is to negotiate a written agreement that both share in writing. Formal meetings should always have written minutes that serve as a record of what was said and what was decided. The trouble with such documents is that they are rarely composed in language that is accessible to children who have attended the meeting, and so can serve as another mechanism for excluding the child and demonstrating to them that the meeting was not really for them but belonged to the adults. It will often be possible, if the adults are only prepared to put themselves out a little, to couch the notes in terms that make sense to the young person. However, where procedures demand formal minutes, a second version of the action plan or key decisions should be written in simple language or other appropriate format (pictures, for example) and given to the child to keep. Ideally this should be co-constructed with the young person themself: this serves as another check that adults and child have the same understanding of what has been agreed. Where the child's view of what should happen has not been agreed, this should be recorded, with the reasons why.

Decision-making is a process, not a one-off event

The thing to remember when following a set of tips like this, is that all the points are interrelated: there is little point in writing a child-friendly care plan at the end of a meeting at which the young person felt totally alienated, or in welcoming them into a meeting for which they are completely unprepared, or to choose between options that they do not understand. A lot of work has to be done with a child before they are ready to take part in formal decision-making processes. It is also the case that they may need to practise making decisions in informal settings first: 'children *learn* to take part in decisions, rather than simply acquiring the ability at a predetermined age' (Thomas 2002, p.196). As parents, foster carers or teachers, therefore, we are helping young people become more responsible and mature if we give them opportunities to make choices of increasing difficulty as they grow, and to deal with the consequences that ensue. Decision-making is a whole-life issue for children. It is also a whole-organization issue for professionals: 'actively involving children is a continuous process facilitated by a participatory culture' (Sinclair 2000, p.5). A number of writers have stressed that children are more likely to have real influence on decisions where the whole organization, not just individual practitioners, support their involvement. Kiely (2005), for example, says that it is not just action plans that should be written in ways that are accessible to children; all the agency's records should be comprehensible to young

'When I looked in my file there were bits I wasn't allowed to read. You know, um – excuse me! Whose file is it? I do feel it's ridiculous.' (Anna)

service-users since they have a right to see what has been written about them: what is needed is a child-friendly organization.

Wright *et al.* (2006) argue that agencies that support children to make decisions in their personal lives – from making choices in their play and leisure or deciding on their own learning, health treatment or care, to getting involved in child protection and family proceedings arenas and having opportunities to make suggestions or complaints about services – should also allow children to influence their own strategies and structures. Children's involvement in agencies' decision-making processes should not be: '"bolt-on" dimensions but should be part of the organisation's infra-structure' (Wright *et al.* 2006, p.21).

Supporting children's involvement in decision-making has to be resourced

The tenth point should by this point be self-evident, since it emerges out of the last nine. Children will not be able to take part in many decisions in a useful and meaningful way without a lot of support. Support takes time, which costs money. That is one reason why Wright and her associates concluded that 'Senior management commitment to participation was the most important action that organisations could take to promote young people's participation' (Wright *et al.* 2006, p.18). Direct work with children is time-consuming and allowances have to be made in practitioners' caseloads if they are to undertake it (Romaine *et al.* 2007). This is even more clearly the case where children have disabilities affecting their ability to communicate (Morris 1998). It takes time to build a trusting relationship with a child who has been maltreated and may have good reason to be wary of adults; such a child may be very confused and so may struggle to articulate their wishes and feelings in a coherent or consistent way (Schofield 2005). Independent advocacy services come at a price. The use of interpreters is not straightforward (Chand 2005), and again carries a cost. Making meetings more child-friendly may require the use of less formal venues and provision of refreshments, and someone has to pay for these. Even providing the software, printers and ink to produce colourful pictorial care plans may entail some organizations in unforeseen expenditure. The expense of effective decision-making is thus far from negligible. However, even more fundamental is perhaps the attitude of the organization, and the encouragement it gives to practitioners to practise in a certain way. Franklin and Sloper (2006), studying participation of disabled young people in decision-making, concluded that practice was fragile:

Participation often rested on individuals with dedication or specific interest... However, without resources, support and management commitment they alone will not change working practices and the ethos of complex organisations. (p.124)

Reflective Exercise 16.1

Where do you stand on what decisions children should be allowed to make at which ages?

Imagine the following scenarios:

- Your five-year-old daughter wants to get her ears pierced to be like her best friend.

- The dentist says your 11-year-old son needs a brace to straighten his teeth. He says he doesn't want it because it will be uncomfortable and make him look stupid, and anyway he doesn't care if his teeth are crooked.

- Your 14-year-old daughter has a boyfriend who is 22, and you think they may be having sex.

How would you respond to these situations? How much say should a child of the stated age have in deciding each issue?

Chapter 17

Wider Spheres of Engagement

The previous chapter concentrated mainly on the involvement of individual children in decisions that affect them personally, but there are a whole range of other decisions that will impact on groups of children and young people and in which those affected should in fairness have a say. As children grow, the locus of their activities shifts from family towards school and wider community. Their degree of democratic involvement in these spheres can be seen as a measure of society's attitude towards children's right to be heard.

Citizenship and schools

Early years settings such as pre-schools and day-care may be the young child's first experience of life outside the home and will shape their expectations in terms of what choices they are offered and how much respect is accorded to their views and, even with the youngest children, effective consultation is possible. Kinney describes a project to consult with children in an early years centre in Scotland. Children's views about how the centre should be run were sought using a range of methods including small group discussions, pictorial sheets, photo-boards and figure play, with unexpected results. The children's views challenged existing practices and led to changes in the way the service was delivered. This process 'made the hidden potentials of children visible' (Kinney 2005, p.127). However it was not without its difficulties as 'some [staff] found it very difficult to engage in the process. For some there was a reluctance to change, for others it was the fear of not knowing what to do or what to think'. Staff training and a 'well thought-through process of change' (p.127) were essential.

Though there are many imaginative examples of involvement, it is clear that children's voices do frequently go unheard within the education system. Alderson (2002), in an international review of research on children's civil rights in schools, provides evidence suggesting that children's participation rights are less respected in the UK education system than in those of other European countries. Citizenship is treated by schools as 'a topic to be taught rather than an identity to be lived' (Alderson 2002, p.1). Mayall (2005) found that London primary school children did not feel that they had any say in how their schools were run or choices in how they spent their time there. Alderson (2002) points out that children excluded from mainstream schooling – and hence prevented from participating in any way – are disproportionately male, black or disabled. Lundy and Kilpatrick (2006), in their study of children's rights in Northern Ireland, also highlight the plight of children with disabilities, who have no statutory right to be heard in the formal process to assess their special educational needs. This can result in them being sent to special schools where the research found they felt isolated and stigmatized and that their views were not respected.

'I didn't want to be at boarding school. I didn't like the idea of living at school. I wanted to be like any normal child.' (Steven)

School councils are often held up as the answer for ensuring pupils have a voice in how schools are run, and are claimed to have benefits for schools and pupils alike (Department for Education and Skills 2004a). There is always a risk, however, of such bodies being tokenistic: much depends on how much influence they are allowed. Hill (2006) found that among Scottish school children opinions about school councils were split: while the 'insiders' (school council members) spoke highly of them, the 'outsiders' (non-members) resented adults taking more notice of the views of those on the council. Begg (2004) studied pupil councils in Norway, where they have been compulsory in all secondary schools since 1949. She found that not many young people were interested in serving on the councils and those that did were mainly from 'secure, well-resourced backgrounds' (p.133). The issues addressed by the councils tended to be relatively trivial – for example, the condition of the school showers. She concluded that notwithstanding Norway's apparently good track record on involving young people there was no room for complacency: young people had a lack of influence despite their opportunities for being heard.

Cairns and Brannen (2005, p.80) reject the representative model of democracy on which school councils are based because it is a 'top-down' model and excludes most young people from involvement: '[School councils] tend to promote participation as an end, rather than a means to an end'. 'Everyone has a right to take part', they assert, participation should not be left to a small number of individuals who may in any case not be representative. They favour rather a participative approach to democracy (see Practice Example 17.1) that is: 'challenging, not only to the dominant discourse on childhood, but also to traditional approaches to political processes generally' (Cairns and Brannen 2005, p.86).

PRACTICE EXAMPLE 17.1 'INVESTING IN CHILDREN'

Investing in Children is an organization, based in the county of Durham in the Northeast of England, that aims to create opportunities for children and young people to influence local policy and service provision. It was established in 1995 and since then has worked with about 7000 children and young people, including those who are disabled or from minority groups, with at any one time as many as 50 special interest groups each addressing an issue that young people have identified as important to them. Groups are young-people-led, but have adult facilitators. Young people provide a reference group for the local council, have been involved in staff recruitment and training and produce a newsletter. Local organizations that can show they listen to children are given 'Investing in Children' membership. There have been a number of changes and improvements in local services in response to young people's lobbying (Wright *et al.* 2006). The project demonstrates that where young people's expert knowledge as users of services is recognized, services can benefit from their involvement. For example, young people with a diagnosis of diabetes researched services for young diabetics in England and Sweden and produced 'an astonishingly comprehensive and well-considered account of their research, in which they compare the pros and cons of the various practices in the two countries' followed by a 'powerful presentation' to local health care managers (Cairns and Brannen 2005, p.83). Their efforts resulted in improvements being made to services in the region.

Participative democracy is harder to control or manipulate than is representative democracy, and thus it is more likely to pose a real threat to existing power bases. The difficulty with 'bottom-up' approaches to democracy, however, is that they tend, as Cairns and Brannen imply, to the anarchic, and this can make systems hard to manage. This is not just a question of power, but also of efficiency. For example, the Bernard van Leer Foundation (2004) quotes an experimental free school in the Netherlands that provided no equipment at all, not even writing materials, until pupils had decided it was necessary, and gave all staff temporary contracts so that the children could have a say in whether or not they remained employed. Not surprisingly, staff recruitment proved difficult!

Alderson's conclusion is that a school council may well have a role to play but it is only likely to have a positive impact if it is trusted and respected by the staff as otherwise it will only breed cynicism. Mechanisms need to be in place to ensure that all pupils feel they can have some input into the council's proceedings, that their concerns can get on to the agenda, and that it can actually influence decisions, otherwise it will be a pointless exercise. There are in any case many other ways of involving young people in decision-making about their education apart from formal councils. Young people have a 'keen interest in mutual respect, equality and justice' says Alderson (2002, p.2), and this can be harnessed to the benefit of all. Behaviour in schools can improve if children are involved in its management: for example, bullying was successfully reduced after finding out from pupils when and where it happened, which made it easier to control. The best discipline occurs in schools where young people have played a part in defining the rules so they feel some ownership and: 'everyone is involved, contributing ideas and working for change' (Alderson 2002, p.2).

Alderson also quotes research that demonstrates that the quality of children's work improves where they have more say in the process and the outcome since their understanding and motivation increase when they are involved in decisions about their learning. May (2005, p.32) supports this view, arguing that democratic teaching techniques where pupils are seen as 'participators in the classroom and contributors to proceedings' enable them to 'understand that their ideas can make a difference'. When staff want to consult with pupils May suggests this should be pupil- rather than staff-led. This could be achieved by using pupils as researchers and by finding out from the children both what issues they want to be consulted on and how they would like to express their views.

Engagement in the community

Many benefits have also been claimed for children's involvement in the decision-making of the wider community. The Forum for Rural Children and Young People (2005, p.4) describes participation as the 'cornerstone of democracy' and says that young people involved in democratic processes at a local level will feel they have a stake in community welfare and so will be less likely to vandalize communal property as well as more likely to become active citizens as adults. Swiderek (2004) argues for political involvement of the young at all levels since this promotes a more child-friendly state and simultaneously militates against young people's disillusionment and disaffection with democratic processes, hence disputes are more likely to be resolved through negotiation than violence.

It is clear that current practice in involving children in community deci-sions, as in other fields, falls short of the good intentions of those promoting it (see Part 1). There is no one best method of doing this: the Bernard van Leer Foundation (2004) describes participation projects from around the world, demonstrating that many approaches can have positive outcomes. One example was a community radio initiative from South Africa: teenagers made programmes in which they interviewed younger children about their views on local issues. This enabled those who lacked the confidence to feed into political processes to be heard. Willow (1998) lists a range of ways in which local councils can ensure they are responsive to younger citizens, from setting up children's councils to listening to pressure groups, and from supporting advocacy services to using young people as trainers for staff. The Forum for Rural Children and Young People (2005) likewise proposes that local planners use a variety of methods to access young people's views. These could include contacting children through local schools; sending child-friendly questionnaires out to their homes; setting up interactive websites and one-to-one interviews targeted at those unlikely to respond to any of these approaches. Their good practice recommendations for involv-ing children include a 'community champion' for children who can act as advocate and go-between with the planners/community leaders. They say that it is important to choose the right forum for involvement: informality is key and meetings with young people need to be specially designed. Younger children can be intimidated by teenagers and may need to meet separately. Respect and trust can be built through giving rewards and responsibilities to young participants, recording the process through photo-graphs or videos and celebrating it using publicity in the local press.

What is really going to motivate young people, however, as we have already noted, is not whether they have been paid a small fee or had their picture in the local paper, it is the belief that they have been able to make a difference. There is no value in involving children if they cannot affect the outcome: participation activity is thus a real test of adult sincerity. Clarity as to the limits of possible influence is essential if participants are not to feel cheated: 'there seems some danger that the wave of participation activity could be followed in short order by a wave of disillusionment among young people' (Sinclair 2004, p.113). This requires that the adults are honest with themselves, and with the children, about the purpose of the exercise. Where any outcomes are likely to be very long term it can be valuable to build in some opportunities for visible shorter-term outcomes so that children can see they have had impact within a manageable time frame (Forum for Rural Children and Young People 2005). A number of writers see responsibility for funding as the key: only when young people have some influence on how the money is spent can they really have an impact on outcomes (Spicer and Evans 2006; Swiderek 2004). Aird (2006) argues that young people (especially those who are socially excluded) should not only be encouraged to get involved practically in projects aimed at community reconstruction, but they should be partners in leading those projects and in decisions about what grants are spent on. Last, but not least, it is also essential to build into any participation project a monitoring process, so that it is clear to all involved what impact the children's involvement has actually had: the *Hear by Right* materials (National Youth Agency 2005) provide one helpful framework for evaluation. *The Evaluator's Cookbook* (NECF 2005) is another very useful resource.

'If you want the Social to do anything you have to be really firm. They'll just say "Oh yeah, we'll do it" and then two years later they won't have.'
(Wayne)

Research with children

The new sociology of childhood (see Chapter 5) was a significant influence on the way research into children was conducted. The title of Christensen and James's (2000) book *Research with Children* illustrates the change: children were no longer to be objects, or even subjects, who had research done 'to' or 'on' them, they were to be viewed as active agents, participating in the research, working *with* researchers to shape the process of the research and sharing in ownership of its outcomes. The research process is seen as an interaction in which its subjects are partners. Central to this approach is the recognition of the individual whose life is being studied as the person who knows most about that life: it therefore demands a degree of humility and a renunciation of status by the researcher. It also calls for some different approaches to research methodology.

The relationship between participatory research and partnership in social-care practice is obvious, and although by no means all research into children is now carried out in a participatory way (Worrall-Davies and Marino-Francis 2007), and indeed this is not the only or always the best way of conducting research (Scott 2000), participatory techniques in research have both borrowed from best child-care practice and promoted developments in practice. Research and practice can thus inform each other. (Everitt *et al.* 1992). Many researchers now involve young people actively in the research process. Kellet (2006) argues that adults are no substitute for children when it comes to researching children's lives – adults belong to another generation, cannot empathize and see the world through an adult filter. What is needed is to use young people as researchers themselves since the data collected will be more valid. It also benefits the young participants, since they gain in confidence and self-esteem.

Participatory research with children can also have positive impacts on policy and service delivery, as Dearden and Becker demonstrate. Their research with young carers had the effect of turning an invisible group into a visible one: 'By giving the young carers a voice and enabling them to share their experiences, the research empowered them and helped them both as individuals and as a group to have their experiences acknowledged and validated' (Dearden and Becker 2000, p.138). Public awareness of the plight of children with caring responsibilities was heightened, funding was increased and as a result the number of support projects for young carers in the United Kingdom increased from two in 1992 to over a 100 in 1998. This led on to participation by young carers in service delivery through being represented on steering committees and involvement in training for professionals. Changes in policy and legislation ensued, and young carers in England and Wales are now entitled to services as 'children in need' under the Children Act 1989, Section 17, or to be assessed as carers under the Carers and Disabled Children Act 2000. 'Social research can thus be both empowering and enabling' (Dearden and Becker 2000, p.140).

Not all research with young people has had such an impact as this appears to have done. Worrall-Davies and Marino-Francis (2007), for example, found very little change resulted from the research into the young people's mental health services they reviewed. They conclude that there must be strong links between researchers and management if change is to result. This conclusion is echoed by Kilkelly (2006) in her study of children's rights in youth courts in Ireland. She concluded that the political context is all-important: the findings of social research are unlikely to be taken seriously where support from policy-makers and managers is not forthcoming. Young offenders, of course, are likely to be viewed as 'villains' and young carers as 'victims', making support for the rights of the former more contentious than providing services to support the latter and research can only play a small role in challenging entrenched societal attitudes.

The literature is full of advice on how to involve young people in social research. Alderson and Morrow (2004) suggest doing a risk–benefit analysis before commencing, since research may have the capacity to harm children

'I got a chance to write something for the local paper about being in care, and Social Services wouldn't let me. They said the publicity would be bad for me personally. If you ask me they were just scared of what I might say about them!' (Anna)

as well as to help them: intrusive techniques may cause embarrassment, distress, humiliation or disappointment. Over-protecting children by preventing them from taking part in research may also be harmful, though, since there are dangers if their voice goes unheard. The analysis needs to consider short- and long-term benefits and risks as well as the probability and severity of each potential harm.

One of the difficulties of involving children in research is that it may not be possible or appropriate to approach them directly to ask if they would like to be involved in the research. Such requests typically have to go through adult gatekeepers (parents, teachers, social workers) who may exclude them without giving the child a choice.

Over-protectiveness of adult gatekeepers is a recurrent theme in research with children. Leeson (2007) had great difficulty getting any access to teenagers in residential care at all so she could undertake her research into care experiences, and then when there was a change of staff, cooperation was withdrawn and part of the planned programme had to be cancelled: 'This served to illustrate quite vividly the power of the adults to control the life of the boys, who had been keen to participate and were disappointed when this did not happen' (p.271). Curtis *et al.* (2004) point out that this is not only hard on young people who want to take part, but it may invalidate results: teachers, for example, can prevent dissenting pupils from contributing to an evaluation and give a false-positive impression. Morris (1998) found this a particular problem when interviewing disabled young people since the adult gatekeepers, in this case care staff at a residential school, sometimes had to be present to interpret for the young people, even when clearly hostile to the research, which may have inhibited the young people's responses. Nevertheless, she concluded that it was better to interview the young people with an inappropriate interpreter than to exclude them from the research altogether.

Once the researcher has gained access to the young people, informed consent has to be sought. This should use age-appropriate written or pictorial materials as well as verbal explanations (Harker 2002) so that participants fully understand what the research involves. Indeed, consent is perhaps better viewed as a process rather than an event, continually renegotiated as the research proceeds (Harker 2002). Confidentiality can also be a tricky issue, as it is in practice. Many young people will be unwilling to engage in research without a guarantee of confidentiality. However this would then present the researcher with dilemmas should abuse or illegal activities be disclosed (imagine doing research with young sex offenders, drug users or asylum-seekers, for example). It is essential to consider these issues carefully in advance and to negotiate and clarify any limits to be set on confidentiality before commencing.

According to O'Kane (2000, p.136): 'the biggest challenge for the researcher working with children is the disparity in power and status between adults and children'. One way of addressing this perennial problem is to offer the child choices: the opportunity to opt out at any stage, but also choices of venue, time and place to meet (Curtis *et al.* 2004); the option of having a supporter with them or not (O'Kane 2000); choices of age, gender or race of interviewer. Research methods chosen need to be appropriate for the questions the research is seeking to answer. They also have to be appropriate for the children being studied. For example, written questionnaires will be inappropriate for those with limited literacy, but interviews may not suit those who are 'not comfortable verbally' (Worrall-Davies and Marino-Francis 2007, p.6). Hill (2006) recommends using a range of methods and where possible offering alternatives to young people about how they are involved. This reduction in the power imbalance by giving young people some choice is: 'a step in engaging young people and making them feel it is possible to make a difference' Curtis *et al.* (2004, p.173) and is therefore politically as well as ethically desirable.

The question of rewards for young people taking part in research is an important one. While the experience may be intrinsically rewarding, children's time is valuable to them (Hill 2006) and it is not ethical to exploit their willingness to be helpful. Curtis *et al* (2004) propose taking the young people out for a pizza as a thank-you payment cum ice-breaker. Others have made a small payment or given a token by way of thanks.

The closing phases of the research are always important, as young people involved in a project and then dropped without further feedback may feel they have been exploited and then abandoned. Hill (2006) points out that while researchers may be very exercised with getting the process of the research right, young people are likely to be more interested in its outcome. In participatory research it is usually recommended that data and findings are shared with contributors throughout the process and that they take part in the subsequent dissemination of results. With children, however, this may not always be practicable, particularly when the time frame of the research is longer than would make sense for children of the age being studied. Harker (2002) recommends debriefing the participants at the end of the project and making sure any necessary support is available to them. She also suggests involving the children themselves in deciding what sort of feedback they would like about the results and when and how they would like to receive it.

Young people, policy and politics

Children have a bigger stake in the future than do older people. That is no doubt why saving the planet appeals so strongly to them. They also, like adults, have a very significant stake in the present. Roughly one in four of the British population is under 18; in parts of the country (for example, Birmingham) the proportion rises to one in three (Willow 1998). In much of the developing world more than half of the population is under 18. It therefore is a question of natural justice that young people should be represented in policy development and in political decision-making processes that shape their present and future lives: 'They like other people have a right to be heard because they are human beings... Practically all activities of councils touch children in some way' (Willow 1998, p.70).

The Australian writers Fattore and Turnbull (2005, p.47) seek to 'challenge orthodox practices and discourses of what constitutes politics and the idea that children are non-political'. Excluding children from conventional political activity is undemocratic, and is based on the mistaken premises that children are incompetent to express their own views and that adults can always be trusted to speak for them. Politics, they argue, should be redefined to encompass the social and cultural: children's role in making decisions within their own families, or in child protection procedures, for example, are both forms of political activity. All political action should be flexible enough to allow for people of different abilities: 'shared understanding is possible between actors of diverse competencies' (Fattore and Turnbull 2005, p.48) and it needs to be accepted that all understandings (including those of adults) are partial. Children can participate in different ways and varying degrees, either directly or indirectly, in political processes. Where this is through adults representing them this must be done in ways that are sensitive to the child's views and that maximize their participation.

Research on children's involvement in policy development at any level indicates that it remains poorly developed (Cavet and Sloper 2004; Spicer and Evans 2006). However, we should not be surprised by these findings given the literature on 'policy networks' – pressure groups and others who take part in influencing government decision-making – claim Tisdall and Davies (2004). Such groups tend to act as 'outsiders' to government, both because they value their independence and because governments see them as anarchic and so will not grant them 'insider' status. Nevertheless, policy-makers invite their limited involvement because their expertise can lead to better policies. Tisdall and Davies describe a two-year-long project involving children and young people with special educational needs in developing policy regarding Scottish special education. The political climate was propitious as the Scottish executive had requested and funded the work and change was on the agenda. The response to the young people's proposals was mixed, however: some of their suggestions were accepted, others ignored or rejected. Overall, there was no radical change in response to the children's views, but there were small, incremental changes that could be built on in future. To achieve more significant impact, the writers suggest, it would be necessary 'to challenge the governance itself so that there were political structures involving children and young people within government' (Tisdall and Davies 2004, p.141).

It is often claimed that if we look to Europe we can see better examples of children's involvement in democratic structures than we will find in the United Kingdom. Aynsley-Green (2004), for example, quotes with approval Scandinavian examples of government taking children's views seriously. Begg (2004) examines Norwegian practice in involving young people in children's councils within local government, however, and is not impressed. Swiderek (2004, p.93) takes a similarly jaundiced view of the German experience at both national and local levels. While there is a proliferation of youth council and youth parliament arrangements: 'The participation of children frequently serves as an alibi for adults – children are used as instruments'.

Strong views are held about the value of different approaches to the involvement of younger people in political processes. Cairns and Brannen (2005) argue persuasively for a model of participative rather than representative democracy. Young people supported by their project to get involved in researching and campaigning on issues that affected them gained in confidence, became more aware of the injustice of a system that failed to listen to them, more sure that they had a right to be heard, and consequently more politically aware. They still did not, however, always achieve their objective of changing policy, since negative attitudes from adults often stood in their way. Being outsiders to the political system was their weakness as well as their strength.

Spicer and Evans (2006) distinguish between 'quantitative' and 'qualitative' participation in strategic processes and highlight that each approach has both benefits and drawbacks. The former approach involves consulting with large numbers of young people on a limited range of issues. Their views can then influence service delivery decisions in predetermined areas. Spicer and Evans describe this approach as more 'democratic' since the views of many can be considered. It is also relatively speedy and cheap and more comfortable for those adults who prefer to avoid the challenge of direct engagement with young people. However, the young people have no sustained involvement and the lack of feedback is disempowering for them.

Alternatively, where there was 'qualitative' involvement of young people in the projects studied (for example, membership of boards, funding committees and reference groups, or involvement in staff interviewing) the young people were directly involved in decision-making, had more real influence and hence felt more empowered. The disadvantages were the small numbers involved, the exclusion of those harder to engage, and the time and resources required to enable children's involvement. Much effort needed to be put into preparing and supporting the young participants; meetings had to be held in the evening, they were longer, had to be more informal and jargon-free. As a result, organizations wanting to involve young people 'must balance the requirement to rapidly deliver their programmes with relatively limited resources with the need to invest considerable time and resources to achieve effective children's participation' (Spicer and Evans 2006, p.186).

PRACTICE EXAMPLE 17.2 INTERVIEWING JOB APPLICANTS

At a family support project run by the children's charity Barnardo's in Cumbria in Northwest England, children who use the project's services take part in staff interviews. Children, generally between 9 and 12 years, but sometimes younger, are invited to help with interviews. If they agree, their project worker prepares them, explaining what the job is the candidates have applied for and emphasizing the importance of not telling anyone the names of those interviewed. It is also explained to the child that their views will influence the outcome but will not necessarily decide it: the final decision of who to appoint rests with the adult panel. The child, in discussion with the project worker, then decides how to conduct their part of the interview. One child decided to devise a 'quiz' for candidates, involving questions from: 'What's your favourite TV programme?' to: 'How would you explain your job to a child?' Another asked candidates to play games with him and then considered a number of questions afterwards, such as: 'Did they allow me to play as I wanted or did they boss me about?' The project worker sits in on the interviews and discusses each candidate with the child afterwards. The child is paid for their help and is sent a card of thanks. Once someone has been appointed to the post a letter is sent to the child telling them who got the job. Children are perceived to have gained a lot from taking part in this process. Perhaps equally importantly, job applicants have commented on the strong message it sends them about children's participation even before they have started working for the organization.

Despite a gloomy overall picture, the literature contains many examples of positive practice. Badham describes how disabled young people in the West Midlands of England campaigned successfully for better access to leisure services locally and for changes to policy nationally. He attributes the group's success to the fact that it was a 'bottom-up' initiative that came from the strongly held views of the young people themselves. There was sustained involvement of supportive adults who operated from a social model of disability, treating the young people as equals and encouraging them to use their own choice of means of communication, which was to make a multimedia CD-ROM of their views and experiences, which was sent to professionals and policy-makers: 'The young researchers themselves took charge of the medium and the message... Lobbying strategies [were] targeted at specific points of influence in the relevant system, in this case a local authority' (Badham 2004, p.150). The outcome was seen to be empowering for the young people, who felt themselves to be instrumental in change.

> 'I enjoy working to get the system changed and I think I can achieve something that way.'
> (Anna)

A survey of the literature can help us identify the approaches that are most likely to bear fruit. Adults who wish to promote young people's participation need to develop their communication skills (Franklin and Sloper 2006). Meaningful involvement of young people in policy development requires a willingness on the part of the policy-makers to listen; there should be clarity about objectives, a flexible approach, adequate resources, training for both staff and young people, inclusion of marginalized groups, feedback about outcomes and evaluation of initiatives (Cavet and Sloper 2004). Effective participation at the macro level is thus about structure and culture as well as about practice: an organization with a culture of participation will be able to evidence participation at all levels (National Youth Agency 2005; Wright et al. 2006).

Important though all these points are, there remains an inherent incompatibility between adults 'allowing' children a say (on their terms) and young people being heard on the issues they want to air (which may be different ones). Tisdall and Davis (2004, p.144) hint at this when they say: 'Ultimately this will not be a gift that adults can give to children but an outcome that children and young people achieve for themselves'. Miljeteig (2005), in an international study of young workers' groups, provides examples of true 'bottom-up' political involvement. The most effective groups, he noted, focused on concrete issues affecting their members, and where adults were involved they were mainly young adults from the same background as group members who took great care not to impose their views on the process. Operating like this, self-help groups in a number of countries in Africa and Latin America have successfully campaigned for better access to education, health and social care for young workers. While groups might be small and local, taken together their numbers were large, and communication networks between them crossed national borders so that together they could be seen as a movement. Respecting young people's democratic right to express their views does not come without challenge, however. In this case, adult policy-makers internationally were very reluctant to accept the young people's view that they had a right to work. 'Are we willing', Miljeteig (2005, p.134) asks, 'to give up power and admit that sometimes young people come up with better explanations and solutions than we do?' This is a question that all adults who believe they favour increased participation for children would do well to ask themselves.

Last Words

'Rabbit's clever,' said Pooh thoughtfully.

'Yes,' said Piglet. 'Rabbit's clever.'

'And he has brain.'

'Yes,' said Piglet. 'Rabbit has brain.'

There was a long silence.

'I suppose,' said Pooh, 'that's why he never understands anything.'

From *The House at Pooh Corner* by A.A. Milne
[1882–1956] (Milne [1928] 1974, p.128)

The young people I interviewed for the 'Listening but not Hearing' study (McLeod 2001) were all troubled to a greater or lesser extent, and some of them were undoubtedly also seen as troublesome by the adults responsible for them. Nevertheless, they were often eloquent in expressing their views and they could speak with considerable wisdom.

> 'I just like to be looked at as a normal kid with a bit of a problem, but not to be regarded as if I've got a mad disease that's catching.' (Tammy)

Much of what they said about adults and communication would have held true for any situation where adults attempt to listen to children: they were, after all, as Tammy indicates above, ordinary young people who just happened to have had some unusual experiences. This concluding chapter aims to highlight some of the main points of the book, but since this is a book about listening to children I will let the young

> 'They've got to really put their minds into what we're thinking and feeling.' (Kerry)

'Every time my social worker comes round he always says "How's school?" and, school, there's nothing to tell you, and I see that as quite an irrelevant subject. If he said "How's everything going?" then there's more to talk about – home and school and everything gives you quite a big subject.' (Patrick)

'Most foster kids need the whole system explaining to them. You just have to pick it up as you go along.' (Alistair)

'If it wasn't for my foster carer I wouldn't have understood anything. He's the one who's sat down with me and said "Here's your choices". If it wasn't for him I'd be bitter. He could win awards.' (Wayne)

'That's the kind of relationship I value: being able to laugh, cry, say what you think.' (Kerry)

'Just being there for you, helping you when you're in trouble, talking with you and trying to sort it out. Take you out just to socialize with you and get to know you.' (Steven)

people make the points for me and will link their points with the briefest of commentaries.

Since it is not always easy to find out exactly what a child's wishes and feelings are, one of the first principles for the adult who wants to hear what children think is to put oneself in their shoes, try to empathize and work out exactly where they are coming from. The second prerequisite is to keep an open mind, avoid prejudging and making assumptions. Open questions will reflect this open mind.

Particularly when children's situations are complex, the practitioner's job can be to explain the things the children do not understand. If they are confused about what has happened to them or what may happen next, young people may feel that their lives are out of control and that they are helpless in the face of events.

Only once a young person fully grasps the options facing them, appreciating both the risks and the benefits of each available course of action, is it possible for them to act in a responsible way and to make wise decisions. Thus, information is the bedrock of involvement in decision-making.

Effective listening to a young person is more likely to be achieved in the context of an ongoing relationship in which trust and rapport can be achieved, rather than in a brief encounter.

Establishing such a relationship is time-consuming. It cannot be rushed. Nevertheless, even the most disaffected of the young people I interviewed could describe what sort of support they valued from a helping professional.

'Having them treat you as an equal, rather than as a little kid, so then you feel you can talk to them, and everything comes out in the open and gets sorted.'
(Robert)

One key feature of a constructive helping relationship is that it is built on respect for the young person as a human being whose perspective is as valid and whose concerns are as important as those of the practitioner. The young people I interviewed repeatedly referred to the concept of 'equality' to express this idea.

'I think everybody's got a right to some say in their future!'
(Kerry)

The notion of equality could be expressed as a partnership through which a child could be empowered. While these young people did not feel powerful – far from it – they had a strong sense of fairness and believed passionately that they had a right to be heard and to contribute to decisions on matters that affected them.

The first word in the book was given to Anna, and I give the last word to her too. In it I think she sums up its central message: that listening is about respect and about empowerment and that it is a question of human rights. When I asked Anna if she had any advice for adults who want to listen to children she said:

'I think I'd have two pieces of advice. First, always remember that the young person's your equal. The second piece would be that it's their life.'

Final Reflective Exercise

Having read this book, what are the things you plan to do or to do differently? Write yourself an action plan.

References

Adoption and Children Act (2002) London: The Stationery Office.

Aiers, A. and Kettle, J. (1998) *When Things Go Wrong: Young People's Experience of Getting Access to the Complaints Procedure in Residential Care.* London: National Institute for Social Work (NISW).

Ainsworth, M., Blehar, M., Waters, E. and Wall, S. (1978) *Patterns of Attachment: A Study of the Strange Situation.* Hillsdale, NJ: Erlbaum.

Aird, G. (2006) 'Children's rights, volunteering and participating.' *Childright 229,* September, 10–14.

Alderson, P. (2002) *Civil Rights in Schools.* London: National Children's Bureau (NCB).

Alderson, P. and Morrow, V. (2004) *Ethics, Social Research and Consulting with Children and Young People.* Barkingside: Barnardo's.

Allerton, M. (1993) 'Am I asking the right questions? – What teachers ask of children.' *International Journal of Early Childhood 25,* 1, 42–8.

Argent, H. (2006) *Ten Top Tips for Placing Children in Permanent Families.* London: British Association for Adoption & Fostering (BAAF).

Aries, P. (1962) *Centuries of Childhood.* Translated from the French by Robert Baldick. London: Jonathan Cape.

Arnstein, S. (1969) 'A ladder of citizen participation.' *Journal of the American Institute of Planners 35,* 4, 214–225.

Austen, J. ([1816] 1966) *Emma.* London: Penguin Classics.

Axline, V. (1969) *Play Therapy.* New York: Ballantyne Books.

Aynsley-Green, A. (2004) 'The Children's Task-force and the National Services Framework: What do they Mean for Children, Young People and Families?' In Lord Justice Thorpe and J. Cadbury (eds) *Hearing the Children.* Bristol: Jordan.

Badham, B. (2004) 'Participation for a change: disabled young people lead the way.' *Children and Society 18,* 2, 143–154.

Barnes, D. (1969) 'Language in the Secondary Classroom.' In D. Barnes, J. Britton and H. Rosen *Language, the Learner and the School.* Harmondsworth: Penguin.

Barrett, H. (2006) *Attachment and the Perils of Parenting: A Commentary and a Critique.* London: National Family and Parenting Institute.

Begg, I. (2004) 'Participation Rights in Norway.' In D. Crimmens and A. West (eds) *Having their Say: Young People and Participation – European Experiences.* Lyme Regis: Russell House Publishing.

Bell, M. (2002) 'Promoting children's rights through the use of relationship.' *Child and Family Social Work 7*, 1, 1–11.

Bennett, C. (1994) 'Who's kidding who? The risks of children's rights.' *The Guardian 2*, 16 March, 1–3.

Berger, N. (1971) 'The Child, the Law and the State.' In P. Adams (ed.) *Children's Rights: Towards the Liberation of the Child.* London: Elek.

Bernard van Leer Foundation (2004) 'Young children's participation: rhetoric or growing reality?' *Early Childhood Matters 103.*

Berry, J. (1972) *Social Work with Children.* London: Routledge and Kegan Paul.

Bolzan, N. (2005) '"To Know Them is to Love Them", But Instead Fear and Loathing: Community Perceptions of Young People.' In J. Mason and T. Fattore (eds) *Children Taken Seriously in Theory, Policy and Practice.* London: Jessica Kingsley Publishers.

Bond, M. (1972) *Paddington Bear.* London: Collins.

Bowlby, J. (1969, 1973, 1980) *Attachment and Loss – Volumes 1–3.* London: Hogarth Press.

Boyden, J. (1990) 'Childhood and the Policy-makers: A Comparative Perspective on the Globalization of Childhood.' In A. James and A. Prout (eds) *Constructing and Reconstructing Childhood: Contemporary Issues in the Sociology of Childhood.* Basingstoke: Falmer Press.

Brandon, M. (1999) 'Communicating with Children and Ascertaining their Wishes and Feelings.' In D. Shemmings (ed.) *Involving Children in Family Support and Child Protection.* London: The Stationery Office.

Brandon, M., Schofield, G. and Trinder, A. (1998) *Social Work with Children.* Basingstoke: Macmillan.

Bray, M. (1991) *Poppies on the Rubbish Heap: Sexual Abuse – the Voice of the Child.* Edinburgh: Canongate.

Brodzinsky, D. and Schechter, M. (eds) (1994) *The Psychology of Adoption.* Oxford: Oxford University Press.

Brontë, C. ([1847] 1996) *Jane Eyre.* Cambridge: Cambridge University Press.

Brown, K. and Rutter, L. (2006) *Critical Thinking for Social Work.* Exeter: Learning Matters.

Buchanan, A. and Ritchie, C. (2004) *What Works for Troubled Children?* 2nd edition. Barkingside: Barnardo's.

Burman, E. (1994) *Deconstructing Developmental Psychology.* London: Routledge.

Bush, M., Gordon, A. and Le Bailly, R. (1977) 'Evaluating child welfare services: a contribution from the clients.' *Social Service Review 51*, 3, 491–501.

Butler, I. and Williamson, H. (1994) *Children Speak: Children, Trauma and Social Work.* Harlow: Longman.

Butler, I. and Williamson, H. (1999) 'Children's Views of their Involvement.' In D. Shemmings (ed.) *Involving Children in Family Support and Child Protection.* London: The Stationery Office.

Butler, I., Scanlan, L., Robinson, M., Douglas, G. and Murch, M. (2002) 'Children's involvement in their parents' divorce.' *Children and Society 16*, 2, 89–102.

Cairns, L. and Brannen, M. (2005) 'Promoting the human rights of children and young people – the "Investing in children" experience.' *Adoption and Fostering 29*, 1, 78–87.

Campbell, T. (1992) 'The Rights of the Minor as Person, as Child, as Juvenile, as Future Adult.' In P. Alston, S. Parker and J. Seymour (eds) *Children's Rights and the Law.* Oxford: Clarendon.

Canadian Nurses Association (CNA) (2002) *Code of Ethics for Registered Nurses.* Ottawa, ON: CNA.

Cancerlink (1993) *Talking to Children when an Adult has Cancer.* London: Cancerlink.

Carers and Disabled Children Act (2000) London: The Stationery Office.

Carr, C. (2007) 'Having a Say: The Student Voice Research Project.' Unpublished Report. Lancaster: Lancaster University.

Carr, S. (2004) *Has Service-user Participation made a Difference to Social Care Services?* London: Social Care Institute for Excellence (SCIE).

Cavet, J. and Sloper, P. (2004) 'The participation of children and young people in decisions about UK service development.' *Child Care, Health and Development 30*, 6, 613–21.

Chand, A. (2005) 'Do you speak English? Language barriers in child protection social work with minority ethnic families.' *British Journal of Social Work 35*, 6, 807–21.

Children Act (1989) London: Her Majesty's Stationery Office (HMSO).

Children Act (2004) London: The Stationery Office.

Children and Young People's Unit (2001) *Learning to Listen: Core Principles for the Involvement of Children and Young People.* London: Department for Education and Skills.

Children (Scotland) Act (1995) London: The Stationery Office.

Chomsky, N. (1959) 'Review of B.F. Skinner's *Verbal Behavior.*' *Language 35*, 26–58.

Christensen, P. (1998) 'Difference and Similarity: How Children's Competence is Constituted in Illness and its Treatment.' In I. Hutchby and J. Moran-Ellis *Children and Social Competence: Arenas of Action.* London: Falmer.

Christensen, P. and James, A. (2000) *Research with Children.* London: Falmer Press.

Cipolla, J., McGown, D. and Yanulis, M. (1992) *Communicating through Play: Techniques for Assessing and Preparing Children for Adoption.* London: British Association for Adoption & Fostering (BAAF).

Clark, A. and Moss, P. (2001) *Listening to Young Children: The Mosaic Approach.* London: National Children's Bureau (NCB).

Clark, A. and Statham, J. (2005) 'Listening to young children: experts in their own lives.' *Adoption and Fostering 29,* 1, 45–56.

Clark, A., Kjørholt, A. and Moss, P. (eds) (2005) *Beyond Listening: Children's Perspectives on Early Childhood Services.* Bristol: Policy Press.

Clarkson, P. (1989) *Gestalt Counselling in Action.* London: Sage.

Cole, C. and Loftus, E. (1987) 'The Memory of Children.' In S. Ceci, M. Toglia and D. Ross (eds) *Children's Eye-witness Memory.* New York: Springer-Verlag.

Coleman, S. and Rowe, C. (2005) *Remixing Citizenship: Democracy and Young People's Use of the Internet.* London: Carnegie Trust.

Corbett, V. (2004) 'Listening to What Children have to Say.' In R. Phillips (ed.) *Children Exposed to Parental Substance Misuse.* London: British Association for Adoption & Fostering (BAAF).

Cox, M. (1991) *The Child's Point of View.* Hemel Hempstead: Harvester Wheatsheaf.

Crittenden, P. (1997) 'Truth, Error, Omission, Distortion and Deception: The Application of Attachment Theory to the Assessment and Treatment of Psychiatric Disorder.' In S. Dollinger and L. Di Lalla (eds) *Assessment and Intervention Across the Lifespan.* Hillsdale, NJ: Erlbaum.

Crompton, M. (1980) *Respecting Children.* London: Edward Arnold.

Cross, C., Goosey, D. and James, G. (1991) 'The wishes and feelings of the child: an expert opinion.' *Journal of Law and Practice 1,* 4, 43–6.

Curtis, K., Roberts, H., Copperman, J., Downie, A. and Liabø K. (2004) '"How come I don't get asked no questions?" – Researching "hard to reach" children and teenagers.' *Child and Family Social Work 9,* 2, 167–75.

Dalrymple, J. (2003) 'Professional advocacy as a force for resistance in child welfare.' *British Journal of Social Work 33,* 8, 1043–62.

Dalrymple, J. (2005) 'Constructions of child and youth advocacy: emerging issues in advocacy practice.' *Children and Society 19,* 3–15.

Daniels, B., Wassell, S. and Gilligan, R. (1999) *Child Development for Child Care and Protection Workers.* London: Jessica Kingsley Publishers.

Davies, G. and Westcott, H. (1999) *Interviewing Child Witnesses Under the 'Memorandum of Good Practice': A Research Review.* London: Home Office.

Davies, G., Wilson, C., Mitchell, R. and Milson, J. (1995) *Video-taping Children's Evidence: An Evaluation.* London: Home Office Research and Statistics Department.

Davis, J., Watson, N. and Cunningham-Barley, S. (2000) 'Learning the Lives of Disabled Children: Developing a Reflexive Approach.' In P. Christensen and A. James (eds) *Research with Children*. London: Falmer.

Dearden, C. and Becker, S. (2000) 'Listening to Children: Meeting the Needs of Young Carers.' In H. Kemshall and R. Littlechild (eds) *User-involvement and Participation in Social Care: Research Informing Practice*. London: Jessica Kingsley Publishers.

Dekleva, B. and Zorga, S. (2004) 'Children's Parliaments in Slovenia.' In D. Crimmens and A. West (eds) *Having their Say: Young People and Participation: European Experiences*. Lyme Regis: Russell House Publishing.

Department for Education and Skills (2004a) *Pupil Participation Guidance. Working Together: Giving Children and Young People a Say*. London: The Stationery Office.

Department for Education and Skills (2004b) *Every Child Matters: Change for Children*. London: The Stationery Office.

Department for Education and Skills (2005) *Common Core of Skills and Knowledge for the Children's Workforce*. London: Department for Education and Skills.

Department of Health (1991) *Children Act Guidance and Regulations*. London: HMSO.

Department of Health (1995) *Child Protection: Messages from Research*. London: HMSO.

Department of Health (1998) *The Quality Protects Programme: Transforming Children's Services*. London: Department of Health.

Department of Health (2000) *Framework for the Assessment of Children in Need and their Families*. London: The Stationery Office.

Department of Health (2001) *Seeking Consent: Working with Children*. London: Department of Health.

Department of Health (2003) *The Integrated Children's System*. London: The Stationery Office.

Department of Health (2004) *National Services Framework for Children, Young People and Maternity Services*. London: Department of Health.

Donaldson, M. (1978) *Children's Minds*. London: Croom-Helm.

Education Act (2002) London: The Stationery Office.

Eide, B. and Winger, N. (2005) 'From the Children's Point of View: Methodological and Ethical Challenges.' In A. Clark, A. Kjørholt and P. Moss (eds) *Beyond Listening: Children's Perspectives on Early Childhood Services*. Bristol: Policy Press.

Elsegood, J. (1996) 'Breaking Bad News to Children.' In B. Lindsay and J. Elsegood *Working with Children in Grief and Loss*. London: Baillière Tindall.

Elsey, S. (2004) 'Children's experience of public space.' *Children and Society 18*, 2, 155–164.

Everitt, A., Hardiker, P., Littlewood, J. and Mullender, A. (1992) *Applied Research for Better Practice*. Basingstoke: Macmillan.

Fahlberg, V. (1994) *A Child's Journey Through Placement.* London: British Association for Adoption & Fostering (BAAF).

Family Law Act (1996) London: HMSO.

Fattore, T. and Turnbull, N. (2005) 'Theorizing Representation and Engagement with Children: The Political Dimension of Child-oriented Communication.' In J. Mason and T. Fattore (eds) *Children Taken Seriously in Theory, Policy and Practice.* London: Jessica Kingsley Publishers.

Forum for Rural Children and Young People (2005) *Participation in Our Village: Involving Children and Young People in the Development of Parish and Town Plans.* London: National Children's Bureau (NCB).

Fraiberg, S. (1972) 'Understanding the Child-client.' In E. Holgate (ed.) *Communicating with Children.* London: Longman.

Franklin, A. and Sloper, P. (2006) 'Participation of disabled children and young people in decision-making within Social Services Departments: a survey of current and recent activities in England.' *British Journal of Social Work 36*, 5, 723.

Freeman, M. (1983) 'The Rights of Children in Care.' In H. Geach and E. Szwed *Providing Civil Justice for Children.* London: Edward Arnold.

Freeman, M. (1992) 'Taking Children's Rights more Seriously.' In P. Alston, S. Parker and J. Seymour (eds) *Children, Rights and the Law.* Oxford: Clarendon.

Fuller, E. (1951) *The Right of the Child.* London: Gollancz.

Garbarino, J. and Stott, F. (1992) *What Children Can Tell Us: Eliciting, Interpreting and Evaluating Critical Information from Children.* San Francisco, CA: Jossey Bass.

Gibran, K. ([1923] 1995) *Prophet, Madman, Wanderer.* London: Penguin.

Gill, T. (2006) 'Childhood Freedoms and Adult Fears: Growing Up in a Risk-averse Society.' Unpublished paper.

Gilligan, R. (1997) 'Beyond permanence? The importance of resilience in child placement practice and planning.' *Adoption and Fostering 21*, 1, 12–19.

Gilligan, R. (1999) 'Enhancing the resilience of children and young people in public care by mentoring their talents and interests.' *Child and Family Social Work 4*, 3, 187–96.

Gilligan, R. (2000) 'The key role of social workers in promoting the well-being of children in state care – a neglected dimension of reforming policies.' *Child and Family Social Work 14*, 4, 267–76.

Gledhill, A. (1989) *Who Cares? Children at Risk and the Social Services.* London: Centre for Policy Studies.

Haddon, M. (2004) *The Curious Incident of the Dog in the Night-time.* London: Vintage.

Hallam, B. and Vine, P. (1996) 'Expected and Unexpected Loss.' In B. Lindsay and J. Elsegood *Working with Children in Grief and Loss.* London: Ballière Tindall.

Harker, R. (2002) *Involving Children in Social Research.* London: National Children's Bureau (NCB).

Harnett, R. (2003) *Peer Advocacy for Children and Young People: Highlight No. 202.* London: National Children's Bureau (NCB).

Harnett, R. (2004) 'Doing peer advocacy: insights from the field.' *Representing Children* 17, 2, 131–141.

Herbert, M. (1981) *Behavioural Treatment of Problem Children.* London: Academic Press.

Hill, M. (2006) 'Children's voices on ways of having a voice: children and young people's perspectives on methods used in research and consultation.' *Childhood 13,* 1, 69–89.

Hillman, M. (2006) 'Children's rights and adults' wrongs.' *Children's Geographies 4,* 1, 61–7.

HMSO (1995) *Looking After Children.* London: Her Majesty's Stationery Office (HMSO).

Hobbs, T., Kaoukji, D. and Little, M. (2006) 'Interview with Lord Laming – reflections on the future of children's services in England and Wales.' *Journal of Children's Services 1,* 1, 58–63.

Holgate, E. (ed.) (1972) *Communicating with Children.* London: Longman.

Holt, J. (1975) *Escape from Childhood.* Harmondsworth: Penguin.

Home Office (1992) *Memorandum of Good Practice in Video-recorded Interviews with Child Witnesses for Criminal Proceedings.* London: Her Majesty's Stationery Office (HMSO).

Home Office, Crown Prosecution Service and Department of Health (2001) *Provision of Therapy to Child Witnesses Prior to a Criminal Trial: Practice Guidance.* London: The Stationery Office.

Home Office, Lord Chancellor's Department, Crown Prosecution Service, Department of Health and the National Assembly for Wales (2002) *Achieving Best Evidence in Criminal Proceedings: Guidance for Vulnerable or Intimidated Witnesses, Including Children.* London: Home Office Communication Directorate.

Howe, D., Brandon, M., Hinnings, D. and Schofield, G. (1999) *Attachment Theory, Child Maltreatment, and Family Support.* Basingstoke: Macmillan.

Hundeide, K. (1985) 'The Tacit Background of Children's Judgements.' In J. Wertsch (ed.) *Culture, Communication and Cognition: Vygotskian Perspectives.* Cambridge: Cambridge University Press.

Ingram, R. and Simm, J. (2006) 'A possible approach.' *Debate* 120, 23–6.

Irish Sports Council (2000) *Code of Ethics and Good Practice for Children's Sport.* Accessed on 22/02/08 at www.irishsportscouncil.ie/code/downloads/ coden.pdf.

Jacobs, G. (2006) 'Imagining the flowers, but working with the rich and heavy clay: participation and empowerment in action research for health.' *Educational Action Research 14,* 4, 569–81.

James, A. and Prout, A. (1990) *Constructing and Reconstructing Childhood: Contemporary Issues in the Sociology of Childhood.* Basingstoke: Falmer Press.

Jewett, C. (1984) *Helping Children Cope with Separation and Loss.* London: Batsford.

John, M. (1995) 'Children's Rights in a Free-market Culture.' In S. Stephens (ed.) *Children and the Politics of Culture.* Princeton, NJ: Princeton University Press.

John, M. (2005) 'Foreword.' In J. Mason and T. Fattore (eds) *Children Taken Seriously: in Theory, Policy and Practice.* London: Jessica Kingsley Publishers.

Johnson, M. and Foley, M. (1984) 'Differentiating fact from fantasy: the reliability of children's memory.' *Journal of Social Issues 40,* 2, 33–50.

Jones, D. (2003) *Communicating with Vulnerable Children: A Guide for Practitioners.* London: Gaskell.

Jordan, B. (2006) 'Well-being: the next revolution in children's services?' *Journal of Children's Services 1,* 1, 41–50.

Keay, L. (ed.) (2006) *Research and Policy Update.* Issue 66, July. Accessed on 22/02/08 at www.rip.org.uk/rpu/2006/detail.asp?id=17.

Kellet, M. (2006) 'Children as researchers: exploring the impact on education and empowerment.' *Childright* 226, May, 11–13.

Kelley, N. (2006) 'Children's involvement in policy formation.' *Children's Geographies 4,* 1, 37–44.

Kenney, C. (1999) 'Using Professional Judgment.' In D. Shemmings (ed.) *Involving Children in Family Support and Child Protection.* London: The Stationery Office.

Kerr, J. (1994) *Out of the Hitler Time: When Hitler Stole Pink Rabbit, Bombs on Aunt Dainty, A Small Person Far Away* (trilogy). London: Collins.

Kiely, P. (2005) 'The Voice of the Child in the Family Group Conferencing Model.' In J. Mason and T. Fattore (eds) *Children Taken Seriously: In Theory and Practice.* London: Jessica Kingsley Publishers.

Kilkelly, U. (2006) 'Operationalising children's rights: lessons from research.' *Journal of Children's Services 1,* 4, 35–45.

King, M. and Piper, C. (1990) *How the Law Thinks about Children.* Aldershot: Gower.

King, P. and Chaplin, P. (1989) *Talking Pictures.* London: British Association for Adoption & Fostering (BAAF).

Kinney, L. (2005) 'Small Voices, Powerful Messages.' In A. Clark, A. Kjørholt and P. Moss (eds) *Beyond Listening: Children's Perspectives on Early Childhood Services.* Bristol: Policy Press.

Kjørholt, A. (2005) 'The Competent Child and the Right to be Oneself: Reflections on Children as Fellow Citizens.' In A. Clark, A. Kjørholt and P. Moss (eds) *Beyond Listening: Children's Perspectives on Early Childhood Services.* Bristol: Policy Press.

Kjørholt, A., Moss, P. and Clark, A. (2005) 'Beyond Listening: Future Prospects.' In A. Clark, A. Kjørholt, and P. Moss (eds) *Beyond Listening: Children's Perspectives on Early Childhood Services.* Bristol: Policy Press.

Klein, M. (1969) *The Psychoanalysis of Children.* London: Hogarth Press.

Kohli, R. (2006a) 'Social work with young asylum-seekers.' *Child and Family Social Work 11*, 1, 1–10.

Kohli, R. (2006b) 'The sound of silence: listening to what unaccompanied asylum-seeking children say and do not say.' *British Journal of Social Work 36*, 5, 707–22.

Kurzt, Z. and Street, C. (2006) 'Mental health services for young people from black and minority ethnic backgrounds: the current challenge.' *Journal of Children's Services 1*, 3, 40–9.

Laertius, D. (1925) *Lives of Eminent Philosophers.* Translated by R. Hicks. London: William Heinemann. (First written third century AD.)

Lamb, M., Sternberg, K. and Esplin, P. (1998) 'Conducting investigative interviews of alleged sexual abuse victims.' *Child Abuse and Neglect 22*, 8, 813–23.

Laming, Lord (2003) *The Victoria Climbié Report.* London: The Stationery Office.

Lansdown, G. (1992) 'Key right is child's right to be heard.' *Childright* 11, November, 4.

Lansdown, R., Burnell, A. and Allen, A. (2007) 'Is it that they won't do it, or is it that they can't? Executive functioning and children who have been fostered and adopted.' *Fostering and Adoption 31*, 2, 44–53.

Leach, R. (2003) *Children's Participation in Family Decision-making: Highlight No. 196.* London: National Children's Bureau (NCB).

Lees, J. (1999) 'Children with Communication Difficulties.' In D. Shemmings (ed.) *Involving Children in Family Support and Child Protection.* London: The Stationery Office.

Leeson, C. (2007) 'My life in care: experiences of non-participation in decision-making processes.' *Child and Family Social Work 12*, 3, 268–77.

LeFrancois, B. (2007) 'Children's participation rights: voicing opinions in in-patient care.' *Child and Adolescent Mental Health 12*, 2, 94–7.

Leoni, J. (2006) 'Communicating quietly: supporting personal growth with meditation and listening in schools.' *Support for Learning 21*, 3, 121–28.

Lewis, A. and Porter, J. (2004) 'Interviewing children and young people with learning disabilities: guidelines for researchers and multi-professional practice.' *British Journal of Learning Disabilities 32*, 4, 191–97.

Lively, P. (1994) *Oleander, Jacaranda: A Childhood Perceived.* London: Viking.

Lloyd Scott, K. (2000) Editorial, *Parents Voice* Issue 1, September.

London Borough of Brent (1985) *A Child in Trust.* London: Borough of Brent.

London Borough of Greenwich (1987) *A Child in Mind: Protection of Children in a Responsible Society. Report of the Commission of Enquiry into the Circumstances Surrounding the Death of Kimberley Carlile.* London: Borough of Greenwich.

London Borough of Lambeth (1987) *Whose Child? The Report of the Panel Appointed to Enquire into the Death of Tyra Henry.* London: Borough of Lambeth.

Luckock, B., Lefevre, M., Orr, D., Jones, M., Marchant, R. and Tanner, K. (2006) *Teaching, Learning and Assessing Communication Skills with Children and Young People in Social Work Education.* Bristol: Policy Press.

Lundy, L. and Kilpatrick, R. (2006) 'Children's rights and special educational needs: findings from research conducted for the Northern Ireland Commissioner for Children and Young People.' *Support for Learning 21*, 2, 57–63.

Macnamara, J. (1972) 'The cognitive basis of language-learning in infants.' *Psychological Review 79*, 1, 1–13.

Maslow, A. (1970) *Motivation and Personality.* New York: Harper and Row.

Masson, J. (1992) *Freud: The Assault on Truth.* London: Fontana.

May, H. (2005) 'Whose participation is it anyway? Examining the context of pupil participation in the UK.' *British Journal of Special Education 32*, 1, 29–34.

Mayall, B. (2005) 'The Social Conditions of UK Childhoods: Children's Understandings and their Implications.' In J. Mason and T. Fattore (eds) *Children Taken Seriously in Theory, Policy and Practice.* London: Jessica Kingsley Publishers.

McLeod, A. (2001) 'Listening but not Hearing: Barriers to Effective Communication between Children in Public Care and their Social Workers.' Unpublished PhD thesis. Lancaster: University of Lancaster.

McLeod, A. (2006) 'Respect or empowerment? Alternative understandings of "listening" in childcare social work.' *Adoption and Fostering 30*, 4, 43–52.

McLeod, A. (2007a) 'Evaluation of 8's to 10's Participation Project: Baseline Survey Report.' Unpublished paper.

McLeod, A. (2007b) 'Whose agenda? Issues of power and relationship when listening to looked-after young people.' *Child and Family Social Work 12*, 3, 278–86.

Melton, G. and Thompson, R. (1978) 'Getting out of a Rut: Detours to Less Travelled Paths in Child Witness Research.' In S. Ceci, M. Toglia and D. Ross *Children's Eye-witness Memory.* New York: Springer-Verlag.

Miljeteig, P. (2005) 'Children's Democratic Rights: What we can Learn from Young Workers Organizing Themselves.' In J. Mason and T. Fattore (eds) *Children Taken Seriously: In Theory, Policy and Practice.* London: Jessica Kingsley Publishers.

Millar, S. (1968) *The Psychology of Play.* Harmondsworth: Penguin.

Milne, A. ([1928] 1974) *The House at Pooh Corner.* London: Methuen Children's Books.

Monckton, W. (1945) *Report by Sir Walter Monckton on the Circumstances which Led to the Boarding Out of Dennis and Terence O'Neill at Banks Farm, Minsterley, and the Steps Taken to Supervise their Welfare.* Cmnd 6636. London: Her Majesty's Stationery Office (HMSO).

Morris, J. (1998) *Don't Leave us Out! Involving Disabled Children and Young People with Communication Impairments.* York: Joseph Rowntree Foundation.

Morris, K. and Shepherd, C. (2000) 'Quality social work with children and families.' *Child and Family Social Work 5*, 2, 169–76.

Morrison, T. (2007) 'Emotional intelligence, emotion and social work: context, characteristics, complications and contribution.' *British Journal of Social Work 37*, 2, 245–64.

Moss, P., Clark, A. and Kjørholt, A. (2005) 'Introduction.' In A. Clark, A. Kjørholt and P. Moss (eds) *Beyond Listening: Children's Perspectives on Early Childhood Services.* Bristol: Policy Press.

Mullin, M. and Singleton, D. (2006) 'NYAS: Representing children and Rule 9.5.' *Family Law* November, *36*, 975–79.

Munro, E. (2001) 'Empowering looked-after children.' *Child and Family Social Work 6*, 2, 129–37.

National Association of Social Workers (NASW) (2006) *Code of Ethics of the National Association of Social Workers.* Washington, DC: NASW.

National Evaluation of the Children's Fund (NECF) (2005) *The Evaluator's Cookbook.* London: National Evaluation of the Children's Fund/Katalyst Tales.

National Youth Agency (NYA) (2005) *Hear by Right.* Leicester: NYA.

New Zealand Teachers' Council (2004) *Code of Ethics.* Accessed on 20/22/08 at www.teacherscouncil.govt.nz/ethics.

Newell, P. (1989) *Children are People Too: The Case Against Physical Punishment.* London: Bedford Square Press.

North West Quality Protects Reference Group (2002) *Guidance to Help Local Authorities Involve Young People.* London: Department of Health.

NSPCC (National Society for the Prevention of Cruelty to Children) (1993) 'Why listening is important.' *Handicapped Adventure Playground Association Journal 8*, 3–5.

Nutley, S., Walter, I. and Davies, H. (2002) *'From Knowing to Doing: A Framework for Understanding the Evidence-into-practice Agenda.'* Discussion Paper 1, St Andrews Research Unit for Research Utilisation. St Andrews: University of St Andrews.

Oaklander, V. (1988) *Windows to Our Children: A Gestalt Therapy Approach to Children and Adolescents.* New York: Gestalt Journal Press.

O'Connell, B. (2001) *Solution-focused Therapy.* London: Sage.

O'Kane, C. (2000) 'The Development of Participatory Techniques: Facilitating Children's Views about Decisions Which Affect Them.' In P. Christensen and A. James (eds) *Research with Children.* London: Falmer.

O'Quigley, A. (2000) *Listening to Children's Views: The Findings and Recommendations from Recent Research.* York: Joseph Rowntree Foundation.

Parenting UK (2007) *Responding to the Review of 'Reasonable Punishment'.* London: Children Are Unbeatable! Alliance.

Parker, J. and Bradley, G. (2007) *Social Work Practice: Assessment, Planning, Intervention and Review.* Exeter: Learning Matters.

Piaget, J. (1959) *The Language and Thought of the Child.* London: Routledge and Kegan Paul.

Pithouse, A. and Parry, O. (2005) 'Children's advocacy in Wales: organizational challenges for those who commission and deliver advocacy for looked-after children.' *Adoption and Fostering 29*, 4, 45–56.

Pocock, D. (1995) 'Searching for a better story: harnessing modern and post-modern positions in family therapy.' *Journal of Family Therapy 17*, 2, 149–74.

Prestage, R. (1972) 'Life for Kim.' In E. Holgate (ed.) *Communicating with Children.* London: Longman.

Pringle, M. Kellmer (1979) 'Children's Rights and Parents' Rights and Obligations.' In S. Doxiadis (ed.) *The Child in the World of Tomorrow.* Oxford: Pergamon.

Prout, A. and James, A. (1990) 'A New Paradigm for the Sociology of Childhood? Provenance, Promise and Problems.' In A. James and A. Prout (eds) *Constructing and Reconstructing Childhood: Contemporary Issues in the Sociology of Childhood.* Basingstoke: Falmer Press.

Pynoos, R. and Eth, S. (1984) 'The child as witness to homicide.' *Journal of Social Issues 40*, 2, 87–108.

Qvortrup, J. (1990) 'A Voice for Children in Statistical and Social Accounting: A Plea for Children's Right to be Heard.' In A. James and A. Prout (eds) *Constructing and Reconstructing Childhood: Contemporary Issues in the Sociology of Childhood.* Basingstoke: Falmer Press.

Rich, J. (1968) *Interviewing Children and Adolescents.* London: Macmillan.

Rinaldi, C. (2005) 'Documentation and Assessment: What is the Relationship?' In A. Clark, A. Kjørholt, and P. Moss (eds) *Beyond Listening: Children's Perspectives on Early Childhood Services.* Bristol: Policy Press.

Rinaldi, C. (2006) *In Dialogue with Reggio Emilia: Listening, Researching and Learning.* London: Routledge.

Roe, R. (1994) 'Silent voice.' *Child Education 71*, 6, 62–3.

Rogers, C. (1979) *Client-centered Therapy.* London: Constable.

Romaine, M., with Turley, T. and Tuckey, N. (2007) *Preparing Children for Permanence: A Guide to Undertaking Direct Work for Social Workers, Foster Carers and Adoptive Parents.* London: British Association for Adoption & Fostering (BAAF).

Rosenbaum, A. (1980) *The Philosophy of Human Rights: International Perspective.* Westport, CT: Greenwood Press.

Rutter, M. (1972) *Maternal Deprivation Reassessed.* Harmondsworth: Penguin.

Rutter, M. (1975) *Helping Troubled Children.* Harmondsworth: Penguin.

Ryan, T. and Walker, R. (2007) *Life Story Work: A Practical Guide to Helping Children Understand their Past.* London: British Association for Adoption & Fostering (BAAF).

Schofield, G. (2005) 'The voice of the child in family-placement decision-making – a developmental model.' *Adoption and fostering 29*, 1, 29–44.

Schofield, G. and Beek, M. (2006) *Attachment Handbook for Foster Care and Adoption.* London: British Association for Adoption & Fostering (BAAF).

Schön, D. (1983) *The Reflective Practitioner: How Professionals Think in Action.* London: Temple Smith.

Scott, J. (2000) 'Children as Respondents: The Challenge for Quantitative Methods.' In C. Christensen and A. James (eds) *Research with Children.* London: Falmer Press.

Searing, H. (2003) 'The continuing relevance of case-work ideas to long-term child protection work.' *Child and Family Social Work 8*, 4, 311–20.

Secretary of State for Social Services (1988) *Report of the Enquiry into Child Abuse in Cleveland.* Cmnd 412, London: HMSO.

Shemmings, D. (2000) 'Professionals' attitudes to children's participation in decision-making: dichotomous accounts and doctrinal contests.' *Child and Family Social Work 5*, 235–43.

Shier, H. (2001) 'Pathways to participation: openings, opportunities and obligations.' *Children and Society 15*, 2, 107–17.

Sidoti, C. (2005) 'The Law and Taking Children Seriously.' In J. Mason and T. Fattore *Children Taken Seriously in Theory, Policy and Practice.* London: Jessica Kingsley Publishers.

Simmonds, J. (1988) 'Social Work with Children: Developing a Framework for Responsible Practice.' In J. Aldgate and J. Simmonds (eds) *Direct Work with Children.* London: Batsford.

Sinclair, R. (1984) *Decision-making in Statutory Reviews on Children in Care.* Aldershot: Gower.

Sinclair, R. (1998) 'Involving children in planning their care.' *Child and Family Social Work 3*, 2, 137–42.

Sinclair, R. (2000) *Quality Protects Research Briefing No 3: Young People's Participation.* London: Department of Health.

Sinclair, R. (2004) 'Participation in practice: making it meaningful, effective and sustainable.' *Children and Society 18*, 2, 106–118.

Skills for Care (2005) *National Occupational Standards for Social Work.* Leeds: Skills for Care.

Slavin, R. (2002) 'Evidence-based Education Policies: Transforming Educational Practice and Research.' *Educational Researcher 31*, 7, 15–21.

Social Services Committee (1984) *Children in Care.* HC 360, London: Her Majesty's Stationery Office (HMSO).

Spicer, N. and Evans, R. (2006) 'Developing children and young people's participation in strategic processes: the experience of the Children's Fund initiative.' *Social Policy and Society 5*, 2, 177–88.

Standbu, A. (2004) 'Children's participation in family group conferences as a resolution model.' *International Journal of Child and Family Welfare 7*, 4, 207–17.

Stephens, S. (1995) 'Children and the Politics of Culture in "Late Capitalism".' In S. Stephens (ed) *Children and the Politics of Culture.* Princeton, NJ: Princeton University Press.

Swiderek, T. (2004) 'The Relevance of a Children's Policy and the Participation of Young People in Decision-making in Germany.' In D. Crimmens and A. West (eds) *Having Their Say. Young People and Participation: European Experiences.* Lyme Regis: Russell House Publishing.

Tammivaara, J. and Enright, D. (1986) 'On eliciting information: dialogues with child informants.' *Anthropology and Education Quarterly 17,* 4, 218–38.

Taylor, C. (2004) 'Underpinning knowledge for child-care practice: reconsidering child development theory.' *Child and Family Social Work 9,* 3, 225–35.

Te One, S. (2006) 'Setting the context for children's rights in early childhood.' *Childrenz Issues 10,* 1, 18–22.

Thoburn, J. (2004) 'Involving Children in Planning and Reviewing Services.' In Lord Justice Thorpe and J. Cadbury (eds) *Hearing the Children.* Bristol: Jordan.

Thomas, N. (2002) *Children, Family and the State: Decision-making and Child Participation.* Bristol: Policy Press.

Timms, J. (1997) 'The tension between welfare and justice.' *Family Law 27,* 1, 38–47.

Tisdall, E. and Davis, J. (2004) 'Making a difference: bringing children and young people's views into policy-making.' *Children and Society 18,* 2, 131–42.

Triseliotis, J., Borland, M., Hill, M. and Lambert, L. (1995) *Teenagers and the Social Work Services.* London: Her Majesty's Stationery Office (HMSO).

Turner, B. (1990) 'Outline of a theory of citizenship.' *Sociology 24,* 2, 189–217.

United Nations (1989) *Convention on the Rights of the Child.* Geneva: United Nations.

Varendonck, J. ([1911] 1984) 'The testimony of children in a famous trial.' *Journal of Social Issues 40,* 2, 26–31.

Veeran, V. (2004) 'Working with street children: a child-centred approach.' *Child-Care in Practice 10,* 4, 359–66.

Velleman, R. and Templeton, L. (2007) 'Understanding and modifying the impact of parental substance misuse on children.' *Advances in Psychiatric Treatment 13,* 2, 79–89.

Walrond-Skinner, S. (1977) *Family Therapy: The Treatment of Natural Systems.* London: Routledge and Kegan Paul.

Ward, D. (2000) 'Totem not Token: Group-work as a Vehicle for User Participation.' In H. Kemshall and R. Littlechild (eds) *User Involvement and Participation in Social Care: Research Informing Practice.* London: Jessica Kingsley Publishers.

Waterhouse R. (2000) *Lost in Care: Report of the Tribunal of Inquiry into Abuse of Children in Care in the Former County Council Areas of Gwynedd and Clwydd.* London: Her Majesty's Stationery Office (HMSO).

Wertsch, J. (ed.) (1985) *Culture, Communication and Cognition: Vygotskian Perspectives.* Cambridge: Cambridge University Press.

Willow, C. (1998) 'Listening to Children in Local Government.' In D. Utting (ed.) *Children's Services Now and in the Future.* London: National Children's Bureau (NCB).

Wilson, J. (1992) *The Story of Tracy Beaker.* London: Transworld.

Wilson, J. (1998) *Child-focused Practice: A Collaborative Systemic Approach.* London: Karnac Press.

Winnicott, C. (1964) *Child Care and Social Work.* Hitchin: Codicote Press.

Winter, K. (2006) 'Widening our knowledge concerning young looked-after children: the case for research using sociological models of childhood.' *Child and Family Social Work 11,* 1, 55–64.

Wittmer, D. and Honig, A. (1991) 'Convergent or divergent? Teacher questions to 3-year-old children in day care.' *Early Childhood Development and Care 68,* 1, 141–8.

Woodhead, M. (1990) 'Psychology and the Cultural Construction of Children's Needs.' In A. James and A. Prout (eds) *Constructing and Reconstructing Childhood.* London: Falmer Press.

Worrall-Davies, A. and Marino-Francis, F. (2007) 'Eliciting children's and young people's views of child and adolescent mental health services: a systematic review.' *Child and Adolescent Mental Health 13,* 1, 16–18.

Wright, P., Turner, C., Clay, D. and Mills, H. (2006) *The Participation of Children and Young People in Developing Social Care.* London: Social Care Institute for Excellence (SCIE).

Yarrow, M. and Waxler, C. (1979) 'Observing Interaction: A Confrontation with Methodology.' In R. Cairns (ed.) *The Analysis of Social Interactions – Methods, Issues and Illustrations.* Hillsdale, NJ: Lawrence Erlbaum Associates.

Youth Justice and Criminal Evidence Act (1999) London: The Stationery Office.

Subject Index

Author Index